COZUMEL

Liza Prado & Gary Chandler

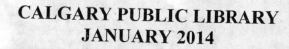

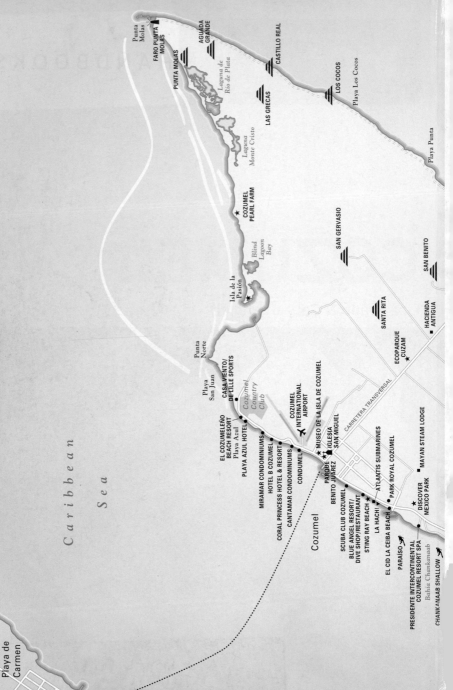

ISLA COZUMEL

Caribbean Sea

Playa de Carmen

Cozumel

Punta Molas
FARO PUNTA MOLAS
PUNTA MOLAS
AGUADA GRANDE
CASTILLO REAL
Laguna de Río de Plata
LOS COCOS
Playa Los Cocos
LAS GRECAS
Laguna Monte Cristo
Playa Punta
COZUMEL PEARL FARM
Blind Lagoon Bay
SAN GERVASIO
SAN BENITO
Isla de la Pasión
SANTA RITA
HACIENDA ANTIGUA
ECOPARQUE CUZAM
Punta Norte
CARRETERA TRANSVERSAL
Playa San Juan
CASA VIENTO/ DE L'ILLE SPORTS
Playa Azul
Cozumel Country Club
COZUMEL INTERNATIONAL AIRPORT
EL COZUMELEÑO BEACH RESORT
PLAYA AZUL HOTEL
MIRAMAR CONDOMINIUMS
HOTEL B COZUMEL
CORAL PRINCESS HOTEL & RESORT
CANTAMAR CONDOMINIUMS
CONDUMEL
MUSEO DE LA ISLA DE COZUMEL
IGLESIA SAN MIGUEL
PARQUE BENITO JUAREZ
ATLANTIS SUBMARINES
PARK ROYAL COZUMEL
MAYAN STEAM LODGE
SCUBA CLUB COZUMEL
BLUE ANGEL RESORT/ DIVE SHOP/RESTAURANT
STING RAY BEACH
LA HACH!
EL CID LA CEIBA BEACH
DISCOVER MEXICO PARK
PARAISO
PRESIDENTE INTERCONTINENTAL COZUMEL RESORT SPA
Bahía Chankanaab
CHANKANAAB SHALLOW

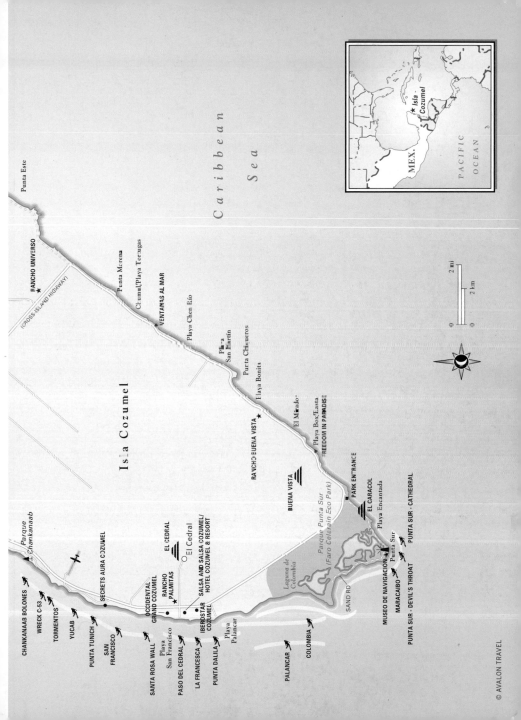

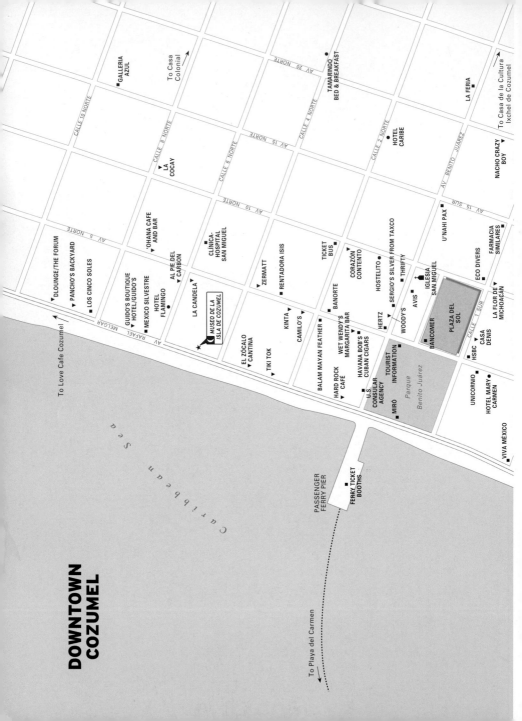

DOWNTOWN COZUMEL

Caribbean Sea

To Playa del Carmen

PASSENGER FERRY PIER

FERRY TICKET BOOTHS

To Love Cafe Cozumel

AV RAFAEL MELGAR

CALLE 10 NORTE
CALLE 8 NORTE
CALLE 6 NORTE

AV 5 NORTE
AV 10 NORTE
AV 15 NORTE
AV 20 NORTE

CALLE 4 NORTE
CALLE 2 NORTE

AV BENITO JUÁREZ
AV 15 SUR
CALLE 1 SUR

GALLERIA AZUL

To Casa Colonial

TAMARINDO BED & BREAKFAST

To Casa de la Cultura Ixchel de Cozumel

LA FERIA

HOTEL CARIBE

NACHO CRAZY BOY

LA COCAY

DLOUNGE/THE FORUM
PANCHO'S BACKYARD
LOS CINCO SOLES
GUIDO'S BOUTIQUE HOTEL/GUIDO'S
MEXICO SILVESTRE
HOTEL FLAMINGO

OHANA CAFE AND BAR

AL PIE DEL CARBON

CLÍNICA-HOSPITAL SAN MIGUEL

LA CANDELA

MUSEO DE LA ISLA DE COZUMEL

ZERMATT

RENTADORA ISIS

TICKET BUS

CORAZON CONTENTO

U'NAHI PAX

FARMACIA SIMILARES

EL ZOCALO CANTINA

KINTA

CAMILO'S

TIKI TOK

BALAM MAYAN FEATHER

WET WENDY'S MARGARITA BAR

BANORTE

HERTZ

HOSTELITO

SERGIO'S SILVER FROM TAXCO

THRIFTY

WOODY'S

AVIS

ECO DIVERS

IGLESIA SAN MIGUEL

HARD ROCK CAFÉ

HAVANA BOB'S CUBAN CIGARS

U.S. CONSULAR AGENCY

MIRO

TOURIST INFORMATION

Parque Benito Juárez

BANCOMER

PLAZA DEL SOL

LA FLOR DE MICHOACÁN

HSBC

CASA DENIS

UNICORNIO

HOTEL MARY CARMEN

VIVA MÉXICO

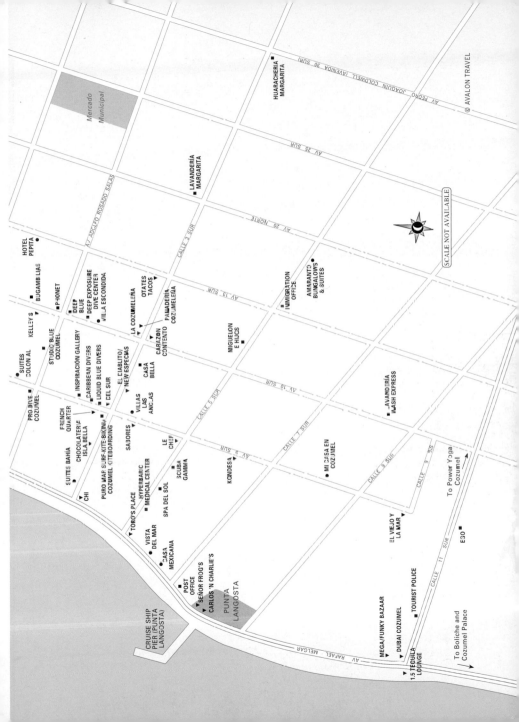

Contents

DISCOVER
Cozumel

All around Isla Cozumel, the Caribbean Sea glitters a hundred shades of blue. To the west, across a channel that's 16 kilometers (10 miles) wide, is Mexico's famous Riviera Maya, with its spectacular beaches and all-inclusive resorts. To the east is the Caribbean Sea, with its blue-white waves rolling onto Cozumel's shore. Cozumel itself is broad and flat—a limestone pancake whose one high point wouldn't clear a five-story building. More than 30 ancient Maya ruins are ensconced in the island's low dense forest, while beneath the dry green covering is a vast network of caves and caverns, the fifth-longest cave system in the world. Cozumel's shoreline alternates between thick white sand, tangled mangrove forest, and long stretches of hard black stone.

Of course, Cozumel is most famous for what is underwater. The Mesoamerican Reef, the world's second-longest coral roof, stretches from the Yucatán Peninsula to the Bay Islands of Honduras. The reef is glorious, especially right in front of Cozumel, composed of over a dozen species of coral that sport every color imaginable. The reef supports many times that number of plants and sea creatures, from clown fish to spiny lobsters to sojourning sea turtles. It's no surprise that Cozumel is a diving and snorkeling paradise, not only for its rich coral and sealife, but also for the warm clear water and variety of underwater environments, including winding mazes, broad plateaus, and plunging walls.

And Cozumel is no less interesting above water. San Miguel de Cozumel, the island's main town, is truly a tale of two cities: Cruise ships dock just south of town, their passengers forming a human river on San Miguel's main drag, flowing slowly down a channel of jewelry stores, souvenir shops, and open-air restaurants. But just a few blocks inland from the promenade is an entirely different Cozumel: a small, friendly community where old folks sit at their windows and kids play soccer in the streets. The town's main plaza is a gathering place for the community, including on weekend evenings, when there's live music and dancing and street carts selling corn cobs on a stick.

Cozumel's interior and far eastern shore are yet another world, lacking even power lines and telephone cables. Heavy surf makes most of the eastern shore dangerous for swimming, but you can easily spend a day beachcombing and relaxing on the unmanicured beaches and lunching at small restaurants overlooking the sea.

As one of Mexico's largest islands, it shouldn't be surprising to discover that Cozumel is so multifaceted. But it's hard not to marvel at how stark the differences are. Come for the diving and snorkeling, but leave time to experience a side of Cozumel you may not have expected.

words of wisdom at the bottom of the pool at Hotel B Cozumel, on the island's northwest shore

Planning Your Trip

Where to Go

Isla Cozumel

Cozumel's pristine coral reefs and crystalline water attract divers the world over; fewer people realize the island also has a scenic national park, numerous beach clubs, a tournament golf course, even an important Maya ruin. Travelers also can beat the cruise ship crowds by heading to the east side's isolated beaches and dramatic surf. Most people arrive by ferry—it's just a half-hour ride from Playa del Carmen—but there's also an airport with both domestic and international arrivals, and all of those cruise ships.

DOWNTOWN COZUMEL

Downtown Cozumel doesn't have a beach-front, but it does have just about everything else: Its main drag, along the waterfront, is packed with pricey shops catering to the masses of cruise ship passengers who disembark a short distance south. Just inland are the colorful homes and simple shops typical of native Cozumeleños. Downtown is where ferries to and from Playa del Carmen dock, and it's where you'll find useful services like dive shops, grocery stores, laundry, Internet

IF YOU HAVE . . .

- **ONE DAY:** Snorkel or dive in the morning and head to the east side for lunch and beach time in the afternoon.

- **THREE DAYS:** Add another dive or snorkel excursion, plus visits to San Gervasio ruins and Parque Punta Sur.

- **ONE WEEK:** Add a third or even fourth day of snorkeling or diving, R&R at a beach club, plus a visit to the Museo de la Isla de Cozumel and a mainland excursion to Playa del Carmen or Cobá.

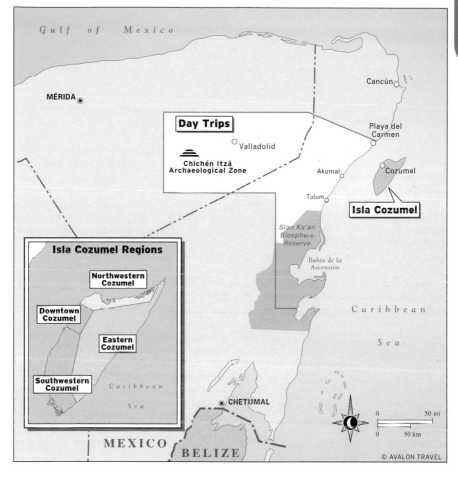

Gulf of Mexico

MÉRIDA

Cancún

Day Trips

Playa del Carmen

Valladolid

Chichén Itzá
Archaeological Zone

Akumal

Cozumel

Tulum

Isla Cozumel

Sian Ka'an
Biosphere
Reserve

Bahía de la
Ascensión

Isla Cozumel Regions

Caribbean

Northwestern
Cozumel

Sea

Downtown
Cozumel

Eastern
Cozumel

Southwestern
Cozumel

Caribbean

Sea

CHETUMAL

0   50 mi

0   50 km

MEXICO / BELIZE

© AVALON TRAVEL

shops, medical centers, and more. It's got a variety of hotels, from hostels to dive resorts to upscale B&Bs, and restaurants for all tastes and budgets. Most of the island's nightlife is in the downtown area, and that, too, ranges from sports bars to discotheques to live music and dancing on the town's main plaza.

NORTHWESTERN COZUMEL

The northwestern shoulder of Cozumel is probably the most overlooked part of the island. Most visitors have their eyes on the shopping and restaurants downtown, and on the beach clubs dotting the southwest shore. Adventurous types head to the east side, leaving the northwest side quiet and crowd-free. (The exception is Isla de la Pasión, which is one of Cozumel's more popular shore excursions for cruise ship passengers, but guests there merely zip through the northwest en route to the island.) There's less sand on the northwest—most of this coastline is ironshore—but there are still a handful of small but pleasant beach clubs, plus some great waterfront nightclubs. The sunsets, of course, are spectacular. And the northwest happens to be Cozumel's hub for sports beyond underwater ones: golf, fishing, kiteboarding, and stand-up paddling. And unlike the east, the northwest has a handful of excellent lodging options, including condos and the island's best boutique hotel.

SOUTHWESTERN COZUMEL

If it's beaches you're after, Cozumel's southwest is the place to go. Sheltered from the open ocean waves, the southwest shore has glassy smooth water and long stretches of thick white sand, perfect for relaxing and soaking up the sun. Not surprisingly, virtually all of Cozumel's all-inclusive resorts are along this coastline, ranging from super deluxe to bargain basement. Most of the island's beach clubs are along the southwest coast, too; they cater primarily to cruise ship passengers on the island for just a day, but are also a good option for independent travelers looking for some beach time. Families enjoy Parque Chankanaab, a large ecopark with beaches, swimming pool, zipline, snorkeling tours, even dolphin programs. The southwest shore also has some inland attractions, namely horseback riding and the town of El Cedral, with a small Maya ruin, a good tequila tour, and a pleasant central plaza with souvenir stands.

EASTERN COZUMEL

Believe it or not, the entire eastern side of Cozumel (the world's second most popular cruise ship port!) is all but untouched, with just one hotel, a handful of restaurants and beach bars, and no telephone wires or power cables. One reason is that the eastern shore,

facing the open ocean, is pounded by heavy surf, making swimming and wading difficult and even unsafe. It's also an important sea turtle nesting ground, which prevents most large-scale development. Independent travelers are the main beneficiaries, as the east side offers an escape from Cozumel's highly developed western shore. The coastal road hugs the shore, with plenty of spots to pull over for sightseeing, beachcombing, or to just lay out a towel and dig into a good book. A handful of beach restaurants have fresh meals and restrooms, and a few spots along the east side are shielded from the waves and are popular with local families. The east side also has a good horseback riding operator, a hacienda giving tequila tours, and (farther inland) the island's best and biggest Maya ruin, San Gervasio.

Day Trips

Day trips to the mainland are easy with frequent daily ferry service between Cozumel and Playa del Carmen. There's plenty to do in Playa del Carmen itself, including golf, shopping, enjoying the beaches, or treating yourself to a nice meal. You even can stock up at Walmart if you'll be on Cozumel for a longer period. There are plenty of car rental agencies, and the main bus station is just steps from the ferry dock, making trips beyond Playa easy, too; check out Maya ruins at Tulum, Cobá, or even Chichén Itzá, or one of the Riviera Maya's large ecoparks, including Xcaret and the new Xplor. For an unforgettable snorkeling or diving experience, book a trip to one or more cenotes (freshwater sinkholes and caverns).

When to Go

Considering weather, prices, and crowds, the best times to visit Cozumel are late November-mid-December and mid-January-early May. You'll avoid the intense heat June-August, the rain (and possible hurricanes) in September and October, and the crowds and high prices around the winter holidays.

The big caveats with those periods are spring break (March/April) and Semana Santa (the week before Easter), when American and Canadian students, and then Mexican tourists, turn out in force and prices spike temporarily.

Be aware that certain attractions—like

a temple pyramid at San Gervasio, Cozumel's most important Maya ruin

Carnaval or the Feria del Cedral—are only available during specific months. Even many year-round activities like sportfishing and kiteboarding are better or worse according to the season.

Before You Go

Passports and Visas

American travelers are required to have a valid passport to travel to and from Mexico. Tourist visas are issued upon entry; you technically are allowed up to 180 days, but agents often issue just 30 or 60 days. If you want to stay longer, request the time when you present your passport. To extend your visa, visit the immigration office (Av. 15 Sur at Calle 5, tel. 987/872-0071), which is open 9am-1pm Monday-Friday. There are immigration agents at the airport, too, open 7am-9pm daily.

Vaccinations

No special vaccines are required for travel to Cozumel, but it's a good idea to be up-to-date on the standard travel immunizations, including hepatitis A, MMR (measles-mumps-rubella), tetanus-diphtheria, and typhoid.

What to Take

Bring to Isla Cozumel what you would to any beach destination: light cotton clothing, hat, sunscreen, sunglasses, flip-flops, etc. Beach and underwater buffs should bring two or even three swimsuits, plus snorkel and dive gear if you've got it. Water shoes come in handy wherever the beach is rocky, while tennis shoes and bug repellent are musts for the Maya ruins. Consider bringing a light sweater or jacket for cool evenings, and a nice outfit for outings to nicer restaurants or to attend church services. Finally, it's always smart to bring an extra pair of glasses or contacts, prescription medications, birth control, and a travel clock. If you do leave anything behind, no worries—there are plenty of stores and pharmacies on the island.

The Best of Isla Cozumel

A week goes by fast in Cozumel. If you enjoy water sports like scuba diving, snorkeling, kiteboarding, or stand-up paddling (or have ever wanted to learn one), you've come to the right place, and can easily dedicate several days just to that. Cozumel has a number of interesting dry-land attractions too, including Maya ruins, horseback riding, museums, and more. Playa del Carmen is a short ferry ride away, with great beaches and shopping of its own, and is a jumping-off point for trips farther afield, like Chichén Itzá or family-friendly eco-parks. And, of course, you'll want to spend a couple of days just relaxing on the beach; Cozumel's sun 'n sand options range from lively beach clubs to locals' favorites on the isolated east side.

Day 1

Arriving in Cozumel, spend some time settling into your hotel, then take a stroll around downtown. You've got two main goals: soaking up the island's laid-back vibe and selecting a dive shop. Once accomplished, you can relax over a nice dinner.

Day 2

Diving, diving, diving. (Or snorkeling, snorkeling, snorkeling.) Depending on your interest and experience, this could occupy one day or several. Both sports are surprisingly tiring, so plan on taking it easy (and drinking plenty of water) between plunges and afterward.

Day 3

If you're not on a diving or snorkeling tour, spend the day circling the island. Parque Punta Sur (Faro Celarain) is not to be missed, with an interesting museum and lighthouse, and a lovely beach with excellent snorkeling; plan on spending a few hours there. Cozumel's undeveloped

A naturally protected pool makes Playa Chen Río the best swimming and family beach on Isla Cozumel's east side.

eastern shore has a lot of places to just pull the car over and admire the view or grab a bite to eat; Playa Chen Río is especially nice, with a restaurant and protected cove for swimming. Back in town, Cozumel's history museum is a nice way to spend an hour or so before drinks and dinner.

Day 4

Take a day to partake in some of Cozumel's dryland activities. San Gervasio, Cozumel's largest and most important Maya ruin, is well worth a morning visit. A second ruin, El Cedral, is located in a pleasant little town, where there's also an interesting tequila tour. Horseback riding or ATV tours are another option. Alternatively, plan to take the ferry to Playa del Carmen; you can spend the day there or book a rental car to visit cenotes and Maya ruins farther afield.

Day 5

Remember, you shouldn't dive within 24 hours of a flight. Snorkeling is okay though, or you can try something totally different, like fishing or stand-up paddling. This also would be a great time to treat yourself to a day at a beach club, or at family-friendly Parque Chankanaab. One last day for fun and sun before returning to reality!

Day 6

A day to do some final shopping, whether for gifts and souvenirs, or something more lasting like folk art or jewelry. Snorkeling hounds could take a quick dip before heading home.

Tequila comes in all shapes, sizes, and colors.

Cozumel's Best Beaches

the road into Parque Punta Sur, a large natural reserve with excellent beaches and snorkeling

Cozumel may not have the drop-dead-gorgeous beaches of Tulum or Cancún, but there are still plenty of spots to enjoy the sun and sand. And for what Cozumel's beaches lack in pure aesthetics, they make up for with character: Some have great snorkeling right from shore, others have impressive surf, and each has a different ambience, from raucous beach clubs catering to cruise ship passengers, to quiet family-friendly spots popular with locals and expats.

- **Isla de la Pasión** (page 43): The beach here is spectacular, a kilometer-long (0.6 mile) stretch of pure white sand, backed by palm trees and kissed by turquoise water. It's not just *like* a Corona commercial, it actually *is* one, having served as the set for one of the beer company's early ads. The trouble is that it's a private island (though the beach is public), and getting there pretty much requires shelling out US$40-65 per person for a four-hour beach package.

- **Playa San Francisco** (page 45): Covering approximately three kilometers (1.9 miles) of Cozumel's calm southwestern coastline, Playa San Francisco has water as smooth as glass and thick white sand that feels like powdered sugar between your toes. It's accessible via several beach clubs (*club de playa* in Spanish), which offer the convenience of restrooms, restaurants, lounge chairs, and

umbrellas, and (depending on the beach club) extras like swimming pools, dive shops, and other beach activities.

- **Parque Punta Sur** (page 48): Parque Punta Sur has a long lovely beach, a wide strip of golden sand bending gently into the distance. One part of the beach is used by cruise ships passengers on package tours, with a buffet restaurant and volleyball courts. A separate area appeals more to independent travelers, with a changing area, lounge chairs, a basic eatery, and a water sports kiosk. The snorkeling just offshore is outstanding—some of the best shore snorkeling on the island, in fact. The beach is part of a sprawling national park that covers most of Cozumel's southern tip, and also has a historic lighthouse and interesting maritime museum.

- **Playa Chen Río** (page 50): Most of Cozumel's east side has surf that's too rough for swimming, but Chen Río is different, thanks to a long rocky arm that blocks the waves and forms a calm natural pool. Add to that a semicircle of thick golden sand and a nearby restaurant, and Chen Río is easily the best place on the east side to have a beach day. On Sundays, Chen Río is a popular spot for locals and their families, which can be a refreshing change of pace from the tourist-only spots elsewhere.

It's not hard to see why Cozumel is one of the world's best scuba diving destinations.

Diving and Snorkeling Guide

Dozens of dive and snorkeling sites encircle the island, from shallow "platform" reefs to deeper "edge" reefs; beyond the edge reefs, the sea floor drops away dramatically, making for deep, fast wall dives. Cozumel is well known for its drift dives, with the Gulf Stream providing a moderate (1-2 knot) south-north current at most of Cozumel's sites. As the name suggests, drift diving is when a current pulls you through the dive; it can be surprisingly difficult to manage, especially for beginning divers, so most dive shops take novices to sites where the current tends to be mild. As you gain experience, drift diving can be a fast and fun adventure.

Below are descriptions of some (but far from all) of the more popular dive sites around the island. You can request certain dives or, more generally, ask that the dive shop not return to the same place twice, especially if you'll be diving with the same shop for several days. Bear in mind, though, that a variety of factors go into a dive shop's decision of where to take their groups on any given day (including weather, current, and a group's overall skill level), so it's not always possible to honor all such requests. As always, it's worth discussing the issue upfront, as part of your process for selecting a dive shop.

Coral Reefs

Cozumel's coral reef—and the world class diving and snorkeling it provides—is the main reason people come to the island. The reef was designated a national marine reserve more than two decades ago, and the waters have thrived under the park's rigorous protection and clean-up programs. Hurricanes can cause significant damage to reef systems, snapping off coral and sponges with their powerful surge and smothering large sections under layers of sand and debris. But hurricanes are nothing new to Cozumel or its reef, and reports of catastrophic damage from recent record hurricanes were greatly exaggerated. (Rising seawater temperatures are a far more serious problem.) Cozumel's underwater treasure remains very much alive, supporting a plethora of creatures, its seascapes as stunning as ever.

AIRPLANE WRECK

A 40-passenger Convair airliner lies on Cozumel's seabed, about 65 meters (213 feet) from the shore near El Cid hotel. Sunk in 1977 for the Mexican movie production of *Survive II,* the plane has been broken into pieces and strewn about the site by years of storms. The site itself is relatively flat, though with parrot fish, damselfish, and a host of sea fans and small coral heads, there's plenty to see. With depth ranges of 3-15 meters (10-49 feet), this is a good site for snorkelers.

PARAÍSO

Just south of the international pier, and about 200 meters (656 feet) from shore, lies Paraíso, an impressive three-lane coral ridge. Medium-size coral—mostly brain and star—attract sergeant majors, angelfish, grunts, squirrel fish, and snappers. This site also is popular for night dives because of its proximity to hotels, which means less time on the boat. Depth ranges 5-13 meters (16-43 feet). Snorkeling is decent near the shore, but be very careful of boat traffic.

DZUL-HÁ (AKA THE MONEY BAR)

Located off the old coastal road (Km. 6.5), Dzul-Há is one of the best spots for DIY snorkeling, with small coral heads and sea fans that support a colorful array of fish like blue tangs, parrot fish, and queen angels. Steps lead into the ocean, where depths range 3-10 meters (10-33 feet). You can rent snorkel gear on-site for US$14, including the marine park fee (US$2).

CHANKANAAB SHALLOW

True to its name, this section of reef is shallow (maximum 12 meters/39 feet) and has very mild currents, making it a good spot for beginner divers. Look for eels hiding in the coral heads, in addition to numerous species of fish. Chankanaab Shallow is also popular as a second dive and for nighttime diving, when you're likely to see spiny lobsters and the occasional octopus. The reef is located in front of Parque Chankanaab.

Divers relax between dives on an isolated pier on Isla Cozumel.

Rich sealife and warm crystal-clear water make Cozumel a great place for snorkeling.

CHANKANAAB BOLONES

Farther offshore than Chankanaab Shallow, this large sandy plateau is 18-24 meters (60-80 feet) down and dotted with coral heads. It's a rewarding dive for novice and advanced divers alike, with an incredible variety of sealife, including eels, rays, and numerous different types of coral, and with relatively little current. The biggest coral formations are in deeper water along the site's outer margin.

WRECK C-53

Most dive "wrecks" aren't wrecks at all, but decommissioned ships that are intentionally sunk to serve as artificial reefs and unique destinations for divers. That's the case with Wreck C-53: a 56-meter-long (184-foot) minesweeper from the Mexican navy that was sunk in a sandy patch just south of Parque Chankanaab in June 2000. The huge ship rests in 24 meters (80 feet) of water, but rises a full 9 meters (30 feet) above the sea floor. Large holes have been cut in the sides, and a guideline has been installed along the safest route through the ship's interior. Note that there's a maximum 4-to-1 diver-to-dive master ratio inside the ship. Besides the thrill of exploring the doomed ship itself, Wreck C-53 is a good spot to see large fish like barracuda and grouper.

TORMENTOS

At this site divers can see about 60 coral heads, each decorated with an assortment of sea fans, brain and whip corals, and sponges. Invertebrates like to hide out in the innumerable crevices—look for flamingo tongue shells, arrow crabs, and black crinoids. Lobsters like the scene, too—keep your eyes peeled for them, especially at the north end of the site. Depth ranges 5-15 meters (16-49 feet). The site is popular with photographers.

YUCAB

A perfect drift dive, Yucab has archways, overhangs, and large coral heads—some as tall as three meters (10 feet)—that are alive with an incredible array of creatures: Lobsters, octopus, scorpionfish, banded coral shrimp, and butterfly fish can almost always be found here. Videographers typically have a field day. Depth ranges 5-15 meters (16-49 feet).

PUNTA TUNICH

Punta Tunich usually has a 1.5-knot current, which makes it an excellent drift dive. The site itself has a white-sand bottom with a gentle downward slope that ends in a drop-off. Along the way, the reef is dotted with finger coral and elephant ear sponges. Divers regularly encounter eagle rays, barracuda, sea horses, bar jacks, and parrot fish. The depth ranges 5-18 meters (16-60 feet).

SAN FRANCISCO

San Francisco isn't the most famous of Cozumel's wall dives, but a remarkable one all the same, with far less traffic than other spots. It's a south-north drift dive, hugging a moderately inclined wall covered with a dense array of coral, sponges, and sea fans. The wall begins at a depth of 12 meters (39 feet), where a rugged crest has overhangs and crevices, and is home to myriad fish, eels, and other sealife; you may even see sea turtles, also perusing the wall's rich banquet. The wall slopes to a depth of 24 meters (80 feet) before plunging abruptly into the blue-black abyss.

SANTA ROSA WALL

With a sensational drop-off that begins at 22 meters (72 feet), this spectacular site is known for its tunnels, caves, and stony overhangs. Teeming with sealife, it's home to translucent sponges, mammoth sea fans, file clams, horse-eyed jacks, fairy basslets, gray angelfish, and black groupers. Strong currents make this a good drift dive, especially for experienced divers. Depth ranges 5-27 meters (16-89 feet).

PASO DEL CEDRAL

A strip reef lined with small corals like disk and cactus, this site attracts large schools of fish including blue-striped grunts and snapper—perfect for dramatic photographs. Southern stingrays often are seen gliding over the sandy areas just inside the reef. Depths range 10-20 meters (33-66 feet).

divers returning from a two-tank dive

LA FRANCESCA

Nurse sharks and eagle rays can sometimes be spotted at this shallow, easygoing dive site. Located slightly up-island from the more famous Palancar and Colombia sites, La Francesca is a long, colorful section of reef with many fun features like crevices and swim-throughs, where you're sure to spot crabs, shrimp, and other crustaceans. It's a south-north drift dive, but the current here is usually quite mellow. La Francesca is an especially good spot to practice underwater photography, with its unique structural features, manageable current, and abundance of coral, fish, and other sea creatures.

PUNTA DALILA

This is another good spot for aspiring photographers, with a shallow profile for maximum bottom time, a mild northerly current, and a visually striking combination of sandy floor, mature coral, and numerous caves and crevices. A huge variety of marine creatures call Punta Dalila home, including crabs and lobsters (look for them hiding under overhangs), myriad fish, and even the occasional nurse shark.

PALANCAR

This spectacular five-kilometer-long (3.1-mile) dive spot is actually made up of five different sites—Shallows, Garden, Horseshoe, Caves, and Bricks. It is known for its series of enormous coral buttresses. Some drop off dramatically into winding ravines, deep canyons, and passageways; others have become archways and tunnels with formations 15 meters (49 feet) tall. The most popular site here is Palancar Horseshoe, which is made up of a horseshoe-shaped series of coral heads at the top of a drop-off. All the sites, however, are teeming with reef life. Palancar ranges in depth 5-40 meters (16-131 feet).

COLOMBIA

An enormous coral buttress, Colombia boasts tall coral pillars separated by passageways, channels, and ravines. Divers enjoy drifting past huge sponges, anemones, and swaying sea fans. Larger creatures—sea turtles, groupers, nurse sharks, and southern stingrays—are commonly seen here. The site is recommended for experienced divers. Depths range 5-40 meters (16-131 feet).

PUNTA SUR–DEVIL'S THROAT

Devil's Throat is one of the more popular and thrilling features of the huge Punta Sur wall, located at the far southern end of the island. Just reaching Devil's Throat is a kick, with a huge cave in a coral head leading to a smaller cavern. There, a small opening marks the beginning of Devil's Throat: a narrow tunnel, angling downward at a 45-degree angle, lined with red sponges. The opening is at a depth of 24 meters (80 feet), and the exit at 39 meters (128 feet); it takes less than a minute to pass through, but is an unforgettable experience. Once out of the throat, you'll zigzag through an upward-sloping maze of coral, with even more tunnels and overhangs to navigate, before reaching a sandy plateau at 9 meters (30 feet) that's perfect for ascending. Excellent buoyancy control and air management are required, making this an advanced-only dive.

PUNTA SUR–CATHEDRAL

As the name suggests, the main feature of this dive is a huge cavern that resembles a cathedral, with sunbeams penetrating through cracks and windows in the ceiling. In fact, this whole area is loaded with caverns and soaring coral structures; where the dive typically takes place, there's a virtual wall of mature coral stretching from 12 meters (39 feet) down to more than 30 meters (100 feet). The dive includes weaving in and out of the various enclosures and trenches, staying at roughly 21 meters (70 feet) in depth. Punta Sur is a good area to spot larger marine animals like turtles and nurse sharks, who can cruise for food and prey while remaining well protected in the oversized coral structures here.

MARACAIBO

At the island's southern tip, Maracaibo is a deep buttress reef interspersed with tunnels, caves, and vertical walls. It is known for its immense coral formations as well as for the possibility of spotting large animals—sharks (black tip and nurse) as well as turtles and eagle rays. A deep-drift dive, this site is recommended for advanced divers only. Depths range 30–40 meters (98-131 feet).

Blue Angel is one of many dive resorts on Cozumel, where you eat, sleep, and breathe scuba diving.

How to Choose a Dive Shop

There are close to 100 dive shops on Isla Cozumel, and scores more on the mainland. Choosing just one—and then placing all your underwater faith into its hands—can be daunting.

Safety should be your number-one concern in choosing a shop. Fortunately, the standards in Cozumel and the Riviera Maya are almost universally first-rate, and accidents are rare. But that's not a reason to be complacent. For example, don't dive with a shop that doesn't ask to see your certification card or logbook—if they didn't ask you, they probably didn't ask anyone else, and ill-trained divers are as dangerous to others in the group as they are to themselves.

Equipment is another crucial issue. You should ask to inspect the shop's equipment, and the dive shop should be quick to comply. Although few casual divers are trained to evaluate gear, a good dive shop will appreciate your concern and be happy to put you at ease. If the staff is reluctant to show you the gear, either they aren't too proud of it or they don't see clients as equal partners in dive safety—both red flags.

Of course, the most important equipment is not what's on the rack but what you actually use. On the day of your dive, get to the shop early so you have time to **double-check your gear.** Old equipment is not necessarily bad equipment, but you should ask for a different BCD, wetsuit, or regulator if the condition of the one assigned to you makes you uneasy. Learn how to check the O-ring (the small rubber ring that forms the seal between the tank and the regulator), and do so before every dive. You also should attach your regulator and open the valve, to listen for any hissing between the regulator and the tank, or in the primary and backup mouthpieces. If you hear any, ask the dive master to check it and, if need be, change the regulator. Arriving early lets you do all this before getting on the boat—ideally before leaving the shop—so you can swap gear if necessary.

Feeling comfortable and free to ask questions or raise concerns (of any sort at any time) is a crucial factor in safe diving. That's where a dive shop's **personality** comes in. Every dive shop has its own culture or style, and different divers will feel more comfortable in different shops. Spend some time talking to people at a couple of different dive shops before signing up. Try to meet the person who will be leading your particular dive—you may have to come in the afternoon when that day's trip returns. Chances are one of the shops or dive masters will click with you.

Finally, there are some specific questions you should ask about a shop's practices. Has their air been tested and certified? Do they carry radios and oxygen? Does the captain always stay with the boat? How many people will be going on your dive? How advanced are they? How many dive masters or instructors will there be? And how experienced are they? Above all, be vocal and proactive about your safety, and remember *there are no stupid questions*.

And, of course, have fun!

ISLA COZUMEL

Isla Cozumel is bursting with options of all kinds and for all budgets. Yet it still feels like a traditional Caribbean island, a place with just a single road hugging its coastline, where you can eat at plastic tables on the sidewalk and are sure to bump into people you met on the ferry. It is, at once, a major tourist destination and a charming Mexican town, a place of incredible natural beauty and historical significance, but also just plain fun.

Cozumel is a place to experience and engage. Snorkeling is a fun and easy entrée to Cozumel's amazing underwater world, and virtually every hotel and beach club rents gear and arranges tours. If you've never scuba dived, why not give it a try? It's a surprisingly easy sport to learn, perfectly suited for couples and accessible to people of all ages and physical prowess. Kiteboarding and stand-up paddling are tougher to master, but all the more rewarding when you do. For relaxing on the beach, Cozumel's western shore has calm water and beach clubs for all tastes, from raucous to family friendly, while the eastern shore will appeal to travelers looking for something off the beaten path. Cozumel has two ecoparks: a huge natural reserve on the island's southern tip, with beautiful views and outstanding snorkeling, and a destination park with a pool, beach area, ziplines, and restaurants. Inland, Cozumel's main archaeological site, San Gervasio, and a smaller one in the historic village of El Cedral, are worth visiting, and there are plenty of dryland activities, like horseback riding, ATV excursions, tequila tours, museums, and shopping. Simply renting a car, or

© GARY CHANDLER

HIGHLIGHTS

◖ Museo de la Isla de Cozumel: This small but fascinating museum has displays on all things Cozumel, including the island's geological formation, early Maya occupation, and the impact of recent hurricanes (page 28).

◖ Parque Punta Sur (Faro Celarain Eco Park): Snorkel the colorful ocean reef, or stay above water on the long curving beaches of this scenic nature reserve. Here at the island's southern tip, there's also a small maritime museum, a Maya ruin, and a lighthouse you can climb for a birds-eye view of the gorgeous surroundings (pages 30 and 48).

◖ San Gervasio: Smack dab in the middle of the island, Cozumel's best and biggest Maya ruin is thought to be dedicated to Ixchel, the goddess of fertility; in ancient times, it attracted women from all over the Yucatán seeking her favor (page 35).

◖ Playa Palancar: This low-key *playa* is the mellowest of Cozumel's main beach clubs. Nearby, the massive Palancar reef dive site has something for everyone. No matter where you go, you'll enjoy rich coral and vibrant sealife (page 46).

◖ Playa Chen Río: Heavy surf makes most of Cozumel's east side unswimmable, except here, where a rocky arm forms a calm natural pool. Come midweek to have it all to yourself, or on a Sunday to *convivir* (literally, share life) with local families (page 50).

◖ Scuba Diving: There's truly no better reason to visit Cozumel than to go scuba diving, with spectacular coral reefs, rich sealife, and crystal-clear water (page 60).

◖ Snorkeling: Snorkeling is a great way to experience Cozumel's amazing underwater realm, whether on a tour or right from shore (page 63).

◖ Kiteboarding: Steady wind and surf conditions ranging from rough to relaxed make Cozumel an ideal place for kiteboarders of all levels (page 64).

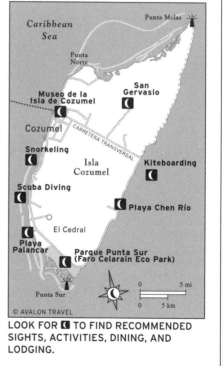

LOOK FOR ◖ TO FIND RECOMMENDED SIGHTS, ACTIVITIES, DINING, AND LODGING.

hiring a taxi, and circumnavigating the island is a popular and memorable way to appreciate Cozumel's many features.

HISTORY

Cozumel has been inhabited since 300 BC and was one of three major Maya pilgrimage sites in the region (the others were Chichén Itzá and Izamal in Yucatán state). The name is derived from the island's Maya name, Cuzamil (Land of Swallows). The height of its pre-Hispanic occupation was AD 1250-1500, when Putún people (also known as the Chontol or Itzás, the same group who built Chichén Itzá's most famous structures) dominated the region as seafaring merchants. Capitan Don Juan

PIRATES OF THE CARIBBEAN

For most of the colonial era, pirates were a major and constant threat to ships and port towns throughout the Yucatán Peninsula. They launched attacks from Laguna Bacalar and Isla Cozumel to present-day Laguna de Términos and Ciudad del Carmen on Campeche's Gulf coast—all serving as virtual pirate colonies. (Cozumel became so popular with pirates that the island, whose native population was decimated early on by disease and slavery, was not repopulated until the 1840s.) Some of the region's more notorious and colorful nemeses include:

Henry Morgan and Jean Lafitte: Pirates who used Isla Cozumel as a refuge and a base to launch attacks on the Yucatecan mainland and various Caribbean islands. Lafitte is said to have often used Isla de la Pasión's safe harbors to hide from pursuers.

Pierre de Sanfroy: A French corsair who occupied Cozumel's small village for several weeks in 1579, making the church his home, including sleeping on the altar, and harassing the local townspeople.

Francisco de Molas: Said to have lived on present-day Isla Holbox for nearly four decades, attacking ships that approached looking for drinking water. The story goes that Molas had an African slave help him bury his treasure, then killed him so that his ghost would watch over the spot. Islanders say a wailing disembodied head haunts the island, and that the name Holbox is an alteration of the Maya term "pool box," or Black Head.

Lorencillo: Born Laurent de Graff, the French buccaneer is best known for attacking Campeche City in 1685 with a pirate army of 700 men and holding the city ransom for two months. According to legend, he was captured in Valladolid after being lured there by a woman he captured on a ship. Held in the Ex-Convento San Bernardino, he was rescued by his crew before authorities could jail or execute him.

Peg Leg: Cornelius Jol was one of the first privateers known to use a wooden prosthetic—and to go by the now-iconic pirate name. Technically an admiral in the Dutch navy, Peg Leg terrorized Spanish and Portuguese ships and ports, including a 10-ship assault on Campeche City in 1663.

Other notable pirates who sailed Yucatán's waters and figure in the region's lore include Sir Francis Drake, John Hawkins, Michel de Grammond, and Jacobo Jackson.

de Grijalva arrived on the island in 1518 and dubbed it Isla de Santa Cruz, marking the beginning of the brutal dislocation of the native people by Spanish explorers and conquistadors. It eventually was overrun by British and Dutch pirates who used it as a base of operations. By the mid-1800s, however, the island was virtually uninhabited. The henequen, chicle, and coconut-oil booms attracted a new wave of people to the Quintana Roo territory (it didn't become a state until 1974), and Cozumel slowly rebounded, this time with a mostly Mexican mestizo population.

Isla Cozumel benefited mightily from the worldwide popularity of Jacques Cousteau's groundbreaking underwater films and television programs of the late 1950s. Although Cozumel was not the setting of those early productions (a commonly held myth), they inspired many similar films, including at least one Mexican movie set in Cozumel that was popular in the United States. More importantly, Cousteau sparked excitement among travelers (and travel agents and magazine writers) for destinations like Cozumel. The island was well known among tourists by the time Cousteau first visited in the 1960s and gained even more exposure with the establishment of Cancún in the 1970s.

PLANNING YOUR TIME

Don't let the cruise ship hubbub on Avenida Rafael Melgar turn you off from the town altogether. Besides the fact that most of the hotels, dive shops, banks, and other services are here, the town itself has much to offer, including a pleasant central plaza and a great museum. Budget a day or two to rent a car and explore the rest of the island, including the beach clubs, Maya ruins, family-friendly ecoparks, and the wild beaches and deserted coastline of Cozumel's eastern side.

ORIENTATION

The town of San Miguel de Cozumel (aka "Downtown Cozumel") is located on the west side of the island. The main passenger ferry lands here, across from the central plaza.

Avenida Benito Juárez is one of the main streets in Downtown Cozumel, beginning at the central plaza, crossing town, and becoming the Carretera Transversal (Cross-Island Hwy.). The highway passes the turnoff to the San Gervasio ruins before intersecting with the coastal road. The coastal road follows Cozumel's eastern shore, which is dotted with a few beach clubs and restaurants. Rounding the southern tip, the road heads north along the west shore before becoming Avenida Rafael Melgar and returning to the central plaza. Continuing north, the road passes turnoffs to the airport and a country club before turning to dirt and eventually dead-ending.

Sights

Cozumel is a vibrant, fascinating place, with sights and attractions that appeal to visitors of all sorts. As an island—Mexico's third largest—surrounded by clear Caribbean waters and encircled by a marine reserve and one of the world's richest coral reefs, it's no surprise to find Cozumel's best attractions have something to do with the ocean. Case in point: the huge national park on the island's southern tip, with a lovely beach and outstanding snorkeling right from shore. Elsewhere, you can interact with dolphins, swim with stingrays, or visit a pearl farm, all with the added bonus of relaxing in the sun and sand as part of your visit. Even at inland attractions, the ocean still looms large, including at two excellent museums (one on the history of Cozumel, another on maritime navigation) and in the island's two impressive lighthouses. And yet Cozumel has plenty of sights that have nothing to do with the ocean, too. Chief among them are the Maya ruins of San Gervasio, considered to be one of the three most important religious pilgrimage sites in the ancient Maya world. A second ruin is much smaller, but is located in a historic village and can be visited as part of a horseback riding or ATV tour. Cozumel also has tequila tours, historic churches, art and history centers, and more and, of course, the town of San Miguel itself, including its attractive central park. Put together, Cozumel has a long and varied list of what-to-do options for anyone visiting the island.

DOWNTOWN COZUMEL
Parque Benito Juárez
Cozumel's central plaza is surprisingly peaceful considering the mass of humanity that disembarks at the ferry pier directly across the street and from the three cruise ship ports just down the road. Few foreign visitors take time to linger in the park itself, which has wood benches, tree-filled planters, a boxy clock tower, and busts of late Mexican president Benito Juárez and the state's namesake, General Andrés Quintana Roo. The city municipal building, occupying most of the plaza's east side, was beautifully restored in 2005, with an airy commercial center on the ground floor and civic offices above. And though the central plaza is in the middle of Cozumel's tourist corridor, it is still a place local families come to stroll about, especially on weekends, when live bands play in the central gazebo, and balloon and cotton candy vendors do a brisk trade.

◖ Museo de la Isla de Cozumel
The town's small but excellent museum, **Museo**

DOWNTOWN COZUMEL WALKING TOUR

Begin and end your walking tour at **Parque Benito Juárez,** the main downtown plaza. It has comfortable shaded benches and convenient shopping in **Plaza del Sol,** an open-air commercial center.

The **passenger ferry pier** is just across the street, with a large, lovely sculpture of swallows in flight. From there, walk north on Avenida Melgar, along the waterfront and past additional sculptures.

Between Calles 4 and 6 is the outstanding **Museo de la Isla Cozumel,** whose exhibits on the island's history and ecology are well worth a stop.

Leaving the museum, continue on Avenida Melgar for another two blocks to **Los Cinco Soles,** one of the best and biggest all-around souvenir and *artesanía* shop on the island.

Walk one block inland and return south on Avenida 10; at Calle 4 you'll pass **Zermatt** with its tantalizing pastries and breads. Continuing south you'll also pass **Kinta,** a high-end Mexican restaurant, and the more low-brow (but no less recommended) **Wet Wendy's.**

Turn left (east) on Avenida Benito Juárez and head one block to **Iglesia San Miguel,** the main church; step in to appreciate its beautiful interior artwork.

For a treat, continue east on Avenida Benito Juárez for two blocks and turn right on Ave-

nida 20. Toward the end of the block is **Nacho Crazy Boy,** serving delicious made-to-order smoothies from the owner's front porch.

Continue south to the corner and then head east, on Calle 1, to Cozumel's small, tidy **Mercado Municipal.** It's a great place to buy fresh fruit or grab something to eat at one of the small lunch stands.

Head back toward the water on Avenida Adolfo Rosado Salas. At the corner of Avenida 5 is **Pro Dive Cozumel,** an excellent diving and snorkeling shop. A block south is **Puro Mar,** also good for swimwear and watersports.

Walk one more block west to the waterfront and Avenida Melgar. This corridor has numerous shops catering to cruise ship passengers, and is often packed with shoppers. For more shopping, head south 2.5 blocks to **Punta Laguna,** a large airy mall across from the **Punta Langosta** cruise ship pier.

To return to Parque Benito Juárez, cut one block inland to Avenida 10, which is quieter than Avenida Melgar and has several great eateries, including **Sabores, Del Sur,** and **New Especias,** all near the corner of Avenida 10 and Calle 3.

Back in Parque Benito Juárez, relax over a cold beer and snacks at **Casa Denis,** the oldest operating restaurant on the island, overlooking on the square.

de la Isla de Cozumel (Av. Rafael Melgar at Calle 6, tel. 987/872-1434, 9am-5pm Mon.-Sat., 9am-4pm Sun., US$3, free child 8 and under), is on the waterfront in what was once a turn-of-the-20th-century hotel. Well-composed exhibits in English and Spanish describe the island's wildlife, coral reefs, and the fascinating, sometimes tortured, history of human presence here, from the Maya pilgrims who came to worship the fertility goddess to present-day survivors of devastating hurricanes. The museum also has a small bookstore and a library. For a good photo-op head to the terrace, which has a great view of the main drag, ferry pier, and—on a clear day—Playa del Carmen.

Iglesia San Miguel

Cozumel's main church, **Iglesia San Miguel** (Av. Benito Juárez at Av. 10, tel. 987/872-0972, 7am-noon and 2pm-8pm Mon.-Sat., 7am-9pm Sun.), is not one of the soaring stone cathedrals found in many other Mexican cities, but it's quite lovely all the same. The church has a high arched entryway and facade, yet is strangely easy to miss. Its location doesn't help: a short distance off the main plaza (rather than right on it) and at the busy intersection of the pedestrian walkway and Avenida 10. Step inside and you're treated to a quiet oasis of soft light and warm colors, with attractive tile floors and long wooden pews.

ISLA COZUMEL

© LIZA PRADO

Cozumel's pleasant, busy central plaza

The church is relatively new, completed in 1946 following a long campaign by the Mary Knoll sisters for its construction. The island's original church was destroyed in 1915 during the Mexican Revolution. A small statue of Saint Michael, said to have been unearthed by early island residents and which is the source of the town's name, is housed here.

NORTHWESTERN COZUMEL
Cozumel Pearl Farm

Located on a remote private island on Cozumel's northern shore, the **Cozumel Pearl Farm** (cell. tel. 984/114-9604, www.cozumel-pearlfarm.com, US$110 pp) is a new and fun place to spend a day and learn about these unique nature-made jewels. The six-hour trip includes touring the farm's facilities to learn how and why pearls form, how they are farmed and harvested, and snorkeling around the underwater installations. A barbecue lunch on the beach is included, plus time for relaxing in hammocks and "power snorkeling"—snorkeling while being tugged by a boat. Service is

friendly and professional; transportation also is included.

SOUTHWESTERN COZUMEL
◖ Parque Punta Sur
(Faro Celarain Eco Park)

Better known as Parque Punta Sur, **Faro Celarain Eco Park** (Carr. Costera Sur Km. 27, tel. 987/872-0914, www.cozumelparks.gob.mx, 9am-5pm daily, US$10 adult, US$5 child over 8) is a massive natural reserve on the southern tip of Cozumel. The park spans thousands of acres of coastal dunes, beaches, mangroves, and wetlands, and extends well out into the ocean, including large areas of coral reef. It's home to a vast array of land and sea creatures, including 30 types of seabirds and some huge crocodiles that live in the park's large inland lagoons. Toward the entrance, there's a small Maya ruin known as El Caracol, which dates to AD 1200, plus the park's famous lighthouse (which you can climb for great views) and a small but rewarding maritime museum. At the park's long, lovely beach—about a kilometer

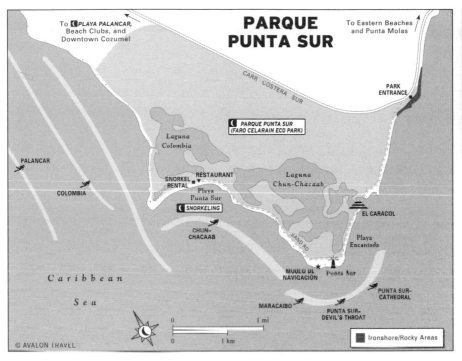

PARQUE PUNTA SUR

To **C** *PLAYA PALANCAR,*
Beach Clubs, and
Downtown Cozumel

To Eastern Beaches
and Punta Molas

PARK
ENTRANCE

CARR COSTERA SUR

C PARQUE PUNTA SUR
(FARO CELARAIN ECO PARK)

*Laguna
Colombia*

PALANCAR

COLOMBIA

SNORKEL
RENTAL

RESTAURANT

*Laguna
Chun-Chacaab*

*Playa
Punta Sur*

EL CARACOL

C SNORKELING

CHUN-
CHACAAB

*Playa
Encantada*

SAND RD.

C a r i b b e a n

S e a

MUSEO DE
NAVIGACIÓN

Punta Sur

PUNTA SUR-
CATHEDRAL

MARACAIBO

PUNTA SUR-
DEVIL'S THROAT

0   1 mi

0   1 km

Ironshore/Rocky Areas

© AVALON TRAVEL

past the lighthouse—there are beach chairs, restrooms, a small eatery, and a shop to rent snorkel gear (US$10) and kayaks. The snorkeling here is outstanding—the last time we were here we saw lobsters, puffer fish, and a huge array of tropical fish; there also is a dramatic sea fan "forest" that waves gently in the current. To get to it, and the best section of the bay for snorkeling, head to the western end of the bay. The staff at the rental kiosk can point out the easiest route to get there, with markers in the ocean and on land.

Most visitors are cruise ship passengers arriving on package tours, but it's perfectly easy to visit independently; there's even a separate area away from the volleyball nets and buffet lines for people arriving on their own. You'll need a car—there used to be shuttle service into the park, but no longer—and you should arrive no later than 1pm in order to take full advantage of all the park has to offer.

EL CARACOL

Located inside Parque Punta Sur, El Caracol is a small, conch-shaped structure that dates to AD 1200. It's believed to have been a lighthouse where Maya used smoke and flames to lead boats to safety. Small openings at the top of the structure also acted as whistles to alert Maya to approaching tropical storms and hurricanes. Admission to the park includes access to the ruin; visitors only interested in visiting the ruin must still pay full price.

MUSEO DE NAVIGACIÓN

Another interesting site within Parque Punta Sur is the Museo de Navigación, an excellent little maritime museum located next to the lighthouse. The displays include the history of regional trading, shipbuilding, piracy, and even an homage to the park's lighthouse keepers. Signage is in English and Spanish. Admission to the park includes entrance to this museum.

© LIZA PRADO

approaching the lighthouse at Cozumel's outstanding Parque Punta Sur

Parque Chankanaab

Some 9 kilometers (5.6 miles) south of town, **Parque Chankanaab** (Carr. Costera Sur Km. 9, tel. 987/872-0914, www.cozumelparks. gob.mx, 8am-5pm daily, US$21 adult, US$14 child under 12) is a national park that operates mainly as a beach club and water park; that is to say, more Xcaret than Punta Sur. A visit here includes sunbathing by the pool, snorkeling in the ocean, relaxing in a hammock, and watching the sea lion and dolphin shows (included in the ticket price). **Dolphin Discovery** (toll-free Mex. tel. 800/727-5391, www.dolphindiscovery.com) has a facility within the park, with various interactive programs with dolphins, as well as manatees and sea lions, for an additional fee. Reserve in advance or right upon arrival, as spots fill up fast. Chankanaab also has a fully equipped dive shop on-site, plus two thatch-roofed restaurants, a handful of gift shops, lockers, and restrooms. Chankanaab may be a bit commercialized for independent travelers—consider

Punta Sur instead—but it's a great option for families looking for an easy all-day option.

Stingray Beach

Families with kids are sure to enjoy **Stingray Beach** (Carr. Costera Sur Km. 2.8, tel. 987/872-4932, www.stingraybeach.com, 7am-5pm, last tour at 3pm, US$59 adult, US$34 child). An interactive experience, it starts with a half-hour stingray "encounter," where you can hold, feed, and pet stingrays in a shallow enclosure. Stingrays are silky smooth yet surprisingly strong and agile, and holding one is like holding a giant, squirming bar of soap. You spend the next half hour snorkeling in a larger, deeper (9-18 feet) area, which is filled with stingrays and myriad tropical fish. Needless to say, the experience is best when you're part of a smaller group; ask which days are slowest when you book. Afterward, you're welcome to hang out in the small beach club, though it's rather exposed to the nearby roadway.

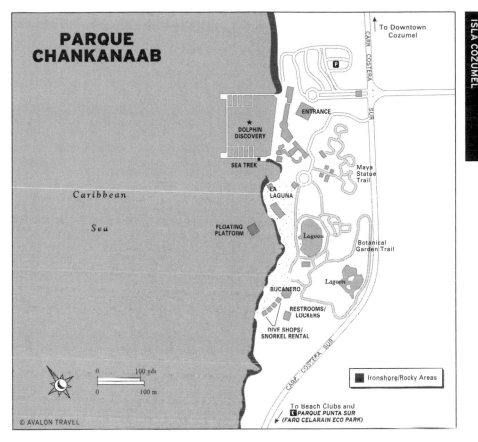

El Cedral

El Cedral is the "other town" on Cozumel, a sleepy village south of San Miguel that's home to a modest Maya structure of the same name as well as a small historic church. It's got a pleasant central plaza and a large *palapa* where souvenir stands are normally set up. Tour operators, including horseback riding guides, often bring visitors to town to visit the ruin and church, and to peruse the souvenirs.

Although overshadowed by San Miguel today, El Cedral is actually the older settlement on the island. It was here that a group of 18 families of indigenous Christian converts fled in 1847 to escape persecution by fellow Maya during the War of the Castes. They came bearing a small wooden cross known as Santa Cruz de Sabán (Holy Cross of Sabán) and founded their church and village alongside a Maya temple that they discovered just inland from their landing site. The group was led by Casimiro Cárdenas, whose descendants still serve as caretakers, or *mayordomos,* of the temple and church; there's a statue of Don Casimiro in the central plaza.

El Cedral is famous for its Fiesta de la Santa Cruz (Festival of the Holy Cross), a 10-day blowout celebration of the Catholic holy cross that begins April 24 and culminates on May 3. The celebration includes food, music,

© H.W. PRADO

A dolphin takes a bow at Parque Chankanaab's interactive dolphin park, Dolphin Discovery.

dance, performances, rodeo, and fireworks aplenty, and even some traditions of distant Maya origin. The party is open to everyone, including tourists, and makes for a fun and fascinating outing if your visit happens to coincide with it.

To get to the town, look for a well-marked turnoff just south of Playa San Francisco that leads 5 kilometers (3.1 miles) to the village. El Cedral's Maya ruin (8am-5pm daily, free) is small and underwhelming, though it still bears a few traces of the original paint and stucco. The church is directly adjacent and contains the original wooden cross borne by El Cedral's founders.

Tequila Tours

Tequila is not produced in Cozumel. For one thing, the soil isn't suitable for growing the huge blue agave cacti from which tequila is made. No less importantly, like champagne in France, the famous drink can only be legally manufactured in select areas of Mexico, mostly in the western state of Jalisco (including the town of Tequila). But you can still learn about how tequila is made at interesting and worthwhile "tequila tours" around the island, where you'll also get a chance to sample unique and high-end varieties.

Mi Mexico Lindo (El Cedral, tel. 987/869 1909, 8am-5pm Mon.-Sat., free) has two locations, but the one in the small community of El Cedral has a more agreeable atmosphere. (The other is along the coastal highway south of town.) English-speaking guides walk you through a leafy garden with various tools, machines, and displays related to tequila production, from colonial times to the modern day. The half-hour tour ends with a sampling of the mother distillery's best products, including terrific "infused" tequilas, with flavors like *jamaica* (hibiscus) and even coffee.

Hacienda Antigua (Cross-Island Hwy. Km. 9, tel. 987/869-4677, 9am-5pm daily, US$14) has a more formalized tour, crossing first through a small field of agave plants to an open-air display of artifacts related to tequila production, from clay urns used by indigenous

© LIZA PRADO

the church at El Cedral, a small town with a long and fascinating history

people to ferment local fruits, to the three-stage copper distilleries introduced by the Spanish. Tastings and an opportunity to buy some bottles follow. It's an interesting and informative tour, with a more spacious tour area, but it's hard to justify spending US$14 when others offer essentially the same thing for free. Last tour is at 4pm.

Discover Mexico Park

Discover Mexico Park (Carr. Costera Sur Km. 5.5, 8am-4pm Mon.-Sat., US$20 adult, US$10 child) boasts hundreds of enthusiastic reviews from visitors, but we're hard pressed to understand the appeal. Exhibits include a video on Mexican history, scale-models of various iconic Mexican structures (the cathedral in Mexico City, the pyramid at Chichén Itzá, etc.), a gallery of Mexican folk art, and, of course, plenty of opportunities for eating, drinking, and shopping. The center's tour guides are peppy and well informed, and Mexican art never fails to impress, but the overall experience is too gimmicky to be truly satisfying.

EASTERN COZUMEL
◖ San Gervasio

San Gervasio (www.cozumelparks.org.mx, 8am-4pm daily, US$8) is Cozumel's primary Maya ruin, the largest of more than 30 archaeological sites identified around the island. It's the only ruin that's a full-fledged visitor's attraction; two other sites—El Cedral, located in a village of the same name, and El Caracol in Punta Sur National Park—are small but interesting stops as part of a visit to their surrounding areas. The rest of Cozumel's ruins are unexcavated, inaccessible, or both.

Archaeologists believe the area around San Gervasio was populated as early as AD 300 and remained so through the general Maya collapse (AD 800-900) and well into the Spanish conquest. Most of the structures that can be visited date from the city's later eras; that is, from AD 1000 and later, periods known as the Terminal Classic and Post-Classic periods. Early archaeologists excavating the ruins found a crypt containing 50 skeletons along with numerous Spanish beads; the bodies are thought to be

IXCHEL AND THE PILGRIMAGE TO CUZAMIL

According to ancient Maya faith and cosmology, the goddess Ixchel ruled over matters of fertility, childbirth, and healing. She appears in some texts as an old woman holding an upturned pot, with water pouring from it, which may represent a pregnant woman and the bursting of the amniotic sac. Ixchel is also associated with the moon, which is not unrelated to questions of fertility, and appears in some texts as a young woman holding a rabbit (a common symbol for the moon).

That Ixchel meant different things to different people is no surprise: She was venerated by Maya, especially women, throughout Mesoamerica and over centuries. The common thread in Ixchel devotees was the need to take a pilgrimage, at least once in one's life, to Ixchel's shrine and sanctuary on the island of Cuzamil (the island's Maya name).

It's believed that hundreds of thousands of Maya women, possibly millions, made the journey to Isla Cozumel. They came from as far away as Campeche and Tabasco, converging on the natural inlet and port of Pole, known today as Xcaret. There, the pilgrims would have boarded long dugout canoes to make the 12-mile trip from the mainland to the island. It would have been a dangerous journey, buffeted by powerful currents and sudden winds.

Once on the island, the women would likely have followed raised stone roads called *sacbé* to the inland temple-city known today as San Gervasio. Archaeologists are puzzled why the temples at San Gervasio are so modest, considering their apparent significance; theories abound, but the answer remains a mystery. It's unlikely the pilgrims lingered—just a day or two, enough time to address the goddess, leave an offering, and gather strength for the long journey home.

© H.W. PRADO

remains of a small temple or residence at San Gervasio, Cozumel's most accessible Maya ruin

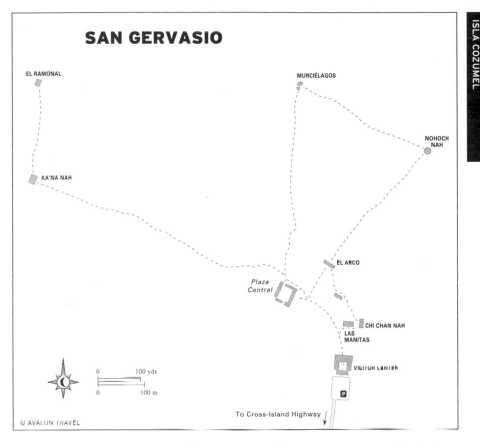

SAN GERVASIO

EL RAMONAL

MURCIÉLAGOS

NOHOCH NAH

KA'NA NAH

EL ARCO

Plaza Central

CHI CHAN NAH

LAS MANITAS

VISITOR CENTER

P

To Cross-Island Highway

0   100 yds

0   100 m

© AVALON TRAVEL

those of 16th-century Maya who died from diseases brought by the conquistadors.

Most of San Gervasio's buildings are modest by Maya standards, stout square affairs with even shorter than normal doors. This style, known as *oratorio*, is common throughout the island and almost certainly developed in response to climatic imperatives: Anything built here needed to withstand the hurricanes that have pummeled Cozumel for millennia. It may also be a reflection of Cozumel's role as a trading hub; the island is crisscrossed with stone roadways known as *sacbé*, and it stands to reason the leaders here were more concerned with transporting products than constructing grand temples.

The entire site at San Gervasio is quite large, with four separate zones spanning several square kilometers. Visitors are restricted to just one zone, but there's still a lot to see. The public area has three building groups—Las Manitas, Plaza Central, and Murciélagos—with over a dozen structures in all. The clusters are connected by trails through the forest, tracing the routes of the original *sacbé*.

LAS MANITAS

Entering the site, the first group of buildings includes one of the site's most famous structures. Las Manitas (Little Hands) got its name for the red handprints still visible on one of its walls. Archaeologists believe Las Manitas was a royal

© H.W. PRADO

San Gervasio was one of the most important religious pilgrimage sites in the ancient Maya world.

residence used by one of San Gervasio's kings, Ah Huneb Itza, and possibly others. It has an older inner room and a newer, more open outer room; most likely, the newer part was added simply to provide the royal residents more space and comfort. Just east of Las Manitas is the diminutive structure called **Chi Chan Nah** (literally, "small house"). The smallest structure in San Gervasio, its exact purpose is unknown, though it was likely used as a private chapel for whoever was living in Las Manitas. Nearby is a platform dubbed **La Tumba** (The Tomb), named for the large crypt discovered beneath it.

PLAZA CENTRAL
Bearing left, the trail leads to the Plaza Central, which served as the seat of power in San Gervasio's latest era, from AD 1200 onward. Surrounding the courtyard are various low structures, in various states of decay. Entering the plaza from the direction of Las Manitas, the building on your right is known as **Las Columnas** (The Columns), named for the series

of columns that likely held up a wood-beam roof. The building probably served as a residence or gathering place, though archaeologists also discovered several tombs beneath its floor.

Many more remains were found in a mass grave in front of a structure known as **El Osario** (The Ossuary, or Bone Room), located on the southern side of the central plaza. El Osario itself is a relatively modest structure, and probably served as a temple for ceremonies and rituals. In front of it, a mass grave contained more than 50 bodies. The presence of Spanish beads suggests the victims died of smallpox, which swept across the island not long after the first European contact, devastating the native population.

Past El Osario, in the southwest corner of the plaza, is **El Palacio** (The Palace), another large structure with columns and open on one side that likely served as a place for public gatherings and pronouncements. Nearby is a structure called **Los Murales,** named for the fading murals that were visible when archaeologists first documented the site. Shadows of red, yellow, and black are still visible in some areas.

KA'NA NAH

A pathway leads west from the central plaza to San Gervasio's largest and most important structure, a large pyramid-like temple known as Ka'na Nah (Tall House). It's widely believed to have been a shrine to Ixchel, the Maya goddess of fertility, and as such would have been a major destination for pilgrims arriving from all over Mesoamerica. In its heyday, the temple was covered in stucco and painted red, blue, green, and black. Hints of red and blue are still visible in a few spots.

The general decrepitude of this structure (and others at San Gervasio) may strike some as odd. After all, most date to AD 1200 or later—quite recent in archaeological terms. Structures at certain other sites show far better workmanship, especially the cutting and fitting of stones, and they remain in much better shape today, despite being hundreds of years older. It's tempting to blame hurricanes, but there's a far more direct culprit: stucco. Developed rather late in the Maya timeline, the Maya used it with gusto, covering structures large and small with a hard smooth cap that could then be painted in bright colors. There was no longer a need for the underlying stones to be so precisely cut and fit, and Maya masonry declined. Of course, over the centuries, the stucco eventually wore away, leaving many newer structures appearing older than their pre-stucco predecessors.

MURCIÉLAGOS

Returning to the central plaza, a trail heading north leads 500 meters (0.3 mile) to the Murciélagos (Bats) group. This was the royal residence before Las Manitas was built. The circular structure adjacent to Murciélagos is called **Pet Nah,** and likely served as a place for private ceremonies and rituals.

NOHOCH NAH

The path continues to another building, this one known as Nohoch Nah (Large House). Built atop a platform, it's a boxy but serene

temple. With an interior altar, the temple might have been used by religious pilgrims to make an offering upon entering or leaving San Gervasio. It was originally covered in stucco and painted a multitude of colors.

EL ARCO

Continuing on the same path back toward the site's entrance, you'll pass through El Arco (The Arch), which served as an entrance to (or exit from) this section of the city. The Maya never developed a "true" archway, which uses a keystone, but managed to construct remarkably resilient arches using the corbeled method of stacking flat stones on either side of an opening, each stone slightly overlapping the previous one, until they meet in the middle (or can be spanned by a long capstone).

PRACTICALITIES

San Gervasio is located in the middle of the island, just off the Cross-Island Highway at Kilometer 7.5. It is open 8am-4pm daily. Admission is US$8.

Guides can be hired at the visitors center for a fixed rate: US$20 for a one-hour tour in Spanish, English, French, or German. Prices are per group, which can include up to four people. Tips are customary and are not included in the price.

Faro Punta Molas

Gnarled but functional, Faro Punta Molas is a red- and white-striped lighthouse rising dramatically from the rocky northeastern tip of Cozumel. It is all the more striking for the long journey that's typically required to even lay eyes on it. This is the forgotten corner of Cozumel; the only road here is an unpaved track that extends 20-something miles through coastal scrub forest and is infamous for its deep ruts and wheel-swallowing sand traps. Getting there by boat is easier, of course, and a few dive shops will swing by if they're going to dive sites on Cozumel's northern or eastern side. The lighthouse is manned by Mexican soldiers, who will usually allow visitors to climb to the top to snap a few photos and take in the bracing views. Punta Molas is named after Miguel

Molas, a 19th-century Spanish soldier and cartographer who mapped the island. Contrary to some claims, Punta Molas is not the easternmost point of Mexico—that distinction goes to the southeastern tip of Isla Mujeres, which beats Punta Molas by a hair.

Castillo Real

Castillo Real is a partially excavated Maya ruin

with a temple, two chambers, and a lookout tower. It is believed to have been a watchtower to protect against approaching enemies. It's located on the remote northeastern corner of the island, along the sand road leading to Punta Molas. The road is quite treacherous—even ATVs and motorcycles can have trouble making it. Ask at the tourist office for the latest before making any plans to head up there.

Beaches and Beach Clubs

Cozumel isn't famous for its beaches, but it is not without several beautiful stretches of sand. The best beaches are on the protected southwestern coast, with soft white sand and calm azure waters. These are occupied by large beach clubs, which have conveniences like lounge chairs, umbrellas, restrooms, restaurants, and water sports; a few even have swimming pools. Most beach clubs charge either a cover or a minimum consumption, but neither is exorbitant. The clubs cater to cruise shippers and range from peaceful and low-key to boisterous and loud. Independent travelers are perfectly welcome too, of course.

The handful of beach clubs on the northwestern coast are much smaller, because the beaches themselves are much smaller. The exception is Isla de la Pasión, a hard-to-reach island with a huge beach used mostly by cruise ship passengers.

Beaches on Cozumel's east side are wild and picturesque, with virtually no development beyond a few small restaurants. The surf can be fierce here, though a few sheltered areas have good swimming and are popular with locals. The municipal government has been steadily improving the road on the east side, including adding signs, stairways, and parking, but it remains a far different experience than the westside beach clubs.

NORTHWESTERN COZUMEL

Cozumel's northwestern shore has a few pocket beaches amid long stretches of ironshore, and

some resorts in this area have created private beaches using containment walls and imported sand. The exception is Isla de la Pasión, a private island sporting a kilometer of white sand that's one of Cozumel's best beaches (and most expensive beach clubs).

Playa Azul

Playa Azul Hotel Beach Club (Zona Hotelera Nte. Km. 4, tel. 987/869-5160, www.playa-azul.com, 10am-6pm Tues.-Sun., US$4.25 minimum consumption) is about as low-key as beach clubs get, with a calm compact beach and a cluster of basic lounge chairs and umbrellas. There's decent snorkeling offshore (watch for areas of very shallow coral), and you can rent needed gear, as well as kayaks and stand-up paddleboards, from the club's small sports kiosk. The nearby swimming pool and second beach area are for hotel guests only, however. The beach is typically uncrowded, especially before 2pm.

Playa San Juan

Tucked behind a long-delayed resort construction project, **Buccanos Beach Club** (Zona Hotelera Nte. Km. 4.5, tel. 987/872-0100, www.buccanos.com, 9am-5pm Sun.-Thurs., 9am-11pm Fri.-Sat., $8.50 minimum consumption) belies its somewhat shoddy surroundings, with a large, clean pool just steps from the beach and a better than average restaurant. The beach here is loaded with shells, and there's good snorkeling right off the shore. (Be aware

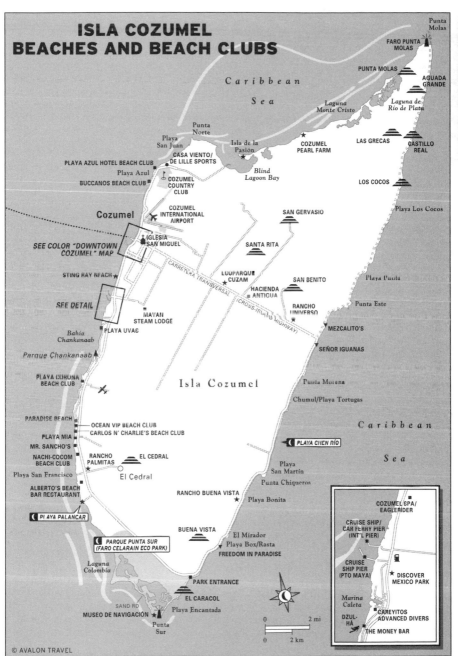

ISLA COZUMEL
BEACHES AND BEACH CLUBS

Caribbean

Sea

Punta Molas

FARO PUNTA MOLAS

PUNTA MOLAS

AGUADA GRANDE

Laguna Monte Cristo

Laguna de Río de Plata

Punta Norte

Playa San Juan

Isla de la Pasión

COZUMEL PEARL FARM

LAS GRECAS

CASTILLO REAL

CASA VIENTO/ DE LILLE SPORTS

PLAYA AZUL HOTEL BEACH CLUB

Playa Azul

Blind Lagoon Bay

LOS COCOS

BUCCANOS BEACH CLUB

COZUMEL COUNTRY CLUB

Cozumel

COZUMEL INTERNATIONAL AIRPORT

SAN GERVASIO

Playa Los Cocos

SEE COLOR "DOWNTOWN COZUMEL" MAP

IGLESIA SAN MIGUEL

SANTA RITA

STING RAY BEACH

CARRETERA TRANSVERSAL

LUUPARQUE CUZAM

SAN BENITO

Playa Punta

SEE DETAIL

HACIENDA ANTIGUA

Punta Este

MAYAN STEAM LODGE

RANCHO UNIVERSO

Bahia Chankanaab

PLAYA UVAS

(CROSS-ISLAND HIGHWAY)

MEZCALITO'S

Parque Chankanaab

SEÑOR IGUANAS

PLAYA CORONA BEACH CLUB

Isla Cozumel

Punta Morena

Caribbean

Chumul/Playa Tortugas

PARADISE BEACH

OCEAN VIP BEACH CLUB

CARLOS N' CHARLIE'S BEACH CLUB

PLAYA CHEN RÍO

Sea

PLAYA MIA

MR. SANCHO'S

NACHI-COCOM BEACH CLUB

RANCHO PALMITAS

EL CEDRAL

Playa San Martín

Playa San Francisco

El Cedral

Punta Chiqueros

ALBERTO'S BEACH BAR RESTAURANT

RANCHO BUENA VISTA

Playa Bonita

PLAYA PALANCAR

BUENA VISTA

El Mirador

Playa Box/Rasta

PARQUE PUNTA SUR (FARO CELARAIN ECO PARK)

FREEDOM IN PARADISE

Laguna Colombia

PARK ENTRANCE

SAND RD

EL CARACOL

MUSEO DE NAVIGACIÓN

Playa Encantada

Punta Sur

COZUMEL SPA/ EAGLERIDER

CRUISE SHIP/ CAR FERRY PIER (INT'L PIER)

CRUISE SHIP PIER (PTO MAYA)

DISCOVER MEXICO PARK

Marina Caleta

CAREYITOS ADVANCED DIVERS

DZUL-HÁ

THE MONEY BAR

0   2 mi

0   2 km

© AVALON TRAVEL

ISLA COZUMEL

CRUISING TO COZUMEL

Cozumel is one of the most popular ports of call in the world, receiving an extraordinary number of cruise ships in its ports every year. Cruise ships and their passengers are responsible for a whopping 70 percent of the island's tourism revenue. And yet Cozumel doesn't feel overrun with cruise ship passengers; except for heavy foot traffic along Avenida Melgar, long queues of waiting taxi cabs, and the occasional air horn, it's possible for independent travelers to forget how outnumbered they are. A few stats about this all-important part of Cozumel's landscape and history include:

- Arrival of the first cruise ship: 1968

- Inauguration of the first cruise ship pier: 1980 (International Pier)

- Current ports of arrival: Punta Langosta, Puerto Maya, and International Pier

- Number of cruise ships to arrive per day: 1-8, typically Monday-Saturday

- Cruise ships scheduled to arrive in 2013: 869

- Number of cruise ship passengers scheduled to arrive in 2013: 2,488,000

- Passengers per ship: 560-5,400

- Ratio of passengers to cruise ship staff (approximate): 3:1

- Time spent on the island: 7-10 hours

- Schedule of arrivals (and more): www.cruiseportinsider.com

cruise ships lined up at Cozumel's large piers

© LIZA PRADO

of the current, and hungry fish accustomed to handouts!) Lockers and showers are a welcome feature, and there's kayaking, parasailing, wave runners, even a rock climbing wall. All in all, it's a good value.

Isla de la Pasión

One of Cozumel's loveliest beaches is **Isla de la Pasión** (no phone, www.isla-pasion.com, US$65 adult, US$40 child), a privately owned island and beach club just off Cozumel's north shore. Although marketed almost exclusively to cruise ship passengers, anyone can sign up for a package tour, which includes a buffet, open bar, and free beach activities. The beach is gorgeous—one of Corona's beer commercials was filmed here—and the island is covered, oddly enough, with wispy pine trees. (Scientists believe their seeds somehow came from the Atlantic coast of the United States.) The price is a bit steep, but the main bummer is you only get four hours at the beach.

It's possible, though not easy or really recommendable, to visit Isla de la Pasión on your own; the beach itself is public, after all, and you can stay as long as you like. From the northern end of Avenida Rafael Melgar, a dirt road continues 5 kilometers (3.1 miles) past a water treatment plant to the port at Bahía Ciega. (The road isn't bad, but drive carefully as your rental vehicle's insurance is probably void here.) At the port, ask around for a fisherman to take you across (around US$10, 20 minutes). Be sure to arrange a time for him to return and cross your fingers he's got a good memory; otherwise, you'll be left begging a ride back with a tour group. Bring food, water, and an umbrella—you won't be allowed to use the beach club facilities, but there's plenty of beach to lay out a towel. If you do book a tour, you can save US$20 per person by getting to the port yourself.

SOUTHWESTERN COZUMEL

The majority of beach clubs are clustered on Playa San Francisco, a three-kilometer (1.9-mile) stretch of white-sand beach that begins just south of the Aura Cozumel all-inclusive resort. Another beach, Playa Palancar, is farther south, near the tip of the island, and has a beach club of the same name.

The Money Bar

The Money Bar (Carr. Costera Sur Km. 6.5, tel. 987/869-5141, www.moneybarbeachclub.com, 8am-10pm daily, no cover) sits alongside one of the best shore snorkeling sites on the island, Dzul-Ha, which makes it a popular stop. By itself, though, it's a nice restaurant with amazing sunset views and an assortment of packages that makes spending a half day here easy. Packages start at US$30 with "The Peso" (includes a guided snorkel tour, lunch, and a cocktail) and run to US$95 with "The Yen" (includes a 2-tank dive trip, a 30-minute massage from a licensed masseuse, lunch, and a cocktail). Meals, drinks, and activities also can be ordered à la carte; happy hour features 2-for-1 drinks 5pm-7pm, and there's live music most Sundays starting at 6pm. There's not much of beach here, but if your plan is

© GARY CHANDLER

Isla de la Pasión is a popular shore excursion for cruise ship passengers.

Beach clubs on Cozumel's south side range from mellow to manic.

© H.W. PRADO

to explore the amazing waters and eat a good meal, this is a great option.

Playa Uvas

Though showing its age, **Playa Uvas** (Carr. Costera Sur Km. 8.5, cell. tel. 987/103-5504, www.playauvas.com, 8am-4pm Mon.-Sat., US$12) is a decent spot if you're looking for beach club amenities but don't need lots of bells and whistles. The beach itself is small and a bit rocky—bring water shoes or prepare to walk on underwater sand bags—but it has plenty of lounge chairs and umbrellas. There's also waiter service that brings finger foods and a full bar to your beachfront perch. A small pool is a nice extra. The cover includes snorkel gear rental, use of the chairs and umbrellas, and a free drink; all-inclusive packages are available, too.

Playa Corona Beach Club

Playa Corona Beach Club (Carr. Costera Sur Km. 10, no phone, 9am-6pm daily, no cover) is more a beach shack restaurant than a club. But it provides access to excellent snorkeling with sea fans, healthy coral formations, lots of colorful tropical fish, and even lobsters just steps from shore. There's no cover charge, but guests are expected to buy something off the menu—ceviche and a cold beer are always a good bet. Clean bathrooms and freshwater showers are pluses. If you're looking for a sandy beach, keep heading south—you'll mostly find ironshore here (bring water shoes).

Playa Mia

Playa Mia (Carr. Costera Sur Km. 14.25, tel. 987/564-0960, www.playamia.com, 9am-6pm daily, US$40 with open bar, US$52 with open bar, buffet, towel, and snorkel gear) is big, busy, and energetic without being crass or obnoxious, like other clubs. The beach is decent, though often very crowded, and there's an excellent beach-side pool. The restaurant-buffet area is cool and pleasant, thanks to a high-peaked tent à la the Denver airport. And there's certainly no shortage of activities: volleyball, table tennis, kids' play structure, massage, snorkeling, parasailing, catamaran rides, water trampoline, even a huge inflatable "iceberg," and more.

Playa San Francisco

Playa San Francisco is Cozumel's longest stretch of white-sand beach, extending for three kilometers (1.9 miles) and accessible through various beach clubs.

OCEAN VIP BEACH CLUB

Ocean VIP Beach Club (Carr. Costera Sur Km. 14.25, tel. 987/869-2250, www.oceanbeachcozumel.com, 8am-9pm daily, US$50 adult all-inclusive, US$40 child all inclusive) tries to offer something for everyone—good lounge chairs and umbrellas for sitting on the beach, kayaks, Hobie cats, and snorkeling equipment for those looking for some activity, a decent restaurant and open bar, a pool for cooling off, and even a grassy area with a playground for little 'uns. It's a pleasant enough place but by trying to please every client, it feels somewhat scattered. If you can live with that for a day—and really, who can't?—this is a great value.

PARADISE BEACH

Paradise Beach (Carr. Costera Sur Km. 14.5, tel. 987/872-6177, www.paradise-beach-cozumel.com, 9am-sunset daily, $10 minimum consumption) has a gorgeous pool and a spacious picture-perfect beach, dotted with palm trees. Oddly, they charge US$2 for beach chairs and US$12 for use of the water sports gear, like kayaks, trampoline floats, paddleboards, and snorkel gear. Nevertheless, it's a lovely and not-too-raucous place to spend a day at the beach.

MR. SANCHO'S

All-inclusives can make life easy, even when you're just going to the beach. **Mr. Sancho's** (Carr. Costera Sur Km. 15, tel. 987/871-9174, www.mrsanchos.com, 9am-6pm daily, US$50 adult, US$45 teen, US$35 child) has a good Mexican restaurant, fairly mellow ambience, and plenty of extras, from snorkeling to massage. The beach is a bit narrow, meaning the lounge chairs are squeezed pretty tightly

together, but it's a lovely spot all the same, and a great option for a no-brainer beach day.

NACHI-COCOM BEACH CLUB

With an upper limit of 100 guests per day, **Nachi-Cocom Beach Club** (Carr. Costera Sur Km. 16.5, no phone, www.cozumelnachicocom.com, 9am-5pm daily, US$55 pp all-inclusive) offers an upscale and low-key beach experience. There's never a need to search for a lounge chair on the long stretch of manicured beach, much less wait for a staff person (they'll even walk out beers to you in the ocean). The all-inclusive plan covers an open bar, a four-course à la carte lunch, hammocks and *palapas*, as well as a well-maintained pool and Jacuzzi. Motorized water sports rentals and snorkeling trips are available for an extra fee. This is a perfect place to spend a day reading, sleeping in the shade, or watching your kids make sand castles.

CARLOS N' CHARLIE'S BEACH CLUB

One in a string of beach clubs on Playa San Francisco, **Carlos n' Charlie's Beach Club** (Carr. Costera Sur Km. 16.5, tel. 987/564-0960, www.carlosandcharlies.com, 10am-4pm daily, no cover) is a loud, bustling place with customers guzzling yard-long drinks and dancing on the tables. The beach is packed with beach chairs and umbrellas, while the water is dotted with ocean toys like water trampolines, wave runner rentals, and banana boat rides. If you're looking to party hard, look no further.

ALBERTO'S BEACH BAR RESTAURANT

Alberto's Beach Bar Restaurant (Carr. Costera Sur Km. 18, tel. 987/876-1394, www.albertosbeachbar.com, 10am-10pm daily, no cover) is a low-frills beach club on a decent stretch of beach near the entrance to El Cedral. There are snorkeling tours (US$40 pp), Jet Ski rentals ($60 for 30 minutes), and even fishing charters (US$335 for 4 hours, US$490 for 6 hours) available. The restaurant serves an extensive selection of fresh seafood; it's a bit pricey for the location (think plastic chairs and peeling paint) but in keeping with

ISLA COZUMEL

© LIZA PRADO

Playa Palancar is a great spot for a low-key beach day.

neighboring clubs. Sunset dinners are especially nice for couples, when the staff lights tiki lamps and sets up tables right next to the ocean. On Tuesdays and Thursdays there's live music 6pm-10pm.

☾ Playa Palancar

With a calm atmosphere to match the calm turquoise waters, **Playa Palancar** (Carr. Costera Sur Km. 19.5, no phone, 8am-5pm daily, no cover or minimum consumption) is just the place to relax in a hammock under a palm tree or dig into a long book while digging your toes into the thick white sand. Playa Palancar has gotten busier over the years, now with music and even parasailing, but it's still the mellowest of Cozumel's main beach clubs. And there happens to be great diving and snorkeling at nearby Palancar and Colombia reefs; an on-site dive shop offers fun dives (US$65/90 one/two tanks) and guided snorkeling trips (US$35-45, 60-90 minutes), with daily departures at 9am, noon, and 2pm. Snorkel gear can be rented separately (US$10), but there's not much to see

close to shore. A *palapa*-roofed restaurant serves classic Mexican seafood and a wide range of drinks (US$5-16). The club is 750 meters (0.5 mile) off the main road.

EASTERN COZUMEL

Cozumel's east side is essentially the opposite of the west: Where the west is mostly developed with pockets of untouched areas, the east is mostly undeveloped with just a smattering of construction. Where the water on the west side is calm and glassy, the ocean on the east side roils and rages, huge slabs of water crashing onto the undulating shore at all angles. And while on the west side you can catch glimpses of the mainland, and huge cruise ships glide by close enough to see the passengers' faces in the cabin windows, the view from the east side is the wide-open ocean, broken only by the occasional far-off ship or approaching storm out on the horizon. This means that while you'll find sandy beaches and restaurant-bars with swinging stools, fresh fish tacos, and cocktails with racy names, the atmosphere on the east side

DEVELOPMENT OF THE NORTHEAST

The northeast corner of Cozumel is a wild and beautiful place that's home to mangroves and micro-atolls: delicate ecosystems vital to the island's bird and fish population. It's an area totally unpopulated by people, with access requiring a four-wheel-drive vehicle and lots of patience.

But untouched doesn't equal forgotten. Cozumel's northeast is the focus of considerable interest, especially by real estate developers and environmentalists. For years, there have been rumors and rumblings of its development, though few hard details. Recently, a US$7 billion project named Punta Arrecifes Resort has gained traction—and attracted critique. A 12.7-kilometer (7.9-mile) strip of beachfront property would include over 600 hotel rooms and villas (expanding to as much as 5,850 units in subsequent phases), two marinas, a golf course, an equestrian center, even a private airstrip. Perhaps to forestall environmental objections, the plans also include a windmill farm and a marine wildlife center.

There are some big players behind the project. The land is owned by the Barbachano family, which owns premier properties throughout the Yucatán (the Barbachanos owned the land upon which Chichén Itzá sits until 2010, when it was sold to the state of Yucatán). The Trump Organization also is rumored to have a hand in the project.

If the project moves forward, it will no doubt create employment opportunities for locals. But is it worth the cost of putting the island's environment at risk? That's the dilemma facing Cozumeleños as they debate the future of the island's last stretch of undeveloped shore.

© LIZA PRADO

Cozumel's scenic and nearly deserted eastern shore is a world apart from the busy western side.

© LIZA PRADO

Punta Sur's long, peaceful beach

is less packaged and more remote—an escape from the ordinary.

(Parque Punta Sur (Faro Celarain Eco Park)

As the name suggests, Punta Sur covers Cozumel's southern point, but the entrance is on the east side and the ambience and appeal is certainly akin to that of the eastern beaches. Officially called Faro Celarain Eco Park, **Parque Punta Sur** (Carr. Costera Sur Km. 27, tel. 987/872-0914, www.cozumelparks.gob.mx, 9am-5pm daily, US$10 adult, US$5 child over 8) is an important natural reserve that happens to have a fine beach and outstanding snorkeling. Because it faces south, the surf tends to be light. There's a small eatery, plus restrooms, changing area, and a kiosk renting snorkel gear.

Playa Box (Playa Rasta)

Playa Box (pronounced Boash, Yucatec Maya for head) is better known as Playa Rasta for the two Jamaica-themed bars that occupy it. Located just past Punta Sur, where the road turns north along Cozumel's eastern shore, it's a rocky stretch of coastline with only a few sandy inlets and the two restaurants blasting reggae at each other. It's not really the best place to spend the day—unless you like rambling on rocks and have a serious craving for jerk chicken and cold beer. (Well, when you put it that way . . .)

El Mirador

Spanish for The Lookout, this is the best place to appreciate Isla Cozumel's dramatic iron-shore formations, including a natural arch and huge exposed bulges of the black jagged stone. Ironshore is formed when waves, wind, and especially microscopic organisms erode the ancient limestone cap that underlies much of the island. Be very careful walking on the iron-shore; flip-flops are not recommended considering how sharp and slippery it can be.

Playa Bonita and Punta Chiqueros

Playa Bonita is another picturesque curve of

SEA TURTLES OF THE YUCATÁN

All eight of the world's sea turtle species are considered endangered, thanks to a combination of antiquated fishing practices, habitat destruction (particularly of the beaches where they nest), and a taste for turtle products. Four turtle species—hawksbill, Kemp's ridley, green, and loggerhead—nest on the shores of the Yucatán Peninsula and, until relatively recently, were a common supplement to the regional diet. Turtles make easy prey, especially females clambering on shore to lay eggs. They are killed for their meat, fat, and eggs, which are eaten or saved for medicinal purposes, as well as for their shells, which are used to make jewelry, combs, and other crafts.

Various environmental protection organizations have joined forces with the Mexican government to protect sea turtles and their habitats; they maintain strict surveillance of known nesting beaches to stop poaching and have developed breeding programs, too. This, in combination with laws that prohibit the capture and trade of sea turtles or their products, has tremendously increased awareness in Mexico about the need to protect these creatures.

On Isla Cozumel, travelers can volunteer to help monitor sea turtle nests and help release hatchlings into the sea. Nesting season runs May-September, and during that period volunteers join biologists on nighttime walks of Cozumel's beaches, locating and marking new nests and helping to move vulnerable eggs to protected hatcheries. July-November, volunteers help release hatchings into the sea. This typically happens at sundown, and involves encouraging turtles to move toward the water (without touching them) and scaring off birds in search of an easy meal.

Dirección Municipal de Ecología y Medio Ambiente (Calle 11 at Av. 65, tel. 987/872-5795) is the governmental agency that monitors Cozumel's sea turtles and manages volunteer opportunities. It maintains a **mobile visitors center** (9:30am-2pm and 3:30pm-5:30pm daily May-Nov. only, free) in a small trailer, usually parked on the roadside near Playa San Martín on the eastern side of the island. Inside are a handful of aquariums, Plexiglas-enclosed nests, and more; stop by for information on upcoming beach walks and hatchling releases, or just to learn a little more about these highly endangered creatures. There is no fee to look around or to volunteer, though donations are appreciated. Spanish is useful but not required.

© LIZA PRADO

sea turtle hatchlings waiting to be released into the sea

ISLA COZUMEL

© LIZA PRADO

Playa Chen Río is protected by a long, rocky spit, making it the east side's best place for swimming.

sand with plenty of room to lay out a towel and soak in the sun. Heavy surf usually makes swimming here inadvisable, but it's definitely dramatic. The northern end of the beach is Punta Chiqueros, where a small **beach bar and restaurant** (no phone, 10am-5pm daily) serves hamburgers, fresh fish, and other standards at decent prices.

Playa San Martín

A wooden stairway leads from the road down to the beach at this long scenic windswept beach. There are a handful of permanent *palapa* umbrellas near the stairway that are popular with couples and families, but otherwise you're likely to have the beach virtually to yourself. As elsewhere on the east side, think twice about wading and swimming here, as the surf is strong and unpredictable. The waterline is great for beachcombing, loaded with shells, seeds, broken coral, and driftwood (and not a small amount of trash, unfortunately). Playa San Martín is easy to miss, as there's just a lone

wooden sign and no parking lot, just a marginal widening of the road.

◖ Playa Chen Río

The best place to swim on the east side of the island is **Playa Chen Río** (1 kilometer/0.6 mile south of Coconuts Bar), where a rocky spit blocks the waves, forming a huge natural pool, and lifeguards are on duty on weekends. Quiet during the week, it's lively and bustling most Sundays, when local families turn out in force. **Restaurant and Bar Chen Río** (no phone, 11am-6pm daily, US$12-26) is located here, but the prices are quite high, so it's not uncommon to see families with coolers and baskets and even small grills.

Chumul (Playa Tortugas)

About six kilometers (3.7 miles) south of the Carretera Transversal intersection is Chumul, also known as Playa Tortugas, a broad beautiful beach on the north side of the Ventanas al Mar hotel. The scenic windswept beach is good for surfing—and has nesting turtles May-November—but it is often too rough for swimming or snorkeling. Still, it makes a good place to watch the wild and crashing waves anytime.

A few steps away is **Coconuts Bar and Grill** (no phone, 10am-sunset daily, US$6-14). Set on a dramatic palm-studded bluff—the only piece of elevated land on the island, in fact—the tables are arranged for diners to enjoy the fabulous views of the beach below and the Caribbean beyond. Classic beach fare is served—ceviche, tacos, nachos—and plenty of cold beer. There's rum punch and live music daily between 2pm and 3pm.

Punta Morena

After lengthy and ambitious construction work, this east-side beach has undergone a major (and majorly impressive) transformation. What was once a scenic but largely unvisited stretch of sand now has an attractive *palapa*-roofed restaurant and beach bar, a breezy shaded area with hammocks, even (gasp!) a small, clean

swimming pool perfect for kids and cooling off. The pool, which has lounge chairs and a view of the ocean, is especially nice considering that the surf here, like elsewhere on the eastern shore, is often too rough for casual swimming and wading. (That said, it can be a good spot for bodysurfing and boogie boarding if you're a strong swimmer and have experience in heavy surf.) The restaurant's food is tasty though quite pricey; drinks aren't cheap either, but at least they're big and strong enough that you don't feel ripped off.

Mezcalito's and Señor Iguanas

These two low-key restaurants—**Mezcalito's** (no phone, www.mezcalitos.com, 9am-sunset daily) and **Señor Iguanas** (no phone, 8am-6pm Mon.-Sat., 9am-6pm Sun.)—are located side-by-side, right where the Carretera Transversal hits the coast. Longtime Cozumel institutions, they have similar menus (ceviche, fried fish, hamburgers, US$7-15), drinks (beer, margaritas, and tequila shots,

© LIZA PRADO

Mezcalito's is one of just a handful of restaurants and clubs on Cozumel's east side.

US$2.50-5), and services (beachside chairs, hammocks, and *palapas,* free if you buy something from the restaurant). Boogie boards also are available for rent at Señor Iguanas (US$5 for 2 hours)—a lot of fun if you can handle the rough surf.

Road to Punta Molas

Cozumel's northeastern shoulder is its long lost coast, the wildest and least visited part of the island. The 25-kilometer (15.5-mile) stretch from the Carretera Transversal north to Punta Molas includes coastal dunes, scrub forest, and deserted beaches, plus the ancient Maya site of **Castillo Real** at around the 22-kilometer (14-mile) mark. This untended coast also is the final resting spot of a shockingly large amount of trash and jetsam, an ugly reminder

of civilization in the one place on the island it ought to be easy to forget.

The road itself is a challenge—four-wheel drive is essential to avoid becoming mired in deep sand—and hurricanes and other storms can render it impassable. The area also is at the center of a bitter, on-again off-again land dispute and is occasionally closed without warning.

If you do go, be aware that there are no facilities whatsoever, or any other people most of the time. If you plan to camp, take plenty of water and food, a flashlight, extra batteries, bug repellent, and a mosquito net. Remember, too, that most car insurance policies (including all policies sold by rental agencies on the island, regardless of the vehicle) specifically exclude this and other dirt roads from coverage.

Entertainment and Events

Cozumel is no longer the super-sleepy island it once was, though it may never entirely shake its laid-back Caribbean vibe (not that we would ever want it to!). As tourism increases, so does the demand for entertainment, and Cozumel has an ever-growing array of options. Drinking always figures prominently, of course, and Cozumel has sports bars, tequila lounges, and no shortage of beach bars and clubs serving creative (and copious) cocktails to guests in swimsuits. Dancing and live music are also popular, and Cozumel's options range from techno to Latin clubs, and from free concerts in the plaza to a part-cooking, part-dancing tour called (what else?) "Salsa and Salsa." For folks after something more low-key, there's a movie theater and regular cultural events at venues around the island.

Like the rest of Mexico, Cozumel celebrates a number of national and religious holidays too, including Independence Day (Sept 16), Day of the Dead (November 2), and, of course, Christmas and New Year's Eve and Day. However, it's one of few places in the country to really celebrate Carnival (late February), and

has a unique festival in late May honoring the founding of the small village of El Cedral by Maya refugees.

NIGHTLIFE

If clubs and partying are an essential part of your trip, you might consider basing yourself in Cancún or even Playa del Carmen, rather than Cozumel, which simply doesn't have the monster clubs and too-cool lounges of its sister cities. That's not to say Cozumel is sleepy: It's got a good and growing number of bars, lounges, and clubs serving visitors of all tastes. One oddity of the cruise ship industry is that, in ports of call like Cozumel, some of the heaviest partying happens during daylight hours, when cruise ships disgorge thousands of tourists eager to stretch their legs and see some new faces. Cozumel's beach clubs can get raucous, and sports bars (of which there are many) do a brisk trade all day long. But the island doesn't shut down once the cruise ships leave. There's a large enough contingent of locals, expats, and overnight visitors to support a handful of bars, lounges, and nightclubs,

©H.W. PRADO

mariachi performance

some open into the wee hours. Most night-spots don't charge a cover; if they do, it's on select nights, like when there's a live band or celebrity DJ.

Nightclubs

Tiki Tok (Av. Rafael Melgar btwn Calles 2 and 4, tel. 987/869-8119, www.tikitokcozumel.com, 9am-2am Mon.-Wed., 10am-4am Thurs.-Sun., no cover) sports a hodgepodge of beach-isle decor, from Polynesian lamps to Jamaican carved masks and figures. The plastic tables and chairs are a killjoy, but the upstairs patio, complete with sandy floor and gorgeous sea views, is a nice touch. A live salsa band gets the crowd moving Friday and Saturday nights, starting at around 10:30pm.

Love Cafe Cozumel (Av. Rafael Melgar at Blvd. Aeropuerto, tel. 987/107-1252, 10am-midnight daily) is a large open-air *palapa* with wood floors and spectacular views, especially at sunset. It's best known as a place to go for live reggae; at the time of research, a hot local band was packing the place Wednesday-Sunday, with

a DJ most other nights. Fridays are all-you-can-drink for US$8.

El Zócalo Cantina (Av. Rafael Melgar btwn Calles 2 and 4, tel. 987/869-1213, 7pm-4am Wed.-Sun.) is an eclectic 2nd-floor cantina with long high tables and music and dancing most nights including live salsa (11pm-2am Fri.-Sat.). Special events are commonplace too, from major sports games projected on a huge screen to surprise happy hours where everyone drinks for free.

Dubai Cozumel (Av. Rafael Melgar at Calle 11, tel. 987/119-9691, 10pm-5am Thurs.-Sun.) is a traditional nightclub playing a variety of music, from techno to Mexican ballads, with breaks in between for karaoke. Come get your five minutes of fame at Dubai, where anything can happen.

Bars
CLASSIC AND RESTAURANT BARS
Woody's (Plaza Central, Av. Juárez btwn Av. 5 and 10, no phone, www.woodyscozumel.net, 9:30am-midnight, no cover) started out as a

© LIZA PRADO

dancing in Cozumel's main plaza

dinky little bar on the main plaza. Nowadays, under new management (the owners are often there, helping out) Woody's is one of the island's most popular bars, with dozens of plastic tables set up along the pedestrian walkway. There's live music every day starting at 7pm, sometimes even earlier.

Its name comes from a Hawai'ian concept of extended family, including more than just blood relations, and that's precisely the vibe you get at **'Ohana Cafe and Bar** (Av. 5 btwn Calles 6 and 8, cell. tel. 987/105-5154, www. ohanacozumel.com, 7am-midnight daily, evenings only in the low season). This welcoming restaurant-bar has an appealingly laid-back atmosphere, with great food and drinks (try the peanut margaritas). There's also live music most weeks, Thursday-Saturday starting at 8pm.

El Diablito (Calle 3 Sur btwn Avs. 5 and 10, tel. 987/869-7947, 6pm-2am daily except Wed.) is a fun, trendy bar that shares a building with New Especias Italian restaurant. The bar is on the bottom floor, with red and black decor befitting its name (Spanish for Little Devil). The

stairway leading to the restaurant is painted with puffy clouds, and the bar food sent down is indeed heavenly (tasty panini and fritattas feature prominently on the menu). Out front are tables and a mural featuring Mick Jagger on a chopper.

Toro's Place (Av. Rafael Melgar at Calle 5, cell. tel. 987/115-1062, www.toroscozumel. com, 9am-11pm daily, no cover) is right on the main drag and up on the 2nd floor, so views of the waterfront (and clear over to Playa del Carmen) are outstanding. The food and drinks here aren't too shabby either, and there's salsa dancing on the weekends. Despite being in the heart of tourist row, Toro's always has a refreshing mix of locals and tourists.

The world's smallest **Hard Rock Café** (Av. Rafael Melgar near Av. Benito Juárez, tel. 987/872-5271, www.hardrock.com, 10am-1am daily) has ocean views during the day and live music starting at 10pm Friday and Saturday. The food is unremarkable—order drinks and, maybe, an appetizer. If you're still collecting them, T-shirts are sold at the boutique up front.

For a spring break atmosphere all day—and year—long, head to the Punta Langosta shopping center, where **Carlos 'n Charlie's** (Av. Rafael Melgar at Calle 9, tel. 987/869-1647, www.carlosandcharlies.com/cozumel, 10am-1:30am Mon.-Fri., 11am-1:30am Sat., 5pm-1:30am Sun.) and **Señor Frog's** (Av. Rafael Melgar at Calle 9, tel. 987/869-1658, www.senorfrogs.com, 10am-1am Mon.-Fri., 10am-4am Sat.) make driving beats, drink specials, and dancing on tables the norm.

LOUNGE BARS
1.5 Tequila Lounge (Av. Rafael Melgar at Calle 11, tel. 987/872-1537, 9pm-5am Thurs.-Sat.) is a modern lounge bar overlooking the ocean. It has low couches and chairs, outdoor decks, and house music playing in the background. Specialty shooters are the way to go, though the premium martinis pack a punch. Ladies night typically is on Thursday.

Though it's located on the 2nd floor of The Forum shopping center, **DLounge** (Av. Rafael Melgar at Calle 10, no phone, 9am-5pm Mon.-Thurs., 9am-3am Fri.-Sat.) somehow manages to ooze cool, specializing in mojitos, top-shelf margaritas, and perfectly chilled martinis. Sunset views are spectacular, with the curving bay, calm waters, and twinkling lights of the city. Also come here late night for live music on most Fridays and Saturdays, starting at 11pm.

OCEANFRONT BARS
Also known as "Rasta Bar," **Freedom in Paradise** (Playa Box, no phone, www.bobmarleybar.com, 10am-sunset daily) is a Cozumel institution, a reggae-themed restaurant-bar serving great bar grub and drinks to the sounds of Bob Marley, Peter Tosh, and more. Located just north of the entrance to Parque Punta Sur and featuring a bright green and yellow paint job—it's all but impossible to miss no matter which direction you're driving.

Perennially packed, **La Hach!** (Carr. Costera Sur Km. 2.9, tel. 987/869-8403, www.lahachcozumel.com, 9:30am-1am Mon.-Tues., 9:30am-3am Wed.-Thurs., 9:30am-4am Fri.-Sat., no cover) is just steps from the cruise ship

ports, making it a convenient and popular stop for cruise ship passengers. But its gorgeous sunsets and live reggae and classic rock (beginning at 11pm most nights) help draw in even independent travelers. The food is just okay—stick to the drinks, which are 2-for-1 all day.

SPORTS BARS
French Quarter Sports Bar (Av. 5 btwn Calles 3 and Rosado Salas, no phone, www.fqcozumel.com, 10am-midnight Wed.-Thurs. and Sun.-Mon., 10am-2am Fri.-Sat., no cover) has a slew of flat-screen TVs so guests can catch just about any game (or fight, or race, or match) they're missing back home. Every night has a different spin: Thursday is Ladies Night, Friday is 80s dance-off, and Sunday is happy hour prices all day. Food and service are a bit uneven, but it's a fun place all the same.

Wet Wendy's Margarita Bar (Av. 5 Nte. btwn Av. Benito Juárez and Calle 2, tel. 987/872-4970, 10am-11pm Mon.-Thu., 10am-midnight Fri.-Sat.) is your classic expat island bar, with usual features like Monday Night Football, giant bacon burgers, and a jocular atmosphere. But it's famous for its huge hand-crafted margaritas, potent creations that look more like sundaes than cocktails and range from mango and strawberry to avocado and cucumber-jalapeño.

Pitched as a "Husband Day Care Center," **Kelley's** (Av. 10 btwn Calles 1 and Rosado Salas, tel. 987/878-4738, www.kelleyscozumel.com, noon-11pm Mon. and Wed.-Fri., 11am-11pm Sat., 10:30am-11pm Sun., no cover) is an outdoor sports bar with 12 screens airing major sporting events, including pay-per-view. As expected it also pours Guinness. Be sure to pay with pesos, as the exchange rate is set at 10:1, regardless of the market. Decent, but pricey, American and Irish food are available, too.

BAR ALTERNATIVES
Cozumel Bar Hop Tour (Carr. Costera Sur Km. 14.5, tel. 987/872-2294, www.cozumelbarhop.com, US$57) takes guests on a four-hour barhopping tour of the east side of the

island, starting around noon. The bus picks up passengers in downtown and takes them in a comfy air-conditioned bus to restaurant/bars at Punta Morena, Chumul (aka Playa Tortugas), Playa Bonita, and Playa Box (aka Playa Rasta). Each stop begins with a complimentary shot—typically a mixed drink—and lasts about one hour (pay-as-you-go drinks and food). A cheery host keeps the party going between stops, typically leading a rousing rendition of "YMCA," with everyone participating. All in all, this is more a chauffeur service than a tour, but it provides a safe and fun way to drink while exploring the east side. You might even make a new friend or two.

Spanish for "bowling," the evenings-only **Boliche** (Av. 5 btwn Calles 13 and 15, tel. 987/878-4321, 8pm-midnight Thurs. and Sun., 8pm-4am Fri. and Sat.) is a 10-lane bowling alley housed in a bright, modern building. There's a full bar and pool tables on the mezzanine level plus a snack bar, too. It's a good option, especially on a rainy night or if you're looking for an activity to go along with your drinks.

THE ARTS

It's safe to say that the Riviera Maya's cultural outlets don't equal those of other cities in Mexico, like Mérida, Guadalajara or Mexico City. The emphasis on resorts, beaches, and nightlife simply doesn't translate into demand for cultural outlets like museums, galleries, and live theater. Cozumel fits the mold, with just two small museums (albeit good ones) and little in the way of fine arts or arts-related festivals. Music is something of an exception, with a number of innovative musicians performing in local venues, mostly bars, and a long tradition of live music and dancing in the central plaza, hosted by the city. It's reasonable to think Cozumel's arts scene will grow richer and more complex as the island's population and economy does the same. Until then, art lovers have little choice but to keep their expectations in check (or book an off-island excursion to Mérida!).

Cultural and Music Performances

Every Sunday evening, the city hosts an **open-air concert** in the central plaza. Locals and expats come out to enjoy the show—put on a clean T-shirt and your nicest flip-flops, and you'll fit right in. Concerts typically last two hours, beginning at 8pm in the summer, 7pm in the winter. Simple food stands selling homemade flan, churros, and other local goodies set up around the park these nights, too.

Casa de la Cultura Ixchel de Cozumel (Av. 50 btwn Av. Benito Juárez and Calle 2 Norte, tel. 987/872-1471, www.casadelaculturaixchel. blogspot.com, 9am-5pm Mon.-Fri.) hosts free concerts, movies, and art exhibits year-round. If you'll be on the island for an extended (or permanent) stay, consider taking one of the many classes offered in dance, art, music, drama, and creative writing. There also is a wide selection of children's classes available.

Cinema

You can catch relatively recent releases at **Cinépolis** (Av. Rafael Melgar btwn Calles 15 and 17, tel. 987/869-0799, www.cinepolis.com. mx, US$5.25 adult, US$4.25 child, US$3.25 before 3pm and all day Wed.), a multiplex located in the Chedraui shopping center, on the southern end of town.

FESTIVALS AND EVENTS

Cozumel celebrates all the major civic and religious holidays the rest of Mexico does, from Independence Day to Semana Santa. It also has some unique festivals of its own, namely the Day of the Cross celebration, with Maya influences, at El Cedral, and Carnaval, a nod to the island's Caribbean roots, plus sporting events like fishing tournaments and even an official Ironman race.

January

January 6 is **Día de los Tres Reyes,** or Three Kings Day. This is traditionally the day when Mexican children receive their Christmas gifts (just as baby Jesus did), though the practice is quickly falling out of use and shifting

ISLA COZUMEL

©GARY CHANDLER

Carnaval in Cozumel is celebrated with parades and dancing in the streets.

to Christmas Eve. On the evening of the 5th, children leave out their shoes, under which gifts are left while they sleep. In addition to gift giving, extended families also enjoy a *rosca de reyes*, a fruitcake in the shape of a crown with a tiny figurine of baby Jesus baked into it. The person who receives the piece with the figurine in it is then responsible for hosting a dinner on February 2, Día de la Candelaria.

February

Día de la Candelaria is a religious holiday celebrating the presentation of baby Jesus. Typically, a tamale feast is held this day, hosted by the person who, on Día de los Tres Reyes (January 6), ate a slice of fruitcake with a hidden figurine of baby Jesus baked into it.

Carnaval is celebrated big on Isla Cozumel. Taking place the week before Ash Wednesday (dates vary), it consists of a winding parade of floats and participants in costumes dancing in the streets. It ends with a huge party in the central plaza.

March

Benito Juárez's Birthday on March 21 is a national holiday. One of the most beloved historical figures, Juárez is Mexico's only indigenous president. He served five terms and, among other things, is remembered for making education free and mandatory for all Mexican children.

Semana Santa is the week before Easter (dates vary), when religious processions go hand in hand with Mexicans hitting the beach. It's considered high season, so if you travel to Cozumel during this period, book early and expect higher prices than normal.

April

The **Feria del Cedral** is celebrated in the namesake village beginning around April 23 and culminating on May 3, the Day of the Holy Cross. Traditionally, the festival entails daily prayer sessions and ends with a dance called the Baile de las Cabezas de Cochino (Dance of the Pigs' Heads). The festival, started by a survivor of the

CARNAVAL IN COZUMEL

You'd be forgiven for forgetting that the blow-out parties of Carnaval are actually religious in origin. The word comes from the Latin phrase *carne vale*, or "farewell to meat," and is celebrated in many traditionally Catholic countries just before the deprivations of Lent, like not eating meat, kick in. Carnaval celebrations vary by city and country, but typically involve costumes, music, parades, dancing, and drinking—that is, all-out partying—for days or weeks, culminating on "Mardi Gras," or "Fat Tuesday."

Carnaval is not widely celebrated in Mexico—it's more of a South American and Caribbean thing—though Isla Cozumel is one of a handful of places that does (Mazatlán and Veracruz are others). For three or four days in February, the island stops to party, with teams of dancers competing for prizes, parades with elaborate floats and costumed people tossing candy and Mardi Gras beads to onlookers, big-name musicians, and an abundance of street food and drinks and general revelry. It all comes to a head on Fat Tuesday with a lively parade down Avenida Melgar that feeds into a massive dance party in the central plaza. The celebration officially ends that night with the burning of "Juan Carnaval," an effigy representing the excesses of the previous days.

The party is open to all, of course—young and old, locals and tourists—and is a safe, fun, and family-friendly event. Hotels can book up, though, so make reservations early.

Caste War to honor the power of the cross, has morphed over the years into a somewhat more secular affair, with rodeos, dancing, music, and general revelry.

May

Every May, Cozumel hosts a popular sportfishing tournament known affectionately as the **Rodeo de Lanchas Mexicanas,** or Mexican Boat Rodeo. Anglers from all over Mexico participate—including nearly 200 boats—and international anglers are welcome as long as they register their boats in Mexico. The tournament is timed to coincide with the arrival of big game to Cozumel's waters. Tuna, dorado, marlin, and sailfish are often among the fish caught.

Travesia Sagrada Maya (toll-free Mex. tel. 800/212-8951, toll-free U.S./Can. tel. 888/922-7381, www.travesiasagradamaya.com.mx) is held every year in late May. Meaning the Sacred Maya Crossing, it's a reenactment of how Maya pilgrimages to Cozumel from the mainland may have taken place. It is believed that all Maya, especially women, would have attempted the journey at least once in their lives, in honor of Ixchel, the goddess of fertility. For this modern version, up to 300 men and women, dressed in traditional garb, climb aboard 10-person open-air canoes, fitted with outriggers, for the 30-mile, 7-8-hour paddle across the channel to Chankanaab Park in Cozumel. Visitors and spectators can check out a predawn traditional market at Xcaret, a celebration marking the boats' departure from Xel-Há, and more festivities celebrating their arrival in Chankanaab, usually beginning around 1pm. At both parks, your ticket allows you to remain to enjoy the parks' ordinary attractions. The oarsmen and oarswomen return to Xel-Há the following day, with additional celebrations to mark their departure and arrival.

September

Mexico's Independence Day, or **Día de la Independencia,** is technically September 16, but the celebrations are mostly held during the evening of the 15th. On Cozumel, that means fireworks, food, and general revelry on the central plaza. "Viva Mexico!" is shouted throughout the evening's celebration.

You'd be forgiven for not knowing that the main town on Cozumel is officially called San Miguel. Hardly anyone, local or tourist, calls it that, preferring just "Cozumel" instead. One story, among many, is that the city got its name when construction workers unearthed

© GARY CHANDLER

Feria del Cedral celebrates the Day of the Holy Cross and the founding of El Cedral village.

a centuries-old statue of the winged saint on September 29, or **Día de San Miguel Arcángel,** the very day Saint Michael the Archangel is traditionally celebrated. San Miguel was designated the town's patron saint, and every year September 29 is marked with a citywide celebration, including special masses and religious processions, a rodeo, food stands, music, and general revelry, mostly in and around the central square and San Miguel church.

November

In much of Mexico, including Cozumel, November 1 is known as **Día de los Inocentes,** or Day of the Innocents. It's a day to remember and celebrate children who have died, and is often called Día de los Angelitos (Day of the Little Angels, a common term of endearment for children) for that reason. Day of the Innocents coincides with Día de los Muertos, or Day of the Dead, which is celebrated on November 2 and generally focuses on adults

who've passed away (see below). Families celebrate both days in much the same way, by creating altars, at home or at the cemetery, with flowers, sugar skulls, photos, and other mementos of the deceased. Día de los Inocentes is not to be confused with Día de los Santos Inocentes (Day of the Holy Innocents), which is celebrated on December 28 in most parts of Mexico, and is equivalent to April Fool's Day—a day to play practical jokes.

Día de los Muertos, or Day of the Dead, is celebrated annually on November 2. It's a day when families in Cozumel, and throughout Mexico, go to the cemetery to visit the graves of their loved ones, especially elders. (November 1, Day of the Innocents, commemorates children who have died; see above.) Families construct altars, some quite elaborate, using marigolds, photos, candles, and other decorations. The celebration lasts all day and even overnight, with family members gathering around the grave sites, sharing stories and music, and enjoying the deceased's favorite foods and drinks. And because the entire island commemorates their dead on the same day, Día de los Muertos is as much a community event as a private family affair, and tourists are very welcome to wander around the cemetery, admiring the altars and soaking up the atmosphere, perhaps reflecting on the deceased loved ones in your own family.

November 20 is **Día de la Revolución,** a day celebrating the beginning of the Mexican Revolution in 1910. Parades and parties typically are held throughout this day in Cozumel.

Ironman Cozumel (www.ironmancozumel.com) is the only qualifying event in the Ironman series to be held in Mexico, featuring a course that's as beautiful as it is grueling. The swim (3.8 kilometers/2.4 miles) is certainly the most distinctly *cozumeleño* part, starting and ending at Chankanaab National Park, with gorgeous underwater vistas, and scuba divers and sea creatures observing from below. The bike ride (180 kilometers/112 miles) entails three laps around the island, with lovely sea views but crosswinds strong enough to topple unwitting racers. The run (42 kilometers/26.2 miles) is oddly uninspired, three laps between downtown and the airport, although the sunsets there are spectacular (and you've got until midnight to finish). Ironman Cozumel is usually held in late November and attracts around 2,500 triathletes from around the world.

December

Día de Guadalupe on December 12 is the day when Mexicans celebrate their nation's patron saint, the Virgen de Guadalupe. Religious processions and celebrations in the central plaza mark the day in Cozumel.

Posadas are parties that are celebrated every day December 16-24. They begin as religious processions with songs that retell the story of the birth of Jesus Christ. Arriving at the host's home, half the guests stand outside and sing the part of Joseph asking for shelter, while the others stand inside the house, singing the part of the innkeeper. Eventually, everyone is let inside and the party begins, with food, piñatas, and general revelry.

December 24 is **Noche Buena,** or Christmas Eve (literally Good Night). This is the night when most Mexicans celebrate Christmas with huge parties, dinner after midnight mass, and gift giving.

December 25 is **Navidad,** or Christmas, which is typically a quiet day throughout Mexico, with families spending the day together. In Cozumel, families often spend it on the beach.

Año Nuevo, or New Year's Eve (and Day) is celebrated with big parties and fireworks, often going strong until sunrise on January 1.

Recreation

Cozumel may be a beach destination and major cruise ship port of call, but a great many travelers to this island destination aren't content to spend their vacation simply downing beers and soaking up the sun. They want to get out and do something—and Cozumel does not disappoint. Cozumel is, of course, one of the world's premier scuba diving destinations (the snorkeling's not too shabby either), surrounded by pristine coral reef and blessed with warm crystalline water teeming with sealife. Diving and snorkeling are great ways to get off the beach chair and experience the best of Cozumel, for novices and experts alike. You can enjoy the island's amazing water and shoreline in other ways, too: Stand-up paddleboarding is fun and easy to learn, and the clear waveless waters on Cozumel's west side are uniquely well-suited to the sport. Kayaking and canoeing are also a great way to explore the inland, and several outfitters (and many resorts) rent equipment and offer guided tours. For a bit more adrenaline, try kiteboarding and windsurfing; there are popular put-ins on the northern and southern tips of the island. Good sportfishing is available year-round. For dryland options, Cozumel has good horseback riding, ATV tours, and ziplines, and several outfits offering tours and packages for each, not to mention a Jack Nicklaus-designed golf course and country club. On the mellower side, Cozumel has numerous spas offering treatments of all kinds, including facials and massages, and there are various specialty tours and courses, from cooking classes to walking photography tours. In short, if you're after an active vacation, Cozumel has you covered, no matter what your interest or experience level.

⟨ SCUBA DIVING

Cozumel is one the world's best (and best known) places to scuba dive and snorkel, so it's no surprise that the island is home to dozens of dive shops—more than 100 at last count. Virtually all offer diving, snorkeling, and all levels of certification courses; there are a handful of dive "resorts," too, which offer packages that include lodging, diving, gear, and sometimes food.

Rates can vary considerably from shop

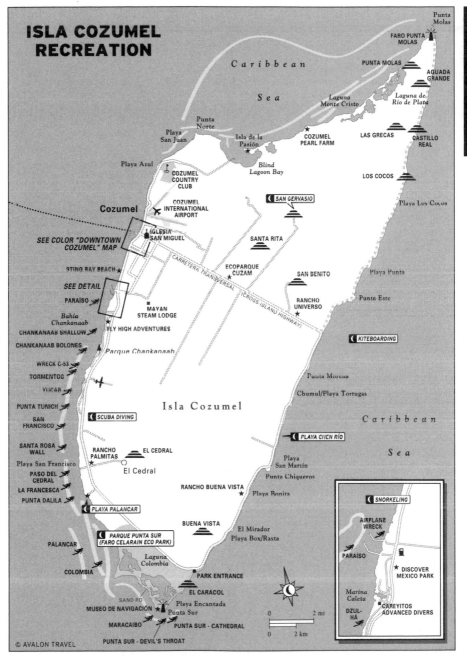

ISLA COZUMEL

ISLA COZUMEL
RECREATION

C a r i b b e a n

S e a

Punta Molas

FARO PUNTA MOLAS

PUNTA MOLAS

AGUADA GRANDE

Laguna Monte Cristo

Laguna de Río de Plata

Punta Norte

Playa San Juan

Isla de la Pasión

COZUMEL PEARL FARM

LAS GRECAS

CASTILLO REAL

Playa Azul

Blind Lagoon Bay

LOS COCOS

COZUMEL COUNTRY CLUB

Cozumel

COZUMEL INTERNATIONAL AIRPORT

SAN GERVASIO

Playa Los Cocos

SEE COLOR "DOWNTOWN COZUMEL" MAP

IGLESIA SAN MIGUEL

SANTA RITA

STING RAY BEACH

CARRETERA TRANSVERSAL

ECOPARQUE CUZAM

SAN BENITO

Playa Punta

SEE DETAIL

PARAÍSO

MAYAN STEAM LODGE

RANCHO UNIVERSO

(CROSS ISLAND HIGHWAY)

Punta Este

Bahía Chankanaab

CHANKANAAB SHALLOW

CHANKANAAB BOLONES

FLY HIGH ADVENTURES

Parque Chankanaab

KITEBOARDING

WRECK C-53

TORMENTOS

YUCAB

PUNTA TUNICH

SAN FRANCISCO

SCUBA DIVING

Isla Cozumel

Punta Morena

Chumul/Playa Tortugas

C a r i b b e a n

SANTA ROSA WALL

RANCHO PALMITAS

EL CEDRAL

PLAYA CHEN RÍO

S e a

Playa San Francisco

PASO DEL CEDRAL

El Cedral

Playa San Martín

LA FRANCESCA

RANCHO BUENA VISTA

Punta Chiqueros

PUNTA DALILA

Playa Bonita

PLAYA PALANCAR

BUENA VISTA

Playa Encantada

Playa Box/Rasta

PALANCAR

PARQUE PUNTA SUR (FARO CELARAIN ECO PARK)

El Mirador

Laguna Colombia

COLOMBIA

PARK ENTRANCE

EL CARACOL

SAND RD

MUSEO DE NAVIGACIÓN

Playa Encantada

Punta Sur

MARACAIBO

PUNTA SUR - CATHEDRAL

PUNTA SUR - DEVIL'S THROAT

© AVALON TRAVEL

0   2 mi

0   2 km

SNORKELING

AIRPLANE WRECK

PARAÍSO

DISCOVER MEXICO PARK

Marina Caleta

DZUL-HÁ

CAREYITOS ADVANCED DIVERS

to shop, and season to season, so be sure to clarify all the details up front. For most of the year, a two-tank fun dive costs US$72-90, plus US$12-35 per day if you need gear. Low-season rates can be significantly lower, and often include gear rental. PADI open-water certification courses (3-4 days) generally cost US$415-535, including all equipment and materials. Most shops also offer advanced courses, Nitrox and night diving, and multi-dive packages. All divers also must pay US$2 per day for marine park admission and to support Cozumel's hyperbaric chambers and marine ambulance; ask if the fees are included in a shop's rates or charged separately.

Dive Shops
OUTFITTERS

Cozumel's diver safety record is good, and there are many competent outfits in addition to those listed here. Consider this list a starting point, to be augmented by the recommendations of trusted fellow divers, travelers, locals, and expats. Most important, go with a shop you feel comfortable with, not just the cheapest, the cheeriest, or the most convenient. Dive shops are generally open 8am-8pm daily, closing during those business hours only if no one's around to run the shop during a dive trip.

- **Blue Angel Dive Shop** (Carr. Costera Sur Km. 2.2, tel. 987/872-1631, www.blueangel-resort.com) is a full-service dive resort, so most clients here are also staying and eating at the resort. Excellent service and by-the-book attention to safety.

- **Careyitos Advanced Divers** (Marina Caleta, tel. 987/872-1578, www.advanceddivers.com) caters to experienced divers, allowing up to 75 minutes bottom time and offering top-notch service. Reserve online or by telephone and just meet the crew at the boat.

- **Caribbean Divers** (Av. 5 at Calle 3 Sur, tel. 987/872-1145, www.caribbeandiverscozumel.com) has been using the same staff and crew for years, with a focus on safety and protection of the marine environment.

- **Deep Blue** (Calle Rosado Salas at Av. 10 Sur, tel. 987/872-5653, www.deepbluecozumel.com) is a long-standing shop with a reputation and track record that keep it busy even through the low season.

- **Deep Exposure Dive Center** (Av. 10 Sur btwn Calles 3 Sur and Rosado Salas, tel. 987/872-3621, toll-free U.S. tel. 866/670-2736, www.deepexposuredivecenter.com) is a small operation with friendly, professional service and many repeat customers.

- **Eco Divers** (Av. 10 at Calle 1 Sur, tel. 987/872-5628, www.cozumel-diving.net/ecodivers) is a relaxed, longtime outfit specializing in small groups and personalized service.

- **Liquid Blue Divers** (no storefront, tel. 987/869-7794, www.liquidbluedivers.com)

DIVE INSURANCE

Although diving and snorkeling accidents are relatively rare on Cozumel, especially among beginning divers, you might consider purchasing secondary accident and/or trip insurance through the **Divers Alert Network** (DAN, toll-free U.S. tel. 800/446-2671, 24-hour emergency Mex. tel. 919/684-9111, accepts collect calls, www.diversalertnetwork.org), a highly regarded, international, nonprofit medical organization dedicated to the health and safety of snorkelers and recreational divers. Dive accident plans cost just US$30-75 per year, including medical and decompression coverage and limited trip and lost equipment coverage. More complete trip insurance—not a bad idea in hurricane country—and life and disability coverage are also available. To be eligible for insurance, you must be a member of DAN (US$35 per year).

ISLA COZUMEL

© 123RF.COM

Scuba diving is a truly otherworldly experience.

has somewhat higher rates than most shops, but it offers small groups and attentive, personalized service.

- **Scuba Gamma** (Calle 5 near Av. 5 Sur, tel. 987/878-4257, www.scubagamma.net) is a mom-and-pop shop (literally) run by an amiable French family. It's one of few shops that's equipped and certified to offer diving and instruction to people with disabilities.

- **Scuba Tony** (no storefront, tel. 987/869-8268, U.S. tel. 303/519-4410, www.scubatony.com) keeps prices low by foregoing a storefront, conducting all business online and in person. Friendly, professional, and highly personalized service.

- **Studio Blue Cozumel** (Calle Rosado Salas btwn Avs. 5 and 10 Sur, tel. 987/872-4414, toll-free U.S. tel. 566/341-1090, www.studioblue.com.mx) is a busy dive shop with good equipment and experienced staff.

◖ SNORKELING

Snorkelers have plenty of options in Cozumel, from cheap-and-easy snorkeling tours to renting gear and exploring on your own, right from shore.

Most dive shops offer snorkeling as well as diving, usually visiting 2-3 sites for a half hour each (US$50-70 pp). Snorkelers often go out with a group of divers and either snorkel in the same general location or go to a nearby site while the divers are underwater. This can mean some extra downtime as divers get in and out of the water, but the advantage is that you typically go to better and less-crowded sites.

For a quick and easy snorkeling tour, stop by one of the booths that flank the ferry pier. These trips are somewhat less expensive (though with larger groups) and can be booked right as you disembark from the ferry. Most offer two tours daily at around 11am and 2pm; some use a glass-bottom boat for extra pizzazz. The standard trip (US$45, including equipment) lasts 2-3 hours, visiting two or three sites, spending 30-45 minutes snorkeling at each one.

© LIZA PRADO

Divers climb aboard for a journey to Cozumel's underwater paradise.

Among many operators vying for your business are **Kuzamil Snorkeling Tours** (tel. 987/111-9333), **Dive Cozumel 1** (tel. 987/869-2591), and **Amazing Cozumel Tours** (no phone).

There are several terrific snorkeling spots near town and just offshore where you don't need a boat or a guide at all. Cozumel's boat drivers are careful about steering clear of snorkelers, but even so, do not swim too far from shore, look up and around frequently, and stay out of obvious boat lanes. If you plan to do a lot of snorkeling, especially outside of established snorkeling areas, consider bringing or buying an inflatable personal buoy. Designed for snorkelers, they are brightly colored and have a string you attach to your ankle or to a small anchor weight, alerting boat drivers of your presence. Also be aware of the current, which typically runs south to north and can be quite strong.

KITEBOARDING

Kiteboarding has quickly and thoroughly morphed from a novelty act to one of the most popular beach sports worldwide. Cozumel is no exception, with a dedicated cadre of kiteboarders and a growing number of options for travelers who want to learn or practice the sport.

De Lille Sports (formerly Kite Cozumel, Casa Viento, Carr. Costera Nte. Km. 7, tel. 987/103-6711, www.delillesports.com) is operated by Cozumel native Raul de Lille, a former Olympic-level windsurfer and now one of Mexico's top kiters and instructors. (He now also offers stand-up paddling, hence the change of name.) Raul doesn't come cheap, but he's an outstanding instructor, not least for his calm demeanor and excellent English. Private lessons are US$125 per hour or US$500 per day. An intensive three-day introductory course includes 15 hours of instruction and costs US$900 per student (maximum 2 students per instructor). For experienced kiters, de Lille offers clinics on kite control, tricks, and other specialties, plus adventuresome tours like downwinding the entire island. Kiting tours in remote areas of the island can also be arranged. Kiteboarding rentals are US$150 per day for a full kit. De Lille

© LIZ ALPRADO

a kiteboarder off Cozumel's northern shore

oversized surfboard-like board and using a long paddle to cruise around. Fitness buffs appreciate the full-core workout SUPing provides, while the elevated perspective allows you to see surprisingly well into the surrounding water—significantly better than in a kayak, in fact. It's not uncommon to see fish, rays, even sea turtles and dolphins swimming below and around you. Numerous resorts have SUP boards available for guests, and a handful of agencies offer instruction, rentals, and tours.

De Lille Sports (Casa Viento, Carr. Costera Nte. Km. 7, tel. 987/103-6711, www.delillesports.com) is operated by windsurfing and kiteboarding legend (and Cozumel native) Raul De Lille, but he's big on SUPing too, even designing his own line of boards. The sports complement each other well: If there's not enough wind for kiting, it's probably perfect for SUPing, and vice versa. SUP instruction runs US$75 per student (2-3 hours, maximum 8 students), while high-quality SUP rentals are US$25 per hour or US$85 per day.

Sports operates out of the Casa Viento (www.casaviento.net), a great hotel north of the center and a short walk from the beach.

Another locally run option is **Cozumel Kiteboarding** (Av. 5 Sur at Calle 3, tel. 987/876-1558, www.cozumelkiteboarding.com). Headquartered downtown in the Puro Mar Surf-Kite-Bikini shop, it offers kiting excursions around the island (4 hours, US$250 for 1-2 people), including to the little-visited northern lagoons: Río de Plata, Monte Cristo, and Blind Bary. Kiteboarding instruction for beginners and more experienced students also is offered.

STAND-UP PADDLING

Stand-up paddling (or "SUPing") is the sport du jour in Cozumel and around the world, and for good reason: It's fun, easy to learn (yet challenging to master), and is a unique way to experience Cozumel's rich coastline and extraordinarily clear waters. The glassy waters on Cozumel's western shore are perfect for the sport, which involves standing upright on an

KAYAKING AND CANOEING

Cozumel's calm, clear waters make it a nice place to kayak. Most **all-inclusive resorts** and some **beach clubs** have a handful of kayaks available for guests to use (free-US$10/hour). If you plan to swim or snorkel along the way—a great way to enjoy little-visited spots on the reef—be sure the kayak has a small anchor to prevent it from floating away.

A tour with Cozumel's one and only canoe outfit, **Mexico Silvestre** (Rafael Melgar 23 btwn Calles 6 and 8, tel. 987/876-0667), is a great way to see remote areas of Cozumel that even many longtime residents have never visited. It's a one-man operation, ably led by Robert Cudney, former director of Cozumel's national marine park and a longtime guide and nature photographer. Tours range from half-day paddles to overnight camping expeditions, mostly visiting areas along Cozumel's remote north and northeastern coastline. You're sure to see a slew of water birds, including herons and roseate spoonbills, and the occasional beefy crocodile. Generous meal spreads are included,

JACQUES COUSTEAU AND COZUMEL

It's a tale told a thousand times over: Cozumel was an unknown backwater until Jacques Cousteau, the globetrotting diver and filmmaker, put the island on the map with a documentary about its remarkable underwater realm.

Nice story; trouble is, it's not true. Jacques Cousteau did indeed produce a break-out underwater film (and companion book) called *Le Monde du Silence (The Silent World)*, which won the top prize at the Cannes film festival in 1956 and became a smash hit worldwide. However, none of the underwater scenes in that film were shot in Cozumel, or even the Americas for that matter. In fact, Cousteau, who famously declared Cozumel to be one of the most beautiful scuba diving sites in the world, did not feature the island in any of his films or TV episodes until the 1970s.

The island does owe a debt of gratitude to the movies, however. In 1957, just a year after *Le Monde du Silence* was released, Mexican filmmaker René Cordova made a black-and-white film called *Un Mundo Nuevo*, which included beautiful underwater footage shot in Cozumel. (The cinematographer was Lamar Boden, who went on to film *Flipper* and the *Sea Hunt* series.) *Un Mundo Nuevo* was later released in the United States with great success, and coincided with a series of media reports about Cozumel as a new and affordable beach destination. Tourism to the island increased dramatically, and permanently.

To be fair, Cordova's film was greatly inspired by *Le Monde du Silence* and frankly never would have been so successful without Cousteau's considerable coattails. Perhaps it was inevitable that Cordova would be overshadowed by Commander Cousteau, by then a genuine global celebrity, especially given the timing and similarities of their films. Still, it was Cordova, not Cousteau, who got a reef named after him, in recognition of bringing Cozumel to the world's attention.

complete with happy hour cocktails. Most people find canoeing more comfortable than kayaking, and all ages and abilities are welcome. Small groups are the norm, so advance reservations are essential.

SPORTFISHING

Cozumel boasts good deep-sea fishing year-round. It's one of few places anglers can go for the grand slam of billfishing: hooking into a blue marlin, a white marlin, a sailfish, and a swordfish all in a single day. It's also got plentiful tuna, barracuda, dorado, wahoo, grouper, and shark.

Albatros Charters (tel. 987/872-7904, toll-free U.S. tel. 888/333-4643, www.albatros-charters.com) charges US$420-450 for four hours, US$500-575 for six hours, and US$575-650 for eight hours. The outfit has a variety of boats, each able to carry a maximum of six anglers. Trips include hotel pickup and drop-off, beer and soda, snacks, bait, and gear.

Other recommended outfits include **Aquarius Travel** (tel. 987/869-1096, toll-free U.S. tel. 800/371-2924, www.aquariusflatsfishing.com), **Chichi Charters** (cell. tel. 987/101-3337, U.S. tel. 214/628-0689, www.chichicharters.com), and **Wahoo Tours** (tel. 987/869-8560, toll-free U.S./Can. tel. 866/645-8977, www.wahootours.com).

GOLF

Jack Nicklaus designed the par-72 championship course at **Cozumel Country Club** (Carr. Costera Nte. Km. 6.5, tel. 987/872-9570, www.cozumelcountryclub.com.mx, 6:30am-6pm daily), located at the far end of the northern hotel zone. Greens fees are US$169 until 12:30pm, when they drop to US$105. Carts are required and included in the rate. In addition to the slightly rolling, moderately challenging course, the club has a driving range, putting and chipping areas, overnight bag storage, a retail shop, and lessons from PGA golf pros. Book online for a discount.

and lockers. Reservations are recommended; minimum eight years old, maximum 240 pounds.

Ecoparque Cuzam

Staff members go the extra mile to give visitors the best possible time at Cozumel's newish ecopark, **Ecoparque Cuzam** (Cross-Island Hwy. Km. 3.8, tel. 987/871-9077, www.ecoparquecuzam.com.mx, 9am-3pm Mon.-Sat., US$50-110), located a short distance from town along the Cross-Island Highway. Count on friendly, funny, yet professional service from employees here, who guide guests of all ages through the park's main activities in a large manicured complex. There's ziplining, including an 80-foot main tower; horseback riding and ATV tours on separate well-maintained trails; and a paintball arena. Half-day combination packages include your choice of two activities and use of the facilities, including a large swimming pool, a smaller pool and play area for kids, showers, lockers, even Wi-Fi. Ecoparque Cuzam is still somewhat off the cruise ship radar (at least for now), so large loud groups are less common than elsewhere.

Cozumel's calm, clear water makes it ideal for kayaking.

ADVENTURE PARKS
Fly High Adventures Zip Line and Eco-Park

The popular zipline park, **Fly High Adventures Zip Line Park** (Carr. Costera Sur Km. 7.2, cell. tel. 998/185-4389, www.cozumelflyhighadventures.com, 9am-3pm Mon.-Sat., US$54) offers nice views of the ocean and docked cruise ships from the highest towers as well as iguanas and birds lurking in the branches, but you may find yourself focused on something else: the over 18 meters (60 feet) of open air under your feet. The park has six towers and six lines in all (stretching 1,400 feet), and a tour here includes two circuits for a total of 12 zips. The lines vary in length and speed; they're fast enough to be a thrill, yet still accessible to all. Every line has a double cable, for safety, and the gear is state of the art. Guided tours run 60-90 minutes, and there's a climbing wall and rope bridges for added fun. The open-air reception area has a snack bar, restrooms,

TOURS
Local and Regional Tours

Part of the locally owned mainland operation Native Choice, **Cozumel Choice** (cell. tel. 983/102-0532, www.cozumelchoice.com, US$85-190 adult, US$75-140 child) offers an excellent alternative to the impersonal and overcrowded tours most cruise ship passengers get roped into. Tours are led by local English-speaking guides, many with Maya roots, and all extremely knowledgeable and passionate about the region's history and culture. The half-day Cozumel tour includes a visit to San Gervasio ruins, followed by an insider's tour of the island's east side, with time for lunch on the beach. Longer tours include visiting Tulum ruins, snorkeling with turtles in Akumal, and others. Transportation and admission are included; reservations are required.

Raise your hand if this sounds familiar: Your camera has about a gazillion features

SPORT- AND GAME FISHING

Isla Cozumel and the Riviera Maya are well known for trolling and deep-sea fishing, while the Sian Ka'an Biosphere Reserve has terrific fly-fishing. Although you can hook into just about any fish at any time of the year, below is information on the peak and extended seasons for a number of top target species. Those fish not listed—tuna, barracuda, snapper, grouper, and bonefish—are prevalent year-round.

SPORTFISHING

Fish	Peak Season	Extended Season	Description
Sailfish	Mar.–June	Jan.–Sept.	Top target species, with a dramatic dorsal fin and a high-flying fighting style.
Blue Marlin	Apr.–Aug.	Mar.–Sept.	Largest Atlantic billfish, up to 500 pounds locally, but much larger elsewhere.
White Marlin	May–July	Mar.–Aug.	Smaller than the blue marlin, but still challenging.
Wahoo	Nov.–Jan.	June–Feb.	Lightning fast, with torpedo-like shape and distinctive blue stripes.
Dorado	May–July	Feb.–Aug.	Hard fighter with shimmery green, gold, and blue coloration; aka dolphin or mahimahi.

FLAT-WATER FISHING

Fish	Peak Season	Extended Season	Description
Tarpon	Mar.–Aug.	Feb.–Oct.	Big hungry tarpon migrate along the coast in summer months.
Snook	July–Aug.	June–Dec.	Popular trophy fish, grows locally up to 30 pounds.
Permit	Mar.–Sept.	year-round	March and April see schools of permit, with some 20-pound individuals.

but you take every shot in "Auto" mode. Don't feel bad—point-and-shoot cameras can take impressive photos all on their own—but the fact is there's a whole world of improved photos within every traveler's reach if they just knew how to use their camera to its full capability. Enter award-winning photographer Tati Biermas, whose **Cozumel Photo Tour** (cell. tel. 987/103-8012, www. cozumelphototour.blogspot.com, US$49 pp) is a fun, informative, and eye-opening way to improve your photography and see Cozumel in a different light. And it's not just getting out of Auto mode, although that's usually a logical starting place. On 3.5-hour walking tours, Biermas helps guests understand and take advantage of framing, lighting, color, depth of field, and more, not to mention how to capture the unique character of a place like Cozumel. She even does underwater photography sessions, on request. Guests of all experience levels, and bearing all types of digital cameras, from simple to pro-quality, are welcome. Reservations are required; bring your own camera and owner's manual.

Horseback Riding

A longtime Cozumel horseback riding operation, **Rancho Buena Vista** continues to impress guests with its personable staff, safe and professional operation, and well-tended horses. Guests are matched with horses according to skill and experience; novices are paired with patient, docile creatures, while those with a background in horses can let the guides know, as there are a few opportunities for galloping. The tour includes riding through a low forest, stopping at a cave occupied by ancient remains (and present-day bats!) and again at El Cedral, a historic Cozumel village and home to a modest Maya ruin (and more than a few souvenir stands, naturally). Most people find the stops interesting—the friendliness and knowledgeableness of the guides certainly helps—while others will wish the time was spent riding.

Located on the inland side of the highway across from Nachi-Cocom Beach Club, **Rancho Palmitas** (Carr. Costera Sur Km. 16, cell. tel. 987/119-1012, 8am-4pm daily) offers two horseback tours. A 2.5- to 3-hour tour (US$40 pp) includes stops at a cavern with a cenote, the archaeological site of El Cedral, and a few unexcavated Maya ruins. A shorter 1.5-hour tour (US$35 pp) leads to the cavern only. Call to set up a tour or just drop in—the last excursion leaves at 3pm.

The moment you walk into the lush grounds of **Rancho Universo** (Cross-Island Hwy. Km. 11.3, cell. tel. 987/119-9828, www.ranchouniverso.com, Tues.-Sun. by appointment), you realize it's not your typical horseback riding

operation. Horses wander freely through the grounds, and an air of calm and tranquility pervade. Part animal sanctuary, part riding school, and part therapeutic retreat, Rancho Universo rescues injured and abused horses from throughout the Yucatán, providing a safe and loving place for animals that have endured the exact opposite. Visits here include much more than climbing onto the horses' backs: Guests help feed and brush the animals, even clean and tidy their stalls. When you do ride, it's with a unique sense of bonding and respect, and the ranch offers daily riding lessons, from beginner to dressage. Some of its horses are trained to participate in horse-based therapy (including riding) for children as young as 18 months and guests with emotional, physical, and neurological challenges.

ATV Excursions

Though catering to cruise ship passengers, **Wild Tours** (Av. 10 Bis btwn Calles 13 and 15, tel. 987/872-5876, toll-free U.S./Can. tel. 888/497-4283, www.wild-tours.com, 9am-7pm Mon.-Fri., 9am-2pm Sat.-Sun.) offers ATV excursions to everyone. Tours include off-roading through the jungle, visiting isolated Maya ruins, and snorkeling at Chankanaab reef (US$70-80 adult, US$110 child with adult, 4 hours; US$58-65 adult, US$90 child with adult, 2 hours). Tours leave from a staging area in front of Carlos 'n Charlie's in Punta Langosta.

Submarine Tour

Atlantis Submarines (Carr. Costera Km. 4, tel. 987/872-4354, www.atlantissubmarines.com, US$99 adult, US$59 child) offers 40-minute underwater excursions near Chankanaab ecopark. The subs have oversized portholes with low seats in a long row down the center. Staff members describe what you're seeing outside. The sub dives as deep as 120 feet; you're sure to see plenty of fish and coral formations, and, if you're really lucky, a shark or sea turtle. It's pretty pricey considering how short the actual tour is, but it's a memorable way for youngsters and nondivers to admire Cozumel's marine riches.

© GARY CHANDLER

Cooking classes at Josefina's Cocina Con Alma begin with a field trip to the market.

Cooking Classes and Food Tours

Josefina's Cocina Con Alma (no phone, talktous@cozumelmycozumel.com, US$69-125 pp, by appointment only) is a small cooking school offering private bilingual instruction in Yucatecan and classic Mexican dishes. Classes begin with a field trip to the market to select fresh ingredients, then it's straight to the kitchen to learn to create a preselected meal. Dishes offered range from *cochinita pibil* (pork marinated in orange juice, achiote, and other spices and baked in banana leaves) and *sopa de lima* (a citrus-based soup with shredded turkey and fried tortilla strips) to *chiles en nogada* (poblano peppers stuffed with meat or cheese and topped with a walnut-based cream sauce and pomegranate seeds) and tamales (seasoned meat, cheese, or vegetables stuffed in a cornmeal dough and wrapped in corn husks). Afterward, students enjoy their creations at a sit-down meal. Chef Josefina gets rave reviews for her expertise and warm manner.

You can guess from this outfit's name— **Salsa and Salsa Cozumel** (Hotel Cozumel & Resort, Carr. Costera Sur Km. 17, cell. tel. 987/100-3161, www.salsaandsalsa.com, by appointment only)—what you'll be doing. You spend the first part of your time learning to make salsa—seven different types, to be exact—plus two different types of margaritas. The latter help with the especially *picante* (spicy) salsas, but also as social lubricant for the next part of the experience: salsa dancing.

Foodies will love **Cozumel Chef** (cell. tel. 987/105-5300, www.cozumelchef.com, by appointment only), a one-woman show run by classically trained French chef Emily Egge. A variety of services are offered: food tours of the lesser-visited establishments on the island (US$60-80, 2-3 hours); gourmet dinner service (US$65/person); and culinary skills classes including filleting a fish, deboning a chicken, and basic knife skills (US$80/person). Upon request, Chef Emily will also provide grocery shopping services so your fridge is stocked with fresh items before you arrive on the island. It's perfect for an off-the-beaten-track island experience.

Chocolates KaoKao Tour (Calle 1-bis, btwn Avs. 80 and 85, tel. 987/869-4705, www.chocolateskaokao.com, tours at 9am, 11am, and 1pm Mon.-Sat., US$11 adult, $5.50 child) offers hour-long "tours" at a family-run chocolate factory that start with a history lesson on chocolate itself, including how ancient Maya revered the cacao tree for its fruit, seeds, and the bitter drink called *chocol-haa* they made from it. You don't get to tour the factory itself, unfortunately, but a detailed presentation (including examples) of the modern chocolate-making process, from fruit to finished product, and the various steps in between, is fascinating all the same. You do get to grind beans using the traditional mortar and pestle, and, of course, there are free samples of KaoKao's various products (and more for purchase) at the end. Reservations are highly recommended, as tours are limited to 12 guests.

SPAS

Cozumel Spa (Condos El Palmar, Carr. Costera Sur Km, 3,8, tel. 987/872-6615, www.cozumelspa.com) gets high marks from visitors and locals alike. A wide range of services include massages for singles or couples (US$50-140), facials (US$50), and specialty treatments like aromatherapy, cold stone massage, and chocolate body wraps (US$50-100).

Spa del Sol (Calle 5 btwn. Avs. 5 and Rafael Melgar, tel. 987/872-6474, www.spadelsolcozumel.com, 9am-7pm Mon.-Sat.) provides a variety of traditional and holistic treatments in its quaint downtown location. Almost a dozen types of massages are offered, including Swedish, Thai, and Aquasana (a treatment performed in open water—who knew?). Acupuncture, Reiki, and ear candling, among other alternative treatments, also are performed regularly. One-hour treatments run US$55-70. Walk-ins are very welcome, and shorter and longer sessions are available, too.

Mayan Steam Lodge (Xcan-Ha Reserve, tel. 987/869-8201, www.temazcalcozumel.com) The word *temezcal* comes from Nahuatl (or Aztec, from central Mexico) and means "steam house," but the ancient Maya of Cozumel and the Yucatán region (and cultures around the world) also used steam lodges as a form of physical and spiritual cleansing. Today, it's a favorite practice of health- and spiritual-minded folks of all stripes, and especially popular in the Riviera Maya. Mayan Steam Lodge has an especially lovely spot to experience this unique treatment, a leafy retreat well inland from Cozumel's busy western shore. A session here begins by addressing the cardinal directions before entering the low, circular brick hut, where the guide leads guests through additional exercises and visualizations, related to ancient Maya beliefs as well as one's own experiences, all intended to further the cleansing and mind-opening process. Afterward, you can take a dip in a nearby freshwater cenote and relax in hammocks with a fresh-made juice.

FITNESS

The most modern gym on the island, **EGO** (Calle 11 at Av. 5, tel. 987/872-4897, 5am-11pm Mon.-Fri., 6am-6pm Sat.) is a full-service facility complete with free weights, weight machines, cardio machines (plus personal trainers to help), and a slew of classes including Pilates, yoga, spinning, and kickboxing. Monthly membership is US$55, while visitors pay US$8 for the day. All that, plus the air-conditioning can't be beat!

Power Yoga Cozumel (Calle 7 at Av. 65 Bis, no phone, www.poweryogacozumel.com, hours vary depending on class schedule) offers all levels of Vinyasa and Hatha classes—group or private—in a large airy space. Instruction is in either Spanish or English and is held early morning and late afternoon Monday-Saturday. Sessions cost $10 but packages are available too, including unlimited classes for US$50 per week or US$130 per month.

Shopping

Retail is a contact sport in Cozumel, where shops compete mightily for the attention and pocketbooks of the thousands of travelers who visit the island on any given day. The vast majority of shoppers are cruise ship passengers, and the main shopping corridor is Avenida Rafael Melgar, right along the waterfront. Cruise ship passengers stream up Melgar from the nearby ports, while tourists arriving by ferry are deposited on the same roadway. Shops along Avenida Melgar range from marble-floored jewelry stores to tacky souvenir shops, and all entice passersby with blasting air-conditioning, free giveaways, and employees at every doorway, ushering you in. Prices are high here, but shops still do a brisk business, in part because so many visitors (especially cruise ship passengers) never leave Avenida Melgar. Travelers who do venture into Cozumel's main plaza, and especially to the city streets beyond, are treated to a wider variety of shops and potential purchases. There are art and handicraft stores, clothing and fashion stores, sporting gear and souvenir stores, music shops, and more. Prices still aren't cheap, but they're not nearly as inflated as along Avenida Melgar.

ART AND *ARTESANÍA*

Los Cinco Soles (Av. Rafael Melgar at Calle 8, tel. 987/872-9004, www.loscincosoles.com, 9am-8pm Mon.-Sat., 11am-5pm Sun.) is a labyrinth-like store at the northern end of Avenida Melgar, filled with quality Mexican folk art from every state in the country: pre-Columbian replicas, *barro negro* (black clay) pottery, colorful *rebozos* (shawls), hand-carved furniture, silver jewelry, hand-carved wooden toys, alabaster sculptures, wool rugs, and more. The prices are higher than others in town, but it's reflected in the quality, and no store can match Cinco

---

BEST COZUMEL SOUVENIRS

Like any tourist destination, Cozumel is overflowing with shops selling souvenirs and other mementos. T-Shirts and jewelry are some of the usual suspects, while Maya replicas, folk art, and more can make for a uniquely Mexican or Cozumeleño gift.

- **T-Shirts:** Cozumel has the same T-shirt offerings so many beach destinations do, from cute and clever to crude and obnoxious, and from dirt cheap to double thickness.

- **Shell Art and Jewelry:** Beautiful, durable, and ubiquitous, shells are a natural raw material for everything from simple necklaces to elaborate etchings.

- **Silver Jewelry:** Mexico has high-quality silver (mined mostly in the central states), and Cozumel shops sell lovely yet affordable silver rings, pendants, earrings, and more.

- **Leather Sandals:** You may need to try on a few pairs to find one that fits, but these traditional handmade sandals can last for years.

- *Artesanía:* Mexico is justly famous for its folk art—colorful, whimsical, artful. Gifts shops have fun cheap stuff, while galleries and certain stores carry beautiful high-quality pieces.

- **Maya Replicas:** Replicas of Maya sculptures, paintings, and other images make a unique and memorable souvenir. Workmanship varies considerably.

- **Feather Paintings:** It's hard not to be impressed by the skill and dexterity required to create these unique pieces of art.

- **Cuban Cigars:** Still the best in quality and flavor. Americans won't be able to bring these home, so you may as well enjoy them on the road.

Soles for selection. The artistry alone makes this a worthwhile stop, but it has enough variety that you're almost certain to find a gift for everyone on your list. There's a smaller satellite shop at the Punta Langosta mall, too (Av. Rafael Melgar btwn Calles 7 and 11, no phone, 9am-8pm Mon.-Sat., 11am-5pm Sun.).

Inspiración Gallery (Av. 5 btwn Calles Rosado Salas and 3, tel. 987/872-8293, 9am-2pm and 5pm-9pm Mon.-Sat.) also specializes in high-quality Mexican folk art, featuring the work of local and regional artists. Here you'll find masks, hand-painted boxes, Maya replicas, paintings, paper art, pottery—the list changes week by week, but the quality and caliber of the *artesanía* is constant.

Airport stores—especially ones at the gate—don't normally make the cut for a guidebook, but **Pineda Covalin** (Cozumel International Airport, Blvd. Aeropuerto at Av. 65, tel. 987/878-4545, www.pinedacovalin.com, hours vary depending on flight departures) is such a special one, it's impossible to leave out. A small boutique shop, it sells luxury items that

integrate indigenous or iconic Mexican art into the design: eyeglasses with Huichol prints, silk ties with Maya glyphs, clutch purses with traditional Chamulan patterns—you'll wish your flight was delayed to be able to browse longer. Staff members have even been known to bring merchandise out to the main ticketing area for guests who don't have a plane ticket but still really want to see and buy the store's one-of-a-kind products. If you're certain to buy an item but won't be leaving the island via the airport, a staff member will bring a small selection of items to your hotel. You can also head to Playa del Carmen, where a much bigger store is located right on the pedestrian walkway (5 Av. btwn Calle 26 and 28, 10am-11pm daily).

Located near the international pier, **Arte de Origen** (Royal Village Mall, Carr. Costera Sur Km. 3.5, tel. 987/857-0725, www.artedeorigen.com, 9:30am-10pm daily) is an upscale *artesanía* shop featuring unique and gorgeous handcrafted items inspired by different Latin American indigenous cultures. There's a wide range of items—tapestries, lacquered boxes,

© H.W. PRADO

Cozumel has fun, colorful folk art for sale.

© LIZA PRADO

Tiny hand-painted figures are one of many kinds of folk art available in Cozumel.

wall art, furniture—from a variety of different countries and regions, all of which makes finding a memento that much easier.

True to its name, which is Spanish for "beautiful house," **Casa Bella** (Calle 3 btwn Avs. 5 and 10, no phone, 9am-6pm Mon.-Sat.) sells beautiful household items created by artisans from around the country. Items include pewter trays, *talavera* pottery, and whimsically painted mirrors. It's easy to imagine them all in your home, though getting some of the larger decorative items home could be a challenge!

Located on a quiet residential street, **Galería Azul** (Av. 15 btwn Calles 8 and 10 Nte., tel. 987/869-0963, www.cozumelglassart.com, 11am-7pm Mon.-Fri.) sells works of art created by local residents, including that of the shop's ex-pat owner Greg Dietrich. The selection changes regularly, of course, but items may include eye-catching handblown glasswork, wood carvings, and paintings on silk, as well as unique poster art and colorful tinwork. Like it or hate it, the artwork at **Miguelon**

e Hijos (Calle 5 Sur btwn Avs. 10 and 15, tel. 987/872-5549, 9am-6pm Mon.-Sat.) is anything but ordinary. The small family-run shop specializes in conch shells delicately carved with intricate portraits and ancient Maya tableaus. Not exactly everyone's taste, but the craftsmanship—each item is carved by hand—is nonetheless remarkable.

Balam Mayan Feather (Av. 5 at Calle 2, tel. 987/869-0548, 10am-10pm daily) trades in a unique and dying art, selling oil paintings created on the feathers of regional birds. Most feathers depict scenes of traditional villages or ancient Maya people, but there is a decent variety beyond that, including tropical flowers and underwater creatures. If you're lucky, an artist will be working on a new feather painting while you're browsing—feel free to watch. Prices range US$30-150.

If you don't mind a hunt, **Unicornio** (Av. 5 near Calle 1, tel. 987/872-0171, 8:30am-8:30pm daily) is a good place to find a hidden treasure. Among the trashy T-shirts and cheap seashell necklaces, you'll find gorgeous *talavera* pieces and traditional wood toys and figurines. It's worth a stop, if you have the time and patience, and bargaining is very welcome.

If you're looking for cheap one-stop shopping, **Viva México** (Av. Rafael Melgar at Calle Adolfo Rosado Salas, tel. 987/872-5466, 8am-9pm Mon.-Sat., noon-8pm Sun.) is a good bet. You'll find iconic Mexican goods—sombreros, zarapes, wood toys, straw purses—and some classic beach-town kitsch, too. It's not exactly a place to find a high-quality gift, much less a one-of-a-kind memento, but it's good for kids or if you're on your way to the airport and need something quick. There's fixed pricing only here.

CLOTHING AND JEWELRY

Miró (Plaza Central, Av. Rafael Melgar at Av. López Máteos, no phone, 10am-9pm Mon.-Sat.) sells high-quality cotton T-shirts and beachwear, most brightly colored or with distinctive Mexican designs. T-shirts run around US$20 apiece, which admittedly is quite a lot more expensive than other shops around

BLACK CORAL: A DISAPPEARING TREASURE

Despite its name, living black coral is not black at all, but a rich blue-green. It's only when the skeleton is stripped and polished that the namesake color emerges. Black coral belongs to a family of coral whose shells are semi-flexible, and colonies grow into beautiful fanlike formations that bend and sway in the current. It's the world's slowest-growing coral, adding just 1-2 *hundredths of a millimeter* per year. (That's 200 times slower than human fingernails.) Black coral is among a handful of coral species recently discovered at extreme depths–300 meters (984 feet) down, and more–far deeper than previously thought possible for coral. And perhaps most remarkable of all was the finding, In 2009, that a colony of black coral near Hawaii is over 4,000 years old, making it the oldest known marine organism.

Vast colonies of black coral once populated Cozumel's waters, and the island was for many years the center of black coral collection and trade. That's less true today, thanks partly to stricter regulation but also to the sad fact that Cozumel's black coral is so diminished–the species is now considered endangered–that poachers have moved elsewhere. Still, black coral from Cozumel retains a certain cachet, and the killing continues. Buying jewelry, souvenirs, and other items made with it only supports its continued destruction–please resist! Saving the black coral that lives in Cozumel's waters is still very possible.

town—no three for US$10 bargains here—but it's a good value considering the superior design and how long the shirts will last you before ending up in the rag pile.

Bugambilias (Av. 10 Sur btwn Calles Rosado Salas and 1, tel. 987/872-6282, 9am-6pm Mon. Sat.) sells traditional handmade linens and clothing, most incorporating embroidery and lace. The quality is excellent, showcasing some of the island's best traditional clothing. Prices range from moderate to high.

If you're in the market for a pair of traditional leather sandals, check out **Huaracheria Margarita** (Av. 30 at Calle 3, no phone, 10am-8pm Mon.-Sat., 10am-2pm Sun.). Among the colorful jellies and flip-flops, you'll find rows and rows of handmade huaraches, many brought from the mainland. The leather inventory is well-priced, especially considering the craftsmanship that goes into making each sandal.

Funky Bazaar (Av. Rafael Melgar at Calle 11, tel. 987/872-5955, 10am-10pm Mon.-Sat.) carries boho women's clothing, most gently used. It's a hidden gem if you forgot to pack a summer dress, shawl, or short shorts. (It's also a good stop if your bags are lost in transit.) For gifts, check out the whimsical paintings and other creations by local artist Beatriz Cornejo; handcrafted jewelry is for sale, too. It's located in the MEGA supermarket complex, next to Office Max.

Sergio's Silver from Taxco (Av. Juárez btwn Avs. 5 and 10, tel. 987/872-7632, www.sergiosilver.com.mx, 10am-8pm Mon. Sat.) is a longtime mom-and-pop shop that specializes in high-end silver jewelry made from silver from Taxco, located outside Mexico City, and the country's silver mining capital. Most of the items are made by local artisans, which means you'll find unique and beautiful pieces of jewelry. Its location just off the main drag also means you'll find a friendly, no-pressure shopping experience. If you don't find what you're looking for here, head to its second location one block east on Juárez between Avenidas 10 and 15 (same phone and hours).

SPORTS GEAR

Pro Dive Cozumel (Calle Rosado Salas at Av. 5, tel. 987/872-4123, 9am-9pm Mon.-Sat., 1pm-9pm Sun.) has the island's largest and most complete selection of snorkel and dive equipment, from various brands of fins, masks, and other basic gear, to specialized items like dive computers and top-of-the-line regulators. It can be a lifesaver for any diver who's left a key item at home, and eye candy for intermediate divers who are just starting to collect diving gear of their own. Prices are certainly higher than what you'd find at home, but sometimes certain purchases just can't wait!

If you're looking for hipster beachwear and gear, check out **Puro Mar Surf-Kite-Bikini** (Av. 5 Sur at Calle 3, tel. 987/872-4483, 9am-9pm Mon.-Sat.). Although it's a fairly small shop, it's jam-packed with everything from bikinis and swim trunks to kiting and surfing gear. This is also a good place to go if you're interested in learning to kiteboard, or, for experienced riders, arranging a kiting tour of the island. The person who owns the shop also owns and operates Cozumel Kiteboarding, one of just a few recommended kiteboarding outfits on the island, and even the mainland.

MUSIC AND SMOKES

Whether or not you play an instrument, **U'nahi Pax** (Av. Juárez at Av. 15, tel. 987/872-5269, 9am-6pm Mon.-Sat.), Maya for The House of Music, is a great little shop with a huge variety of handcrafted instruments from over 37 countries—you'll find everything from rain sticks to guitars. If you'll be on the island for an extended period, ask about music lessons.

If you're in the market for Cubans, or just want to learn more about them, check out **Havana Bob's Cuban Cigars** (Av. 5 btwn Av. Juárez and Calle 2, cell. tel. 987/103-5726, 10:30am-4pm and 7pm-11pm Mon.-Fri.). Selling certified Cuban cigars, the shop has a large walk-in humidor with high-end smokes ranging from slender cigarillos to heavy gauge beauties. Havana Bob's also sells its own popular line of cigars, which are hand-rolled on the island. A full line of desktop humidors, cutters, punchers, lighters, and other accessories are also available for sale. Look for the shop next to Wet Wendy's, where shoppers often head to enjoy their smokes with a stiff drink.

MARKETS

Located in a yellow building on the east side of the main plaza, **Plaza del Sol** (Av. 5 Nte.

btwn Av. Benito Juárez and Calle 1, 9am-8pm Mon.-Sat., 11am-5pm Sun.) houses a labyrinth of small souvenir shops selling everything from bad T-shirts to quality silver jewelry. You'll have to poke around a bit to find items worth buying, but a little perseverance will go a long way, especially if you're on a tight budget.

Reminiscent of a flea market, **La Feria** (Av. Juárez btwn Calles 20 and 25, no phone, 9am-10pm Mon.-Sat., 9am-8pm Sun.) is a mishmash of small vendors selling everything from DVDs to kitchenware. For travelers, it's a great place to buy flip-flops, a travel clock, or a set of cheap headphones for the beach. Bargaining is welcome.

MALLS

Punta Langosta (Av. Rafael Melgar btwn Calles 7 and 11, 9am-8pm daily) is Cozumel's swankiest shopping center. The ultramodern open-air building is home to high-end clothing boutiques, air-conditioned jewelry stores, and fancy ice cream shops. It's a good place to window shop, especially if you want to buy a memento but aren't sure exactly what you'd like.

The Forum (Av. Rafael Melgar at Calle 10, tel. 987/869-1687, 9am-5pm Mon.-Sat.) is a small shopping center on the north side of downtown. It has a handful of fancy jewelry shops, a cigar store, a cowboy boot outlet, and the requisite bad T-shirt and souvenir shops. Prices tend to be a bit higher here than elsewhere, but the marble floors and powerful air-conditioning make it easy to linger.

Located just north of the international pier, **Royal Village Mall** (Carr. Costera Sur Km. 3.5, no phone, www.royalvillageczm.com, 10am-8pm Mon.-Fri., 10am-9pm Sat.-Sun.) is a pleasant open-air mall with tropical plants, a couple of cenotes (no swimming, unfortunately), and lots of upscale shops and cafés. Most are international chain stores like Lacoste and GNC, but there are a few like Arte de Origen and Hecho en Mexico that are only found domestically and feature items you'll be hard pressed to find back home.

No doubt, **Puerto Maya Mall** (Carr. Costera Sur Km. 4, no phone, www.puertamaya.com,

© LIZA PRADO

Cozumel has shops for all budgets.

hours vary depending on daily cruise ship schedules) is geared toward those traveling by cruise ship (it's attached to the international pier), but nonetheless, it's a pleasant pedestrian mall with many of the same big shops from downtown plus some nicer souvenir and knick-knack shops. As you'd expect, prices are somewhat higher, but this is an easy place to shop if you're staying on the south end of the island and don't feel like trekking into town.

Accommodations

Cozumel has a surprisingly wide variety of accommodations, with something for all tastes and all budgets. The downtown area has numerous independent hotels, including popular youth hostels, friendly bed and breakfasts, large commercial hotels, and classy boutique ones. North of the downtown area are several condominium complexes, offering fully furnished units of various sizes. Service and standards at Cozumel's hotels and condos are uniformly high, and several offer extras like free use of snorkeling gear or dry storage for scuba gear. Cozumel has several dive resorts, of course, where packages include lodging, meals, and two or more dives per day with the resort's own dive shop. Less well known are hotels like the one catering to kiteboarders and stand-up paddlers, and another to golfers; like dive resorts, they appeal to travelers who eat, drink, and breathe their given sport, and typically offer package deals on lodging, gear, and more. And while Cozumel lacks the long spectacular beaches of Cancún and the Riviera Maya, it still has plenty of all-inclusive resorts. Most are located on the island's calm southwestern shore, where the best beaches are located, and include both upscale and affordable alternatives. All told, Cozumel has a larger selection

CHOOSING A PLACE TO STAY

Cozumel's accommodations run the full gamut, from hostels and bare-bones hotels to all-inclusive resorts and boutique hotels. Choosing the one that's best for you usually entails juggling competing priorities. Overall, the quality of lodging in Cozumel is quite high, and it's not totally unreasonable to say "You can't go wrong." But the truth is, the hotel you stay in has a major impact on your visit, and it's worth taking time to really think about what sort of lodging will best fit your travel tastes and plans.

Price: This is the first consideration of most travelers, understandably, but price alone can be deceiving. Ask about important details, like whether taxes are included (they can be up to 22 percent!); how many guests are included in the rate (especially for families); and exactly which amenities are (or are not) included in the rate. If you find a too-good-to-be-true deal online, be sure to read through the fine print.

Amenities: Consider which amenities you need or want, and which might save you time and money. Rooms with kitchen may cost slightly more but can save you time, money, and headaches in the long run, especially for families and groups. Most hotels offer free

Wi-Fi, but it's always worth double-checking (including whether it's available in-room or in the lobby only). And if a hotel offers breakfast or other meal plan, be sure to clarify exactly what's included.

Type: Most travelers gravitate toward the type of lodging they're most familiar with, whether small hotels, all-inclusive resorts, or others. While all such options are available on Cozumel, it's worth thinking twice before doing what you always do. Indie travelers may be pleasantly surprised by the convenience all-inclusives offer, especially if there are kids in tow. Resort-goers may find staying at a B&B to be a fun challenge. Longtime budget travelers may want to treat themselves to some nicer digs. Trying out a new type of lodging can be a great change of pace.

Location: The majority of Cozumel's independent hotels are in or near the downtown area, while the resorts are farther afield. Even some independent hotels claim to be a short walk from town, when in fact they're rather removed. Booking a rental car can solve some of these issues (and make exploring the island easier), but be sure to ask about parking.

and variety of accommodations that its size might suggest, and there are several great options within each lodging type and category.

DOWNTOWN COZUMEL
Under US$50

Just one block from the central plaza, **Hostelito** (Av. 10 btwn Av. Benito Juárez and Calle 2 Nte., cell. tel. 987/869-8157, www.hostelcozumel.com, US$12.50 dorm, US$37.50-55 s/d with a/c) is a stylish hostel—Cozumel's only hostel, in fact—with a large coed dorm packed with bunks, lockers, and fans; there are also attached gender-specific bathrooms, with well-kept shower and toilet stalls. Groups of four or more should ask about the air-conditioned dorm with private bathroom—at US$12.50 per head, they're a steal. Private doubles have air-conditioning, minifridge, and TV—they were

being renovated when we passed through, so ought to be in nice condition. Best of all are the outdoor common areas: a fully equipped rooftop kitchen is available for all to use, as is a great lounge and solarium with hammocks for just kicking back. There's free Wi-Fi, too.

Hotel Pepita (Av. 15 Sur btwn Calles 1 and Rosado Salas, tel. 987/872-0098, US$35 s/d with a/c) is a good value for traveler 'tweens on a budget: post-hostel but pre-B&B. The friendly owners keep the rooms very clean, though some of the beds are saggy, and the decor could use some serious updating (think early 1980s in a not-so-good way). All have air-conditioning, ceiling fan, cable TV, minifridge, and two double beds. There's also fresh coffee every morning in the long inner courtyard, which also doubles as a no-frills lounge.

Hotel Caribe (Calle 2 Nte. btwn Avs. 15

and 20, tel. 987/872-0325, US$46-54 s/d with a/c) has a small appealing pool in a leafy central garden—a rare and welcome feature in the ranks of budget hotels. Rooms are plain but clean, with one, two, or three beds, okay bathrooms, and old-school air conditioners. Service can be ambivalent, but you can't argue with the value.

Hotel Mary Carmen (Av. 5 Sur btwn Calles 1 and Rosado Salas, tel. 987/872-0581, US$33 s/d with a/c) is a simple but reliable budget hotel, with a great location on the pedestrian walkway. Rooms have modern decor and are reasonably clean, though the rattling air conditioners and old-school bathrooms could use updating. The owners are friendly and very helpful, though, and you can't beat being just a half block from the central plaza.

US$50-100

Mi Casa en Cozumel (Av. 5 btwn Calles 7 and 9, tel. 987/872-6200, www.micasancozumel.com, US$45-70 s/d, US$160 penthouse) is a terrific boutique hotel and an architectural gem—the curves of the spiral staircase and use of tropical woods are counterbalanced by the triangular patios and angled nooks occupied by whirlpool tubs. All nine units have contemporary Mexican decor, most have a minifridge and cable TV, and a few have kitchenettes. Complimentary continental breakfast is served in a cozy ground-floor dining area. Several units have air-conditioning, while the others were designed for natural ventilation and are quite comfortable with fans only. The split-level penthouse is stunning, with full kitchen, outdoor hot tub, front and rear patios, and great views of downtown. The hotel's lofty structure is equally impressive, but could be difficult for guests who have trouble climbing stairs. Weekly rates are available.

Tamarindo Bed and Breakfast (Calle 4 btwn Avs. 20 and 25 Nte., tel. 987/872-6190 or 987/112-4111, www.tamarindobedandbreakfast.com, US$45-51 s/d with fan, US$57 s/d with a/c and minifridge, US$62 suite with a/c and kitchenette) is a pleasant B&B owned by a friendly French expatriate who lives on-site.

The hotel has seven units bordering a large, leafy garden. Each room is different from the other, from two boxy but comfortable hotel rooms to a whimsical *palapa* bungalow with boho flair. All have cable TV and Wi-Fi. Full breakfast is included for rooms without a kitchenette, and there's a small communal kitchen in the main building. Rinse tanks and storage facilities are provided for guests with dive gear, too. The same owner also rents three apartments and bungalows known as **Tamarindo II** (US$69-79 s/d); located south of the center a few blocks from the water, they've got one or two bedrooms, air-conditioning, kitchen, cable TV, Wi-Fi, and a small pool. Reservations are highly recommended.

Amaranto Bungalows & Suites (Calle 5 btwn Avs. 15 and 20 Sur, cell. tel. 987/106-6220, www.amarantobedandbreakfast.com, US$59 s/d bungalow with a/c, US$65 s/d suite, US$75 s/d suite with a/c) offers seclusion and privacy, while still within easy walking distance from downtown. The obliging stars of the place are the suites, in a three-story tower, each with a sitting area and 360-degree views; the lower unit has air-conditioning, high ceilings, and a modern feel, while the upper one has a *palapa* roof with a lookout tower and rustic-chic decor. There also are three thatch-roofed bungalows with modern bathrooms and a beachy feel. All the rooms have king-size beds, minifridges, microwaves, cable TV, and security boxes. There is a plunge pool on-site—perfect for cooling off after a day in the sun—and Wi-Fi in the small lobby-lounge. Breakfast is included during high season, too. Amaranto doesn't have a full-time attendant, so it's best to reserve in advance to be sure someone is expecting you (otherwise your chances of finding a staff member are hit or miss).

Hotel Flamingo (Calle 6 btwn Avs. Rafael Melgar and 5 Nte., tel. 987/872-1264, toll-free U.S. tel. 800/806-1601, www.hotelflamingo.com, US$79-91 s/d with a/c, US$195 penthouse) offers classy, well-priced rooms with modern furnishings, mosaic tile bathrooms, and colorful Guatemalan decor, all in a quiet north-of-center location. Rooms have powerful

ISLA COZUMEL

DOWNTOWN COZUMEL ACCOMMODATIONS

Name	Type	Price
Amaranto Bungalows & Suites	small hotel	US$59-75
Casa Colonial	condominiums	US$154
Casa Mexicana	hotel	US$90-110
Casita de Maya	guesthouse	US$89-119
Cozumel Palace	all-inclusive resort	US$413-686
Guido's Boutique Hotel	apartments	US$110-130
Hostelito	hostel	US$12.50-55
Hotel Caribe	small hotel	US$46-54
Hotel Flamingo	small hotel	US$79-195
Hotel Mary Carmen	hotel	US$33
Hotel Pepita	small hotel	US$35
◖ Mi Casa en Cozumel	boutique hotel	US$45-160
Suites Bahía	hotel	US$67-92
Suites Colonial	hotel	US$59-67
◖ Tamarindo Bed and Breakfast	bed and breakfast	US$45-62
Tamarindo II	apartment-hotel	US$69-79
Villa Escondida	bed and breakfast	US$90
◖ Villas Las Anclas	condominiums	US$110
Vista del Mar	small hotel	US$78-90

Features	Why Stay Here	Best Fit For
king-size beds, plunge pool	quiet, location	couples, adult travelers, families with older children
2-bedroom units, spacious, daily maid service, pool, hot tub	amenities, private	families, group travelers
views, pool, breakfast	location, discreet	couples, families, business travelers
small size, pool, beach club access, near airport	quiet, personalized attention, opportunity to meet other guests	couples, solo travelers, families with older children
oceanfront location	spa, resort credit	families, couples, solo travelers
ocean view, balcony	private, convenience	families, couples
air-conditioning, private doubles, shared kitchen, solarium	affordable, opportunity to meet other travelers	budget travelers, solo travelers
pool, central garden, air-conditioning	affordable	budget travelers
quiet location, rooftop Jacuzzi, solarium, garden courtyard, breakfast	location, relaxed atmosphere	couples, families
near central plaza, air-conditioning	affordable, location	budget travelers
air-conditioning, minifridge	affordable	budget travelers
modern architecture, whirlpool tubs, kitchenettes, breakfast	private, unique property	couples, adult travelers, families with older children
waterfront, balconies, buffet breakfast	location, affordable	budget travelers
central location, kitchenettes, buffet breakfast	location, affordable	budget travelers
garden, breakfast, kitchenettes, rinse tanks	affordable, personalized service	families, couples, budget travelers
location, kitchen, pool	amenities, private	families, group travelers, couples
adults-only, pool, breakfast, bicycles, snorkeling gear	location, amenities	couples, solo travelers
2-story units, garden, dive shop	location, amenities	couples, families
ocean views, hot tub, continental breakfast	location, amenities	families, couples

air-conditioning, electronic safes, and cable TV. Three common areas provide lots of extra outdoor space for guests—a rooftop solarium with lounge chairs and Jacuzzi, a shady mid-level area with hammocks, and a garden courtyard with tables and chairs. Wi-Fi is available in the lobby and bar areas. Families and groups should consider booking the penthouse, a two-bedroom apartment with a full-size kitchen, private Jacuzzi, even a rooftop grill. Book in advance to get full breakfast at no extra charge.

Located in the heart of San Miguel, **Villa Escondida** (Av. 10 Sur btwn Calles 3 Sur and Rosado Salas, tel. 987/120-1225, www.villaescondidacozumel.com, US$90 s/d with a/c) is an adults-only B&B with just four guest rooms. Each is modern in style, if a bit sparse, with comfortable beds and spacious bathrooms. All look onto a well-tended garden with an inviting swimming pool, lounge chairs, and hammocks. A full-size breakfast is served on the hotel terrace; daily offerings include everything from pancakes to *chilaquiles*. Complimentary bicycles and snorkeling gear also are available to guests.

Vista del Mar (Av. Rafael Melgar btwn Calles 5 and 7 Sur, tel. 987/872-0545, toll-free U.S./Can. tel. 888/309-9988, www.hotelvistadelmar.com, US$78-90 s/d with a/c) is a charming hotel in the middle of a string of tacky souvenir shops. Rooms have muted earth tones, high-end furnishings, inlaid stone walls, and balconies (some with spectacular views of the Caribbean). All have cable TV, minifridges, safety deposit boxes, robes—even turndown service. The hotel's patio also has lots of comfy lounge chairs as well as a hot tub with a mosaic-tile floor—a great space to relax if you don't mind the view of the kitsch below. Continental breakfast, delivered to your room, is included.

Suites Bahía (Calle 3 btwn Avs. Rafael Melgar and 5 Sur, tel. 987/872-9090, toll-free Mex. tel. 800/277-2639, toll-free U.S. tel. 877/228-6747, www.suitesbahia.com, US$67-92 s/d with a/c) and **Suites Colonial** (Av. 5 Sur btwn Calles 1 and Rosado Salas, tel. 987/872-0506, same toll-free tels., www.suitescolonial.

com, US$59 s/d with a/c, US$67 suite with a/c) are sister hotels, renting unremarkable but functional and well-priced rooms. The Colonial is more central, right on the pedestrian walkway, with slightly newer rooms and full kitchenettes. For a bit higher rate, rooms at the Bahía are larger and brighter (especially the ocean-view ones), and still have minifridge and microwave ovens. Neither hotel will win any awards for charm, but units at both are clean and reasonably comfortable, and include air-conditioning, cable TV, Wi-Fi, and (perhaps best of all) buffet breakfast at upscale Casa Mexicana hotel, a third sister located nearby. Both are favorites among longtime Cozumel visitors on a budget.

US$100-150

◖ Villas Las Anclas (Av. 5 Sur btwn Calles 3 and 5, tel. 987/872-5476, www.hotelvillalasanclas.com, US$110 s/d with a/c) is a great option for those who want a little home away from home. Seven pleasantly decorated apartments open onto a leafy, private garden, each with a fully equipped kitchen, a living room, and a loft master bedroom accessed by spiral stairs. Using the built-in sofas as twin beds, the apartments can accommodate up to four people while still not feeling overcrowded (optimally, 2 adults and 2 children). All units also have air-conditioning and Wi-Fi. New owners have brought some welcome updates—a fresh coat of paint, newer TVs and appliances, and a reception area and dive shop in front—while the friendly vibe and great value remain the same.

Guido's Boutique Hotel (Av Rafael Melgar btwn Calles 6 and 8 Nte., tel. 987/872-0946, www.guidosboutiquehotel.com, US$110-130) is less a hotel and more do-it-yourself apartments, but the location, amenities, and price make Guido's an outstanding option. Master suites have king beds, while junior suites have queens; all are spacious, with full-size kitchens, stylish decor, and satellite TV and Wi-Fi. Each has a small balcony overlooking the street and ocean—traffic can get noisy midweek but the views are priceless. The hotel is located just north of the center, above Guido's Restaurant,

© LIZA PRADO

Fully furnished apartments are a great way to save on food and other costs while remaining in the center of town.

one of the island's best. There's no formal reception, so reserve ahead.

Casa Mexicana (Av. Rafael Melgar btwn Calles 5 and 7, toll-free Mex. tel. 800/277-2639, toll-free U.S. tel. 877/228-6747, www.casamexicanacozumel.com, US$90-110 s/d with a/c) is a modern beauty with a soaring interior courtyard and gorgeous views of the Caribbean from the ocean-side rooms, including cruise ships gliding in and out of port. Rooms are attractive and bright, though less inspired than the building itself, with good beds, quiet air conditioners, and updated bathrooms. There is a small infinity pool overlooking the Caribbean on one end of the spacious lobby; it's a little strange to be taking a dip in view of desk staff and inquiring guests, but it's still quite nice. Rates include buffet breakfast in an impressive open-air dining room.

Casita de Maya (Av. 65 Bis. at Blvd. Aeropuerto, tel. 987/869-2606; toll-free U.S. tel. 281/214-1122, www.casitademaya.com, US$89-119 s/d with a/c) is a popular

guesthouse with just four rooms, each with colorful paint, artful decor, and mini-split air conditioners. Come here if you enjoy meeting and mingling with fellow guests, as it's pretty much impossible not to. The expat owner is likewise friendly and attentive, and a fount of information about Cozumel. The hotel's narrow, clean swimming pool is great for cooling off—almost too cold!—and guests have access to Playa Azul beach club. The hotel's location, just blocks from the airport, is a potential drawback. Noise is less an issue than simply getting to and from town—a rental car definitely comes in handy. Free phone calls to the United States and Canada are included; meals are prepared on request.

Over US$150

A long walk from town but worth every step, **Casa Colonial** (Av. 35 btwn Calles 8 and 10, toll-free U.S./Can. tel. 866/437-1320, www.cozumelrentalvillas.com, US$1,075/week villa with a/c) has four fully equipped

NORTHWESTERN COZUMEL ACCOMMODATIONS

Name	Type	Price
Cantamar Condominiums	condominiums	US$241
Casa Viento	small hotel	US$110-190
Condumel	condominiums	US$120-142
Coral Princess Hotel & Resort	resort	US$95-367
El Cozumeleño Beach Resort	all-inclusive resort	US$159-238
(Hotel B Cozumel	boutique hotel	US$216
Miramar Condominiums	condominiums	US$129-180
Playa Azul Hotel	hotel	US$165

Mexican-style villas. All are two stories with two bedrooms, 2.5 bathrooms, a living room, a dining room, a modern kitchen, 32-inch hi-def TV, Wi-Fi, even a washer and dryer. And unlike many longer-term rentals, you still get daily maid service and complimentary concierge service. All villas face a lush courtyard with a large pool and hot tub. Rinse tanks for dive gear are available, too. It's a great rate, especially if traveling in a group of four, for an incredibly comfortable stay.

Cozumel Palace (Av. Rafael Melgar at Calle 17, toll-free U.S. tel. 877/325-1537, www.palaceresorts.com/cozumelpalace, US$413 s/d all-inclusive, US$550-686 suite all-inclusive) offers a typical all-inclusive experience with the huge plus of being a short walk from the action downtown. Rooms themselves are modern with fully stocked minibars, complimentary room service, and Wi-Fi; suites have the added bonus of ocean-view balconies and two-person Jacuzzi tubs. The food options are limited—a snack bar, a buffet, and two à la carte restaurants (dinner only)—which is fine for a long weekend or so. There also is a small spa. The major drawback of the resort is that there is no beach. There are sandy areas and plenty of pool space (stake out a chair early), but if you're looking for beach time, it won't happen here (though the snorkeling is surprisingly good). Resort credit often is part of the package—consider using it to explore the island's beach clubs or its sister resort in Playa del Carmen.

NORTHWESTERN COZUMEL US$100-150

Located just minutes from some of Cozumel's best kiteboarding spots, the aptly named **Casa Viento** (House of Wind, Country Club Estates, tel. 987/869-8220, www.casaviento.net, US$110-190 s/d with a/c) has comfortable rooms and cheerful *mi casa es su casa* service from the live-in owners. Choose between large standard rooms, one- and two-bedroom suites with kitchen, and a honeymoon suite with cupola and great ocean views; all rooms have air-conditioning, Wi-Fi, and look onto

Features	Why Stay Here	Best Fit For
2-bedroom units, ocean views, daily maid service, pool, snorkeling	amenities, oceanfront, proximity to downtown	families, group travelers
on-site kiteboarding school, kitchen, pool	kiteboarding, proximity to beach	couples, families
oceanfront, king-size beds, daily maid service	amenities	couples, families
pool, oceanfront, snorkeling	affordable	families, couples
beach, snorkeling	location, attentive service, affordable	families, couples
ocean views, pool, gourmet restaurant	amenities, great service	couples, solo travelers, families with older children
pool, oceanfront, snorkeling, concierge	amenities, location, attentive service	families, group travelers, couples
ocean views, pool, golf packages, breakfast	beach, nearby golf course	couples, families

a welcoming pool. If you're interested in kiting, Casa Viento also is home base for De Lille Sports, a kiting school and tour operator run by legendary Mexican kiteboarder Raul de Lille. SUPing lessons and rentals are available, too

The intimate **Miramar Condominiums** (Zona Hotelera Nte. Km. 3.4, toll-free U.S. tel. 866/564-4427, www.cozumelvillas.com/miramar, US$129-150 one-bedroom condo, US$180 two-bedroom condo) is a well-maintained complex with units varying in style, though all are updated and very comfortable. There's a fabulous infinity pool overlooking the Caribbean and entry points to the ocean that make snorkeling easy. The staff does a good job of making guests feel welcome—from fresh flowers upon arrival to concierge services like booking rental cars. There's no on-site beach, which is a drawback, but if you enjoy exploring the island, this is a great place to stay. It's especially suitable for families and those traveling in small groups.

Maya stellae decorate the facade of

Condumel (Zona Hotelera Nte. Km. 1.5, tel. 987/872-0892, www.condumel.com, US$120-142 for up to 4 people), an old-school but very agreeable oceanfront condo complex, located a 15-minute walk from downtown. Spacious one-bedroom apartments have king-size beds, Wi-Fi, fully equipped kitchens, and daily maid service. Oversized sliding-glass doors offer awesome views of the Caribbean and incoming airplanes. The coast here is ironshore, so there's just a small patch of sand; steps and a ladder make swimming and snorkeling a breeze. It's popular with longtime visitors to the island, especially couples.

Coral Princess Hotel & Resort (Zona Hotelera Nte. Km. 2.5, tel. 987/872-3200, toll-free U.S. tel. 800/253-2702, www.coralprincess.com, US$95-118 s/d, US$277-367 suite) is an old-school hotel offering a basic resort experience for travelers on a budget. It's kind of like staying at a Best Western with the added bonus of good snorkeling just steps from your room. Relaxing oceanfront is easy too, in the hotel's expansive sandy area, which has plenty

IRONSHORE

Ironshore is the evocative name given to the hard jagged rock that forms much of Cozumel's coastline. It can be incredibly sharp, like a field of upturned knives, and renders large stretches of the shoreline virtually inaccessible (to people, at least). Hotels that front ironshore sometimes fill in sections with sand to create artificial beaches, or else build walkways over it, with ladders and platforms at the water's edge. Still, it has an undeniable beauty, with its dark ashy color and dramatic formations, slashing emerald waves into a frothy white.

Ironshore is a type of karst topography, a class of distinctive seascapes and landscapes caused by erosion, usually in limestone. The entire Yucatán Peninsula, including Cozumel, sits on a massive limestone shelf, and its most fa- mous karst formations are cenotes, a vast system of underground caves and rivers formed by rainwater seeping through the porous bedrock. Ironshore is formed by water erosion too, of course, but its uniquely intricate formations are more directly caused by *bioerosion:* the work of seaborne bacteria, fungi, algae, sponges, and worms boring tirelessly into the coastal rock. The same process, when it occurs in coral, re- sults in fine powdery sand, which is why iron- shore and white-sand beaches so often form near each other.

There's no shortage of ironshore in Cozumel, but the best place to admire it up close is on the eastern shore, especially at El Mirador, a beach where there's a natural ironshore arch and easy access from the road.

© LIZA PRADO

Ironshore is hard, jagged limestone shaped by thousands of years of erosion, partly by wind and water, but mostly by microscopic organisms.

ISLA COZUMEL

of lounge chairs as well as a large pool (like most hotels in this part of the island, there's no beach because of the ironshore). Service is surprisingly attentive—the staff is hardworking and pleasant, which goes a long way in smoothing out the resort's rough edges and making for many repeat customers.

Over US$150

Playa Azul Hotel (Zona Hotelera Nte. Km. 4, tel. 987/869-5160, www.playa-azul.com, US$165 s/d) caters mostly to golfers—guests pay no greens fees at Cozumel Country Club—but has packages for divers and honeymooners as well. Medium-size rooms and more spacious suites all have fairly modern furnishings and large bathrooms—they're not fancy, but the excellent ocean views make up for any deficiencies in decor. The pool is clean and attractive, too. The beach, while well-tended, is small; it can get crowded with day-trippers, especially those from cruise ships.

Oozing cool, ⚓ **Hotel B Cozumel** (Zona Hotelera Nte. Km. 2.5, tel. 987/872-0300, www.hotelbcozumel.com, US$216 s/d) is a boutique hotel that combines midcentury esthetic with traditional Mexican decor. Rooms have clean lines, lots of natural light, and feature gorgeous one-of-a-kind Mexican folk art. All have a balcony or patio and the amenities you'd expect from a high-end place—silent air-conditioning, cable TV, and Wi-Fi. Most have ocean views, too. Outdoors, there's a breezy gourmet restaurant, a great half-moon pool, plus lots of sandy areas with hammocks and beach chairs. The only thing missing is a beach. The waterfront has lots of ironshore, so the hotel has done its best to create plenty of easy entry points to the water.

Located approximately one mile from downtown, **Cantamar Condominiums** (Zona Hotelera Nte. Km. 1.9, toll-free U.S. tel. 866/564-4427, www.cozumelvillas.com/cantamar, US$241 two-bedroom condo) is a

© LIZA PRADO

Cozumel has several classy boutique hotels, like Hotel B Cozumel on the northwest shore.

© LIZA PRADO

Resorts that don't have a natural beach often create one by filling in the rocky shoreline with sand.

nine-unit condominium complex offering two-bedroom, two-bath condos with fully equipped kitchens and daily maid service. Each has a different owner, so decor varies dramatically, but all have ocean-view balconies or patios, air-conditioning, and are steps from an ocean-side pool. Like most of the accommodations north of town, the property is lined with ironshore, but Cantamar has created a small sandy area behind a retaining wall plus a small pier with a ladder for easy access to the water, making snorkeling or swimming easy.

El Cozumeleño Beach Resort (Zona Hotelera Nte. Km. 4.5, tel. 987/872-9530, toll-free U.S. tel. 800/437-3923, www.elcozumeleno.com, US$159 s all-inclusive, US$238 d all-inclusive) is an older all-inclusive offering very basic facilities. The food is passable but with only three options—a snack bar, a buffet, and an à la carte restaurant—it gets tiresome fast. The rooms need updating, but those in the south tower are in much better condition than

the rest. For children, there's a simple miniature golf course, a kids club, and family-friendly movies screened throughout the week. The main reason to stay here is the beach, which is wide and well maintained; it also leads to a nice snorkeling area. The service is friendly and attentive, too. If you don't mind a low-frills vacation and are able to find an online special, this is a decent option. If the rack rate is all you find, your money is better spent elsewhere.

SOUTHWESTERN COZUMEL
US$100-150

A laid-back dive resort, **Blue Angel Resort** (Carr. Costera Sur Km. 2.2, tel. 987/872-0188, www.blueangelresort.com, US$110 s/d) provides all the amenities a diver could want: a reputable dive shop, reliable boats, an on-site dock, and drying racks and lockers for gear. The rooms themselves are modern but basic with polished cement floors, good beds, and updated bathrooms; all have great ocean views.

© LIZA PRADO

palapa-roofed bungalows at Iberostar Cozumel, an all-inclusive resort on Cozumel's southwest shore

There's also an open-air restaurant serving American classics, a well-tended pool on the water, and plenty of shady places to sit back and relax. The only thing missing is a beach. If you can live with that, this a perfect place to stay awhile.

Scuba Club Cozumel (Carr. Costera Sur Km. 1.5, tel. 987/872-0853, toll-free U.S. tel. 800/847-5708, www.scubaclubcozumel. com, US$130 pp all-inclusive) is an old-school dive hotel known for its great packages. It has an on-site dock, outdoor lockers, and drying racks for dive gear. Rooms are very basic–clean and bare bones (good beds and a balcony yes, cable TV and Wi-Fi no). There's a small pool and a man-made beach, too. Meals are typically included in the rate and are served in a bustling dining room with plastic tables and chairs. Not exactly a tropical getaway but perfect if you'll be underwater most of the time anyway.

A small, long-running resort, **El Cid La**

Ceiba Beach (Carr. Costera Sur Km. 4.5, tel. 987/872-0844, toll-free U.S. tel. 866/306-6113, www.elcid.com/ceiba beach, US$90-175 s/d with a/c, US$160-275 pp all-inclusive) is just south of town and overlooks one of the main cruise ship docks. Most guests enjoy watching the giant ships come and go, though some may find it an intrusion. The guest rooms (and resort as a whole) are comfortable but need updating; the elevators and air-conditioning especially could use some attention. There is a smallish pool and sunny beach. Best of all is the snorkeling right in front, with numerous coral heads and even a submerged airplane wreck. The waterfront restaurant serves decent meals, though you're close enough to town that you can easily forgo the pricey meal plan and eat off-resort instead (and make use of the in-room kitchenettes). El Cid sells day passes that are popular with cruise ship crew members, who seem to enjoy the hotel's Wi-Fi as much as any other amenity.

SOUTHWESTERN AND EASTERN COZUMEL ACCOMMODATIONS

SOUTHWESTERN COZUMEL

Name	Type	Price
Blue Angel Resort	dive resort	US$110
El Cid La Ceiba Beach	resort	US$90-275
Iberostar Cozumel	all-inclusive resort	US$200-450
Occidental Grand Cozumel	all-inclusive resort	US$200-420
Park Royal Cozumel	all-inclusive resort	US$144-188
《 Presidente InterContinental Cozumel Resort Spa	resort	US$218-2,250
Royal Club at Occidental Grand Cozumel	all-inclusive resort	US$275-525
Scuba Club Cozumel	all-inclusive dive resort	US$130
Secrets Aura Cozumel	all-inclusive resort	US$243-305

EASTERN COZUMEL

Name	Type	Price
Ventanas al Mar	small hotel	US$94-184

Over US$150

《 Presidente InterContinental Cozumel Resort Spa (Carr. Costera Sur Km. 6.5, tel. 987/872-9500, toll-free U.S. tel. 800/327-0200, www.intercontinentalcozumel.com, US$218-415 s/d with a/c, US$1,080-2,250 suite) may well be the best resort in Cozumel, with sleek sophisticated rooms that offer high-end amenities as well as niceties like twice-daily maid service and turndown service. While the views are of either garden or ocean, all roads lead to a mellow and welcoming pool scene and a great beach, despite the ironshore—thick white sand and calm, turquoise waters with plenty of access points for snorkelers and shore divers. A well-regarded dive shop, two lighted tennis courts, three restaurants, and a full-service spa round out this elegant hotel.

Located on a jungly plot of land fronting the ocean, **Occidental Grand Cozumel** (Carr. Costera Sur Km. 16.6, tel. 987/872-9730, www.occidentalhotels.com/resort/occidental-grand-cozumel, US$200-420 pp all-inclusive) is a classic all-inclusive with the amenities you'd expect—three swimming pools, a gym and spa,

Features	Why Stay Here	Best Fit For
dive shop, on-site dock, pool	amenities	divers
all-inclusive option, pool, beach, snorkeling	amenities	couples, families
beach, pools, several restaurants, activities	affordable, amenities	families, couples
beach, swimming pools, spa, organized activities, several restaurants	amenities, location	families, couples
ocean views, balconies, beach, pools	amenities	families, couples
beach, pool, dive shop, tennis courts, gourmet restaurants, spa	amenities, personalized service	couples, families, business travelers
VIP service, beach, swimming pools, spa, several restaurants	amenities, location, personalized service	families, couples
dive shop, on-site dock, pool	affordable, amenities	divers
adults-only, à la carte dining, "swim up" rooms, beach	facilities, location	couples, adult travelers

Features	Why Stay Here	Best Fit For
off-grid, kitchenette, breakfast, beach	isolated, location	couples, families

lighted tennis courts, and a long list of water sports including snorkeling and diving. There are six restaurants (three are open for dinner only) and organized activities and entertainment throughout the day and evening. Rooms are spread out throughout the resort, though none are oceanfront; the closest to the beach are those in Buildings 16 to 19. For a room upgrade and VIP services, consider staying at the on-site boutique resort, **Royal Club at Occidental Grand Cozumel** (tel. 987/872-9730, www.occidentalhotels.com/resort/royal-club-grand-cozumel, US$275-525 pp all-inclusive). For the extra cash, guests enjoy access to a private pool and restaurant, concierge services, and a bit more pampering.

Iberostar Cozumel (Carr. Costera Sur Km. 17.8, tel. 987/872-9900, toll-free U.S. tel. 888/923-2722, www.iberostar.com, US$200-450 s/d all-inclusive) is a basic all-inclusive with well-kempt, lush grounds. It's a good option if you're traveling on a budget but want a resort experience. The rooms, for instance, are reasonably comfortable but have older amenities; they're located in brightly painted two-story bungalows that are distributed throughout the resort. The beach is wide but has lots of rocky areas—great for snorkeling, not so great for wading (bring water shoes). The food is fine—there's an extensive buffet and snack bar plus two reservations-only restaurants (dinner only)—any longer than four days, though, and the offerings can be tiresome. The service is consistently good, and the activity offerings include water aerobics and yoga. There's also an on-site dive and snorkel shop. All in all, this is a good value if you find an online deal. If you encounter rack rates only, head elsewhere.

The adults-only **Secrets Aura Cozumel** (Carr. Costera Sur Km. 12.9, toll-free Mex. tel. 800/546-7445, toll-free U.S. tel. 800/413-3886, www.secretsresorts.com, US$243-305 pp all-inclusive) is a small all-inclusive resort sitting on a lush oceanfront property. It has features like à la carte dining (no buffets here) and top-shelf drinks. Rooms are spacious and modern, with updated amenities. If you can swing it budget-wise, opt for a "swim up" room, which provides direct access to one of its winding pools through the room's patio door (as in open the door and step right in).

Located near the southernmost cruise ship piers, **Park Royal Cozumel** (Carr. Costera Sur Km. 3.5, toll-free U.S. tel. 800/774-0040, www.parkroyalcozumel.com, US$144 s all-inclusive, US$188 d all-inclusive) is a modern all-inclusive resort with lush, well-maintained grounds and gorgeous ocean views (albeit highlighted with cruise ships). Its 340-plus rooms are located in two towers; they have updated amenities, granite throughout, and glass-enclosed balconies (for the best views, request a room on the 5th floor or higher). A tunnel leads from these towers to a beach club across the street. The resort has a protected beach, two infinity pools, and two whirlpools—though those traveling with young children will especially appreciate the small size and calm waters of the beach. All in all, this a comfortable place to stay and a good value. **Note:** Most of the sidewalks and roads are cobblestone, which may make this a tough resort to navigate for guests with mobility challenges.

EASTERN COZUMEL

The only hotel on the east side of the island, **Ventanas al Mar** (south end of Playa Tortugas, cell. tel. 987/105-2684, www.ventanasalmar.com.mx, US$94-104 s/d, US$164-184 s/d suite) has 12 large rooms and two suites, all with high ceilings and private patios or decks, many with marvelous ocean views. The interiors lack the detailing and upkeep you'd expect at this price but suit the hotel's isolated feel. All have kitchenettes with microwaves; some have minifridges. There's no air-conditioning, as the hotel runs almost entirely on wind and solar power. Fortunately, the constant sea breeze keeps rooms cool. There's a popular restaurant and beach club next door, but you'll probably want a car, as the east side has no ATM, grocery stores, or other services. You can also just embrace the isolation: Many guests spend a week or more without going to town at all. Rates include full breakfast.

Food

Cozumel's food scene is steadily improving, with an ever-increasing variety and quality of restaurants, eateries, cafés, and dessert spots. Like most islands, Cozumel has terrific seafood, always served fresh, from gourmet restaurants with executive chefs to simple eateries operated by local fisherman's cooperatives. (You may be surprised to learn, though, that much of the catch actually comes from around Isla Mujeres because the waters around Cozumel are protected). And the island's popularity with Americans, especially hungry divers, means you'll never want for steak, pasta, burgers, or big breakfasts. But Cozumel's cuisine doesn't stop there (as it once did). Diners now have several high-end options, including outstanding Italian, Argentinean, Mediterranean, Mexican, and contemporary fusion. At the other end of the spectrum, tourists are finally

making their way to some longtime locals' favorites, especially hole-in-the-wall taco joints. A new *chocolateria* and front-porch smoothies spot add to the already long list of irresistible sweets shops. And with so much within walking distance of the central plaza, Cozumel is suddenly a great place to eat out.

MEXICAN AND YUCATECAN

Kinta (Av. 5 btwn Calle 2 and 4 Nte., tel. 987/869-0544, www.kintacozumel.com, 5:30pm-11pm Tues.-Sun., US$10-17) is a chic restaurant serving gourmet Mexican dishes and out-of-sight cocktails. Seating is indoors in a modern, welcoming space or outdoors in a leafy tropical garden. The menu includes such specialties as the chile relleno, a poblano chile stuffed with ratatouille and Chihuahua cheese, and *kamarón adobado*, grilled shrimp marinated

© H.W. PRADO

Forget poolside dining—in Cozumel you can eat on the beach.

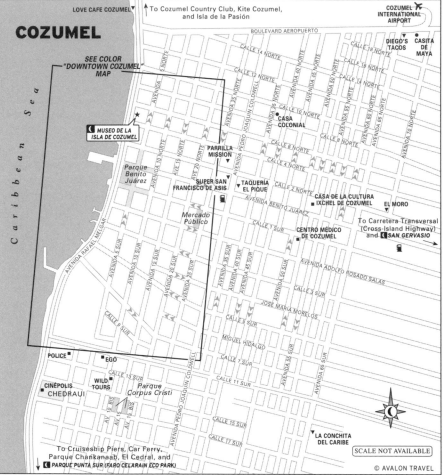

COZUMEL

LOVE CAFE COZUMEL ▼ ↑ To Cozumel Country Club, Kite Cozumel, and Isla de la Pasión

COZUMEL ✈ INTERNATIONAL AIRPORT

BOULEVARD AEROPUERTO

CALLE 14 NORTE

CALLE 18 NORTE   DIEGO'S TACOS   CASITA DE MAYA

CALLE 19 NORTE

CALLE 12 NORTE

CALLE 14 NORTE

SEE COLOR "DOWNTOWN COZUMEL" MAP

Caribbean Sea

CALLE 10 NORTE

● CASA COLONIAL

🏛 MUSEO DE LA ISLA DE COZUMEL

CALLE 8 NORTE

Parque Benito Juárez

PARRILLA MISSION ▼

CALLE 6 NORTE

CALLE 4 NORTE

SUPER SAN FRANCISCO DE ASIS

▼ TAQUERÍA EL PIQUE   CALLE 2 NORTE

Mercado Público

AVENIDA BENITO JUÁREZ

CASA DE LA CULTURA ■ IXCHEL DE COZUMEL   EL MORO ▼

CALLE 1 SUR

CENTRO MÉDICO ■ DE COZUMEL

To Carretera Transversal (Cross-Island Highway) and 🏛 SAN GERVASIO

AVENIDA ADOLFO ROSADO SALAS

CALLE 3 SUR

JOSÉ MARÍA MORELOS

CALLE 5 SUR

MIGUEL HIDALGO

POLICE ■   ■ EGO

CALLE 7 SUR

CALLE 11 SUR

CINÉPOLIS   WILD ■ TOURS   *Parque Corpus Cristi*
■ CHEDRAUI

CALLE 13 SUR

CALLE 15 SUR

CALLE 17 SUR   ▼ LA CONCHITA DEL CARIBE

To Cruiseship Piers, Car Ferry, Parque Chankanaab, El Cedral, and
↓ 🏛 PARQUE PUNTA SUR (FARO CELARAIN ECO PARK)

SCALE NOT AVAILABLE

© AVALON TRAVEL

in achiote with caramelized pineapple salsa. Be sure to try the tamarindo martini—unforgettable! Reservations are recommended.

(Parrilla Mission (Av. 30 btwn Calles 2 and 4, tel. 987/872-3581, www.parrillamission.com, 7am-11pm daily, US$3-14) specializes in tacos, served on delicious handmade corn tortillas and heaped with fresh grilled steak, chicken, or *al pastor* (spicy grilled pork). A self-serve "sides bar" includes not just salsa, cilantro, and lime, but Spanish rice, beans, and grilled onions as well. The rest of the menu is pretty outstanding too, including mole, chiles rellenos, and fajitas, all very reasonably priced. This place is a favorite among locals and a highlight for tourists willing to venture beyond the main downtown area.

The breezy *palapa*-roofed **La Candela** (Av. 5 at Calle 6 Nte., tel. 987/878-4471, 8am-11:30pm Mon.-Sat., US$3-14) offers an extensive lineup of Mexican and traditional Yucatecan dishes in a cafeteria-style setting. Check out what's steaming behind the glass window cases, find a seat, then place your order with your waiter. Lunch specials typically include soup or pasta, a main dish, and a drink (US$5-6).

For some local flavor, **Sabores** (Av. 5 btwn Calles 3 and 5, no phone, noon-4pm Mon.-Sat., US$5-13) is a great family-run restaurant operated out of a bright yellow house. Lunch specials, known across Mexico as *comida corrida*, run US$4-8 and come with soup, fruit drink, and your choice among a selection of traditional main dishes. Dine in the converted living room or under the shade trees in the backyard.

Pancho's Backyard (Av. Rafael Melgar 27 btwn Avs. 8 and 10 Nte., tel. 987/872-2141, www.panchosbackyard.com, 10am-11pm Mon.-Sat., 6pm-11pm Sun., US$11-24) is Mexico epitomized: gurgling fountains, colonial-style decor, live marimba during lunch, and Mexican haute cuisine, including *camarones a la naranja* (orange shrimp flambéed in tequila) and chiles rellenos (peppers stuffed with meat, bananas, and walnut). Though popular with cruise ship travelers, this perennial favorite is big enough that it never feels crowded.

Otates Tacos (Av. 15 btwn Calles Rosado Salas and 3, no phone, noon-11pm daily, US$2-6) is a bustling taco joint serving authentic Mexican grub at nearly street-cart prices. Tacos are just the beginning, served piping hot on tiny corn tortillas; the quesadillas, *tortas* (Mexican-style sandwiches), and *pozole* (pork and hominy soup) are all terrific, and the guacamole is rave-worthy. Service is fast and friendly, with menus in Spanish and English.

Taquería El Pique (Av. Pedro Joaquín Coldwell btwn Av. Benito Juárez and Calle 2, 7pm-midnight daily, US$2-5) is a classic taco joint serving pint-size tacos, chunky guacamole, gooey *queso fundido* (melted cheese for dipping), and more. It's a locals' favorite, though a small stream of expats and tourists make their way here too.

Diego's Tacos (Av. 65 at Blvd. Aeropuerto, 7am-1pm and 7pm-11pm daily, US$4-12) is one of those out-of-the-way cateries where outstanding food and service, and the owners' sheer force of will, have earned it a loyal and enthusiastic following. Located near the airport and car rental shops, this taco shack has just a handful of tables but some of the best tacos around—fish, shrimp, chorizo, and more—and an unfailingly friendly atmosphere.

La Cozumeleña (Av. 10 Sur at Calle 3, 7am-3pm daily) is popular with local families and

---

YUCATECAN SPECIALTIES

Considered among the most distinct cuisines of the country, Yucatecan food reflects the influences of its Maya, European, and Caribbean heritage. Some of the most popular menu items include:

- **Cochinita Pibil:** pork that has been marinated in achiote, Seville orange juice, peppercorn, garlic, cumin, salt, and pepper, wrapped in banana leaves, and baked. It's typically served on weekends.

- **Dzoto-bichay:** tamales made of chaya (a leafy vegetable similar to spinach) and eggs. It comes smothered in tomato sauce.

- **Empanizado:** slices of pork or chicken that has been breaded and fried. This is often served with salad, rice, and beans.

- **Panucho:** handmade tortilla stuffed with refried beans and covered with shredded turkey, pickled onion, and slices of avocado. Like a *salbute* plus!

- **Papadzules:** hard-boiled eggs chopped and rolled into a corn tortilla. It comes smothered in a creamy pumpkin-seed sauce.

- **Poc-Chuc:** slices of pork that have been marinated in Seville orange juice and coated with a tangy sauce. Pickled onions are added on the side.

- **Salbute:** handmade tortilla covered with shredded turkey, pickled onion, and slices of avocado.

- **Sopa de Lima:** turkey-stock soup prepared with shredded turkey or chicken, fried tortilla strips, and juice from *lima*, a lime-like citrus fruit.

dinnertime on Cozumel's main plaza

© LIZA PRADO

professionals, serving classic dishes in a quiet air-conditioned dining area. For breakfast, try *chilaquiles* (fried tortilla strips, scrambled eggs, and chicken doused in green or red salsa) or eggs with *chaya*. Lunch specials include a main dish, like fish tacos or baked chicken, and a drink. There's a bakery next door too, for fresh breads and pastries.

Corazón Contento (Av. 10 Sur at Calle 3, 7am-3pm daily) has a peaceful and welcoming ambience befitting its name (Contented Heart), while the stenciled walls and colorful tile floors are reminiscent of Mérida. Service is friendly, with great bottomless coffee and simple breakfast and lunch specials. Watch out: The bread basket is charged per item, and the chocolate-filled croissants are almost impossible to resist!

Casa Denis (Calle 1 btwn Avs. 5 and 10, 7am-9pm daily, US$3-10) is Cozumel's oldest restaurant, serving up reliable Mexican and Yucatecan dishes since 1945. It's by no means gourmet, but you can't go wrong with standards like *cochinita pibil* (marinated pork) plus a basket of chips, hot homemade salsa, and an ice-cold beer. Breakfasts are pretty tasty, too. The open-air dining area has nice views of the central plaza and the various comings and goings there.

El Moro (Av. 75 Bis btwn Calles 2 and 4, tel. 987/872-3029, 1pm-11pm daily except Thurs., US$8-16) is a longtime family restaurant and a worthwhile venture off the beaten path, popular with locals and tourists alike. It's not fancy by any stretch of the imagination—think linoleum-top tables and fluorescent lights—but the food is good and the servings generous. Specialties include Mexican and Yucatecan classics, and even modern versions of traditional Maya dishes, all at affordable prices.

SEAFOOD

El Viejo y La Mar (Av. 5 Sur btwn Calles 9 and 9 Bis, no phone, noon-8pm daily, US$5-15) is a low-key eatery run by a local fisherman's cooperative, so the fish is especially fresh and well-priced. Whole fried fish is US$9 per

CHILE PEPPERS

It's almost a given that at some point you'll bite into a seemingly innocent quesadilla, or dip a chip into a bowl of salsa, and end up with a raging fire in your mouth. A wide variety of chiles are used to spice food in Cozumel and the Yucatán. Some are mild, even sweet, while others will make you sweat with just a whiff. (In all chiles, the seeds are the hottest part.) Though most waiters will warn you if an item will *pica* (literally, sting), here are some guidelines for chiles—and their *pica*-factor—you're likely to encounter:

· **Pimiento** (bell pepper): benign

· **Chile dulce** (sweet pepper—small, pumpkin shaped, and light green): benign

· **Güero** (light skinned long, light green): mildly hot

· **Chile seco** (dried pepper—comes in *pasilla* and *ancho* varieties): mildly hot

· **Poblano** (medium-size, dark green): ranges from mild to very hot

· **Serrano** (small torpedo-shaped peppers, typically green or red): medium hot

· **Puya** (small, thin red peppers): hot

· **Jalapeño** (small- to medium-size, hard and green, often pickled): hot

· **Chipotle** (medium and rust colored, often dried): hot

· **Morita** (smoked and red): very hot

· **Piquín** (tiny, red, torpedo-shaped): extremely hot

· **De árbol** (literally, from a tree—long, red, thin): extremely hot

· **Habanero** (bulbous, small, and typically green, orange, or yellow): blazing hot

If you take a wrong bite, you'll find some quick relief in a bit of salt, a banana, beer, or milk. *Buen provecho!*

---

kilo (2.2 pounds); a half kilo makes for a hefty meal. There are a dozen different ceviche and cocktail options, and just as many fillets. Eat in the large open-air dining area, or order to go if it's near closing time.

Camilo's (Av. 5 btwn Calles 2 and 4, tel. 987/872-6161, 11am-9pm daily, US$8-16) is a small place offering an abundance of fresh seafood: ceviche, shrimp cocktail, lobster tail, fried fish, grilled fish—you name it, they've probably got it. It's popular with locals, and travelers are beginning to trickle in now, too.

A family-run restaurant, **La Conchita del Caribe** (Av. 65 btwn Calles 13 and 15, tel. 987/872-5888, www.laconchitadelcaribe.com, 11:30am-7:30pm daily, US$9-16) is another locals' favorite, in a spacious location. When ordering whole fish—the house specialty, served grilled or fried—you'll be asked to pick the fish you want out of a cooler by the counter and will be charged according to size. And whether you order fish, shrimp, or other seafood, it was

almost certainly swimming earlier in the day. This is a great off-the-tourist-path option; takeout is also available.

Buccanos at Night (Buccano's Beach Club, Av. Rafael Melgar, buccanos@yahoo.com, 6pm-11pm Fri.-Sat., US$14-22) is only open on Friday and Saturday nights, so anticipation and expectation are a built-in part of the experience. Tables are set up on the beach and alongside the pool (it's a beach club by day) with excellent views of the ocean and sunset, morphing into romantic mood lighting as the sun disappears. The menu, mostly seafood, is reasonably inventive; more importantly, the fish and lobster are super fresh and well prepared, and the service is first-rate.

OTHER SPECIALTIES

La Cocay (Calle 8 btwn Avs. 10 and 15, tel. 987/872-5533, www.lacocay.com, 5:30pm-11pm Mon.-Sat., US$15-22) offers Mediterranean cuisine with flair. The menu changes seasonally, but expect to see dishes

© LIZA PRADO

Fish tacos are a staple on Isla Cozumel: simple, classic, delicious.

like fish of the day with cilantro herb mojo and blue-cheese-filled phyllo dough rolls with black cherry sauce. Seating is in a candlelit dining room or on the breezy garden patio—perfect for a special night out.

(Kondesa (Av. 5 btwn Calles 5 and 7, tel. 987/869-1086, 5pm-11pm Tues.-Sun., US$4-12) may well be Cozumel's classiest restaurant, with its sister restaurant, Kinta (Av. 5 btwn Calle 2 and 4 Nte., tel. 987/869-0544, www.kintacozumel.com, 5:30pm-11pm Tues.-Sun., US$10-17) its closest competition. Seating is in a lush garden with tables under a high *palapa,* on a central wooden platform, or right under the stars. The menu has some classic Mexican and Mediterranean dishes, but is mostly contemporary fusion. The Guacamole Trio and lionfish tortas are popular appetizers and go well with the restaurant's creative cocktails, including mojitos and sangria. The catch of the day is always flavorful and inventive, while homemade churros and coffee make a perfect dessert. Service is impeccable.

Founded in 1978 and passed from father to daughter, **(Guido's** (Av. Rafael Melgar btwn Calles 6 and 8, tel. 987/872-0946, www.guidoscozumel.com, 11am-11pm Mon.-Sat., 2:30pm-9:30pm Sun., US$13-17) is a bit pricey but worth every peso, serving unique Italian-ish dishes like brick-oven baked lasagna, homemade pastas, memorable seafood dishes (like prosciutto-wrapped sea scallops), and excellent sangria and desserts. The leafy courtyard setting makes a meal here all the more worthwhile.

Al Pie del Carbon (Calle 6 at Av. 5, cell. tel. 987/101-2599, 3pm-11pm Tues.-Sun., US$8-16) is a popular Argentinean steak house serving up excellent cuts of beef, plus tasty salads and sides. Steaks are grilled over an open flame and can be enjoyed in the restaurant's air-conditioned dining room or open-air patio. The empanadas, another Argentinean classic, make great appetizers. There's a decent wine list, too.

Cruise ship crew members beeline to **Chi** (above Pizza Hut, Calle 3 at Av. Rafael

Melgar, tel. 987/869-8156, www.chicozumel. com, 9:30am-midnight Mon.-Wed., 9:30am-2am Thurs.-Sat., noon-midnight Sun., US$8-15) for its gorgeous ocean views and extensive pan-Asian menu, including Chinese, Thai, Japanese, and Filipino dishes. The sushi is mediocre (ham nigiri?) but the rest is quite tasty, and a nice change of culinary pace.

Not content to rest on its laurels, **New Especias** (Calle 3 btwn Avs. 5 and 10, tel. 987/869-7947, 6pm-11pm daily except Wed., US$6-18) has a new look, new menu, and new location—sort of. The restaurant occupies just the 2nd floor of the building now, including a narrow patio with street views and a breezy dining area in the rear. That makes room for a lively new bar downstairs, with the idea that guests will migrate from one to the other, and even to the bistro tables set up on the sidewalk in front. The menu, once an eclectic mix of Argentinean, Thai, and Jamaican, is now strictly Italian—and quite good at that.

Del Sur (Corner of Av 5 Sur and Calle 3, tel. 987/871-5744, 5pm-11pm Mon-Sat, US$2-21) serves crispy Argentinean empanadas and hearty steak (plus seafood, chicken, and salads) in a homey and attractive dining room. Order a couple of empanadas as a starter, or several for a full meal; either way, they go great with a cold beer. If you're ordering from the grill, ask for a recommendation from the restaurant's excellent wine list. There's live tango on Fridays.

Le Chef (Av. 5 at Calle 5, tel. 987/878-4391, 9am-11pm Mon.-Sat., US$8-17) is famous for its bacon lobster sandwich: a divine creation, served on a baguette with pesto mayonnaise. (The smoked salmon baguette is also excellent.) The rest of the menu, mostly Mediterranean, includes in-house pasta, fresh seafood with sauces like saffron and creamed spinach, and tasty desserts, like homemade ice cream. Service can be a bit slow, especially considering the small size of the place, but never unfriendly.

Blue Angel Restaurant (Blue Angel Resort, Carr. Costera Sur Km. 2.2, tel. 987/872-0188, 7am-10pm daily, US$6-17) is a dive resort restaurant, which means if you're looking for

fancy cuisine and signature cocktails, you're barking up the wrong tree. Instead, come here for ice-cold beer and comfort food from back home: pork chops, fried chicken, mashed potatoes, spaghetti, and a smattering of familiar Mexican dishes. It's also got spectacular sunsets and live guitar (7pm-9pm Wed.-Sun.).

SWEETS

At **Zermatt** (Av. 5 Nte. at Calle 4, tel. 987/872-1384, 7am-8:30pm Mon.-Sat., 7am-noon Sun., US$1-2.50) you may have to jostle with locals for a crack at the island's best fresh breads, pastries, and other traditional Mexican baked goods.

◖**Nacho Crazy Boy** (Av. 20 Sur btwn Av. Benito Juárez and Calle 1, 8am-11pm Mon.-Sat., 10am-2pm Sun., US$2) serves outstanding juices and smoothies right from the patio of the owner's modest house. Fruits fresh from the market are squeezed and blended on the spot by Nacho Crazy Boy himself, an earnest and interesting guy who makes time for conversation with customers.

La Flor de Michoacán (Calle 1 near Av. 10, 9am-11pm daily, US$1-2) serves cool treats, including *aguas* (fruit drinks), *nieves* (ice cream), and *paletas* (popsicles).

Rave reviews keep the small **Chocolatería Isla Bella** (Calle 3 btwn Av. 5 and Rafael Melgar, tel. 987/564-1075, 1pm-9:30pm daily, US$1-5) hopping. Its friendly owners churn out exquisite handmade chocolates in a variety of flavors, including nutella, vanilla, lime and coconut, a luscious dark chocolate called The Black Panther, and more. New creations and holiday specials are announced on the restaurant's Facebook page, as well as special events, like truffle-making classes: a fun and informative (and tasty!) way to spend a couple of hours.

GROCERIES

Whatever groceries you need, you'll find them and more at **MEGA** (Av. Rafael Melgar at Calle 11, tel. 987/872-3658, 7:30am-11pm daily), the island's largest supermarket.

Chedraui (Av. Rafael Melgar btwn Calles 15 and 17, 7am-10pm daily) also has a little of everything, and is located in the same shopping center as the island's movie theater. **Super San Francisco de Asis** (Av. Pedro Joaquín Coldwell btwn Av. Benito Juárez and Calle 2, 7:30am-11pm daily) is another large supermarket.

For a traditional market experience, Cozumel's **Mercado Municipal** (Av. 25 btwn Calles 1 and Rosado Salas, 7am-3pm daily) has stalls brimming with colorful produce, freshly butchered chickens, eggs, cheese, spices, and more, all at reasonable prices.

DAY TRIPS

While there's plenty to see and do on Cozumel itself, a visit to the mainland Riviera Maya is awfully tempting, too. From Cozumel, Playa del Carmen is just 30 minutes away by ferry, and you could easily pop over there for a day or even an afternoon. Playa is a lively bustling city and a great place for Cozumel-goers to go for a change of pace, a special meal, or any needed shopping, whether in the boutique shops along the pedestrian walkway or at mega-stores like Walmart. But why stop there? If you've got the time, you could easily spend several days exploring the Riviera Maya and its innumerable (and unforgettable) sights and attractions. There are spectacular beaches, of course, from Cancún clear down to Tulum, and opportunities for parasailing, kiteboarding, kayaking, and more. The mainland's Maya ruins are larger and more impressive than Cozumel's and are easy to reach, too: There's Chichén Itzá, of course, with its iconic pyramid and massive ball court; Tulum, with its picture postcard setting; and Cobá, where you can ply the leafy paths on a rental bike and climb to the top of its dizzying main pyramid. The Riviera Maya also is home to scores of cenotes (freshwater sinkholes) whose eerie depths and crystal-clear water make for truly unforgettable snorkeling and diving, for beginners and advanced alike. All of the above are very family friendly, but the Riviera Maya also has large popular "ecoparks" like Xcaret and Xel-Há, where the whole family can spend the day snorkeling, ziplining, sitting by the pool, or at the beach.

© LIZA PRADO

HIGHLIGHTS

◖ Playa del Carmen's Quinta Avenida:
Ever growing yet wonderfully walkable, Playa's 5th Avenue has block after block of tempting restaurants, hipster boutiques, and lively bars. The ferry and bus terminals are at the busy southern end, while the northern end is cooler and quieter, with a distinctive European flair (page 104).

◖ Chichén Itzá Archaeological Zone:
Voted one of the New Seven Wonders of the World, the Yucatán's most famous ruin is all about hyperbole: the iconic star-aligned pyramid, the gigantic Maya ball court, even the crush of bikini-clad day-trippers from Cancún.

Be sure to arrive early to enjoy this singular ancient city (page 128).

◖ Xcaret: The Riviera Maya's elaborate eco-parks are a hit with parents looking for a safe, active, friendly place to take the kids. Xcaret is the most ambitious of them all, with tubing and snorkeling, an aquarium and animal enclosures, an orchid greenhouse, and an end-of-the-day extravaganza performance (page 135).

◖ Bahía de la Ascensión: A huge protected expanse of calm ocean flats and tangled mangrove forests make this a world-class destination for bird-watchers, anglers, and everyday travelers alike (page 138).

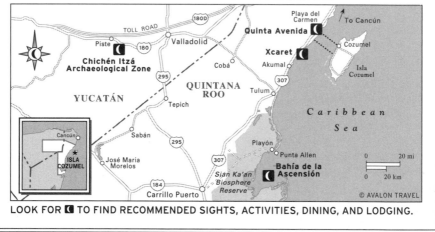

LOOK FOR ◖ TO FIND RECOMMENDED SIGHTS, ACTIVITIES, DINING, AND LODGING.

PLANNING YOUR TIME

Not all day trips are created equal, ranging from a leisurely afternoon to a jam-packed weekend of travel and sightseeing. Planning your trip begins with deciding what you want to do and how long you've got to do it. From there, you can make the necessary arrangements, from time management to transportation.

Playa del Carmen makes for the easiest day trip from Cozumel, and requires virtually no planning. There's frequent ferry service, including well past dark, and no need to think about

renting a car or catching a bus. A day in Playa might include strolling and shopping along Quinta Avenida, a few hours at a beach club, an early dinner back in town, and then a few drinks at a lounge bar before catching the ferry home. For a bit more action, consider adding paddleboard lessons, a sailing-and-snorkeling tour, or even skydiving.

The Riviera Maya's archaeological zones also make great day trips. Tulum is the easiest Maya ruin to reach, located about an hour south of Playa del Carmen. There are frequent buses and

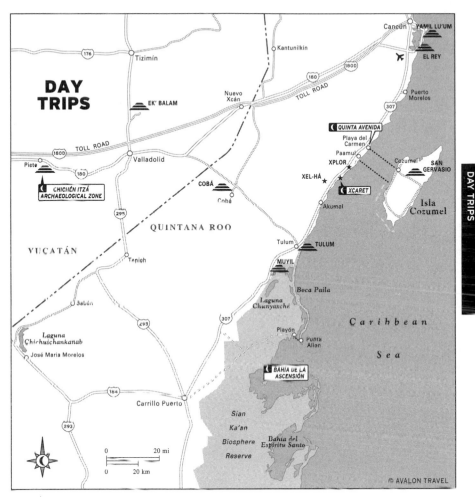

combis between Playa del Carmen and the turn-off for the ruins. Cobá archaeological zone also can be reached by public transportation, but we'd recommend renting a car in Playa. You'll have more time to spend at the ruins themselves, and also be able to hit the nearby cenotes or monkey reserve before heading back. With a car you could even visit Tulum and Cobá in a single (albeit long) day.

Of course, for many people Chichén Itzá is the must-see Maya ruin. Although it's possible to reach Chichén Itzá by bus, a rental car will make the trip considerably less taxing. You'll have more flexibility in terms of when you arrive (the earlier the better, in terms of beating the crowds!), how long you stay at the ruins, and whether to make any stops on the way back.

The Riviera Maya's ecoparks are a great day trip option, especially if you've got kids. Three sister parks (Xcaret, Xplor, and Xel-Há) are each a little different, but all offer convenient all-day all-inclusive packages and a variety of family-friendly activities. Transportation to and from Playa can also be booked, so all you'll have to think about is getting on the ferry from Cozumel. Admission isn't cheap (though you can sometimes get deals by sitting through a timeshare presentation), but the ecoparks are a fun and easy way to spend a day off-island.

Finally, a massive biosphere reserve called Sian Ka'an, located south of Tulum and teeming with birds and sealife, also makes a fascinating day trip. The best one-day option would be to book a tour from an agency in Tulum. Most tours leave around 9am, so plan on an early start to get to Tulum from Cozumel.

Playa del Carmen

Playa del Carmen (or Playa for short) is the easiest day trip from Cozumel: the ferry docks right in town, at the foot of Quinta Avenida (5th Ave.), Playa's main pedestrian walkway. Playa has lovely beaches, great restaurants, and many more stores and services than Cozumel does, from boutique shops to Walmart.

Playa is a mostly walkable town—another reason it makes for a nice day trip. But it's also one of the fastest growing cities in Mexico, and development along Quinta Avenida now extends a solid 40 blocks (and counting); a bike path along 10 Avenida is a smart and welcome addition. And while lounge bars and beach clubs are still the mainstay of Playa's nightlife, the opening of Coco Bongo Playa, an offshoot of the famous Cancún nightclub, has fanned fears of an impending "Cancúnification" of Playa del Carmen.

SIGHTS
◖ Quinta Avenida
Playa's main pedestrian and commercial drag is Quinta Avenida, or 5th Avenue, which stretches more than 40 blocks from the ferry dock northward. Pronounced KEEN-ta av-en-EE-da, you may see it written as 5 Avenida or 5a Avenida, which is akin to "5th" in English. The southern section, especially near the ferry dock, is packed with typical tourist traps: souvenir shops, chain restaurants, etc. North of Calle 10 or Calle 12, and even farther past Avenida Constituyentes, the atmosphere is somewhat cooler and mellower, with more bistros, coffee shops, and high-end boutiques. The north-south division is less stark than it used to

be, with some nice spots opening in the former and plenty of kitsch in the latter. You'll probably walk the length of Quinta Avenida once or twice, and everyone seems to find his or her favorite part. There are excellent beaches virtually the entire length.

Aviario Xaman-Ha
A short distance inside the Playacar entrance off 10 Avenida, the small bird sanctuary **Aviario Xaman-Ha** (Paseo Xaman Ha s/n, tel. 984/873-0593, 9am-5pm daily, US$22 adult, child under 12 free) is home, or a stopover, for more than 60 species of tropical birds, including toucans, flamingos, cormorants, and parrots. Some birds are in enclosures, but many are not, and a stone path meanders through the leafy grounds. It's a pleasant place to spend an hour, though the admission price is ridiculously inflated. If you do go, be sure to bring bug repellent.

BEACHES AND BEACH CLUBS
Playa del Carmen is blessed with gorgeous beaches stretching from the resort enclave of Playacar, south of town, all the way north past the last development. The sand is thick and white, and dozens of yards wide in places, with clear aquamarine water and mild surf. It's a change from several years ago, when a series of large storms and shifting currents left many beach areas thin and rocky.

All along the beach are numerous beach clubs where, for a small fee or for simply ordering something from the menu, you can make use of the lounge chairs, umbrellas, restrooms, even swimming pools and changing rooms. If beach clubs aren't your thing, there are several convenient beaches to lay out your own towel and umbrella.

Playa Tukán (entrance at 1 Av. Nte. at Calle 26) has two popular beach clubs. **Mamita's Beach Club** (end of Calle 28, tel. 984/803-2867, www.mamitasbeachclub.com, 8am-6pm daily) is one of Playa's best known, with thumping music and a lively atmosphere. It's the one place in Playa where topless sunbathing is permitted and common. Just down the beach is **Kool** (end of Calle 26, tel. 984/803-1961, www.koolbeachclub.com.mx, 8am-6pm daily), which is more laid-back and good for a slightly older crowd and families with young children. Both have food service, restrooms, changing areas and lockers, and similar prices: around US$2.50 apiece for chairs and umbrellas, US$15-25 for beach beds and large *palapas*, and US$5-15 for snacks and drinks. Both also have small swimming pools; it's free at Kool, while Mamita's asks for a US$12.50 per person minimum consumption.

Playa El Recodo is the little-used name for the stretch of sand stretching south of the pier at Avenue Constituyentes to Playa's historic lighthouse. The northernmost section, adjacent to the pier, is used to moor fishing boats and is unusable for swimming and sunbathing, but the rest is gorgeous and benefits from relatively little foot traffic. **Lido** (btwn Calle 10 and 12, tel. 984/803-1090, 8am-5:30pm daily, minimum consumption US$12.50, chairs free, beach beds US$8) has cheery lime-green umbrellas and faces an equally smile-inducing beach. The food service here is surprisingly refined, unlike the Plain Jane fare served up at most beach clubs. Next door, **Zenzi Bar** (btwn Calle 10 and 12, 8am-2am daily, minimum consumption US$17 pp) is primarily a restaurant-bar known for its variety of live music, but also has umbrellas and beach beds for rent. Nearby are beach booths offering massages, snorkeling trips, catamaran rides, and more.

Playa El Faro (btwn Calles 8 and 16), named for the large lighthouse (or *faro*) at one end, is a lovely beach that's convenient to

just about everywhere. **Wicky's Beach Club** (at Calle 10, tel. 984/873-3541, www.wickysplayadelcarmen.com, 7am-midnight daily, US$12.50 pp minimum consumption) is an upscale, welcoming spot with beach chairs, a shaded patio with chairs and tables, and a large indoor restaurant area. Food and drinks are excellent, though service can be aloof. Nearby operators can arrange snorkel tours, Jet Skis, and more. Alas, the very enticing swimming pool is for condo guests only.

If beach clubs aren't your thing, there are plenty of spots to claim your own patch of sand. The best are **Playa Tukán** (entrance at 1 Av. Nte. at Calle 26) and **Playa El Faro** (btwn Calles 8 and 16); while both have beach clubs, they also have long lovely stretches of open sand and are popular with independent travelers and locals. Note that Playa Tukán is popular with Europeans, and topless sunbathing is not uncommon. Another option, if you don't mind the walk (or taxi or bike ride), is **Coco Beach;** located between Calles 38 and 46, it's ideal for laying out on your towel, listening to the waves, and chilling out. And just north of there is **Chunzubul Reef,** one of Playa's best spots for snorkeling.

ENTERTAINMENT AND EVENTS

Playa del Carmen's nightlife has long been dominated by bars and lounges, as if deliberately leaving the raucous clubs and discotheques to Cancún. While that's still mostly the case, Playa is definitely getting rowdier, with several major nightclubs and the increasingly boisterous cluster of club-like bars at the corner of 1 Avenida and Calle 12. Note the large signs prohibiting open containers in the streets; although many bars are clustered together, be sure to finish your drink before heading to the next.

Lounges and Bars

With retro tables and armchairs, low beats, and even lower lights, **Diablito Cha Cha Cha** (1 Av. at Calle 12, tel. 984/803-4506, www.diablitochachacha.com, 7pm-3am daily) is

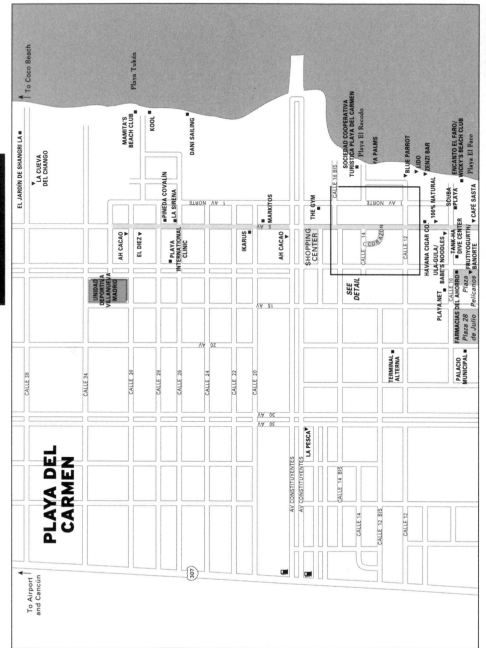

PLAYA DEL CARMEN

To Airport and Cancún

To Coco Beach

Playa Tukán

EL JARDIN DE SHANGRI LA ■

LA CUEVA
DEL CHANGO

MAMITA'S
BEACH CLUB ■

KOOL ■

DANI SAILING ■

AH CACAO ■

EL DIEZ ▼

PINEDA COVALIN ■
LA SIRENA ■

PLAYA
INTERNATIONAL
CLINIC ■

IKARUS ■

AH CACAO ▼

MARKITOS ■

1 AV NORTE

5 AV

UNIDAD
DEPORTIVA
VILLANUEVA
MADRID

SOCIEDAD COOPERATIVA
TURÍSTICA PLAYA DEL CARMEN

Playa El Recodo

YA PALMS

BLUE PARROT ■

UDO ■
ZENZI BAR

ENCANTO EL FARO/
WICKY'S BEACH CLUB ■

Playa El Faro

CALLE 16 BIS

100% NATURAL ■

SCUBA
PLAYA ■

CAFÉ SASTA ▼

THE GYM ■

1 AV NORTE

CALLE 14

CORAZON

CALLE 12

SHOPPING
CENTER

SEE
DETAIL

HAVANA CIGAR CO. ■

TANK-HA
DIVE CENTER ■

ULA-GULA/
BABE'S NOODLES ▼

FRUTIYOGURTH ▼
BANORTE ■

PLAYA.NET ■

CALLE 10

FARMACIAS DEL AHORRO ■

Plaza 28
de Julio

Plaza
Pelicanos ▼

15 AV

20 AV

TERMINAL
ALTERNA ■

PALACIO
MUNICIPAL ■

CALLE 38

CALLE 34

CALLE 30

CALLE 28

CALLE 26

CALLE 24

CALLE 22

CALLE 20

30 AV

30 AV

AV CONSTITUYENTES

AV CONSTITUYENTES

LA PESCA ▼

CALLE 14 BIS

CALLE 14

CALLE 12 BIS

CALLE 12

307

To Airport
and Cancún

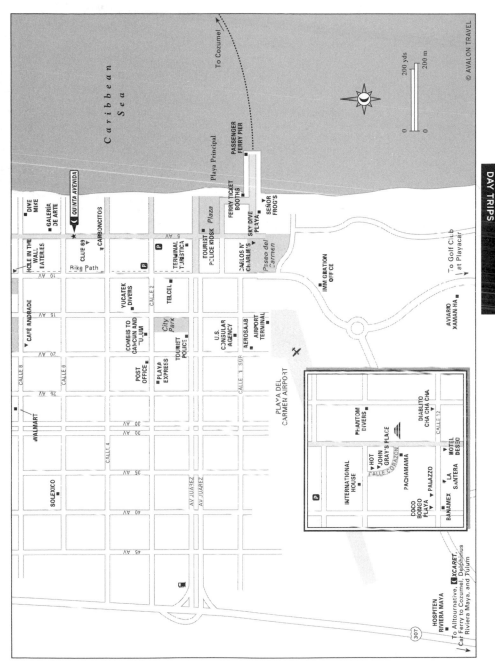

© AVALON TRAVEL

PLAYA DEL CARMEN WALKING TOUR

Debarking from the ferry at the **passenger ferry pier,** turn north at the ticket booths and cut diagonally to Playa's pleasant but little-used **central plaza.**

You'll emerge at the busy corner of Avenida Juárez and **Quinta Avenida** (5th Avenue), Playa's main pedestrian walkway. Walk north on Quinta Avenida, passing numerous restaurants and souvenir shops.

At Calle 8, turn left and walk two blocks to Playa's large civic center park—a sunny stone-paved square with an interesting fountain/installation showing Maya numerals, and city hall on the west side.

If you're hungry, **Café Andrade** (Calle 8 facing the plaza) and **Frutiyogurth** (Av. 10 btwn Calles 8 and 10) serve simple meals and snacks.

Backtrack on Calle 8, past 5th Avenue, to **Playa El Faro,** one of Playa's best beaches. Kick off your shoes and bury your feet in the cool powdery sand.

Back on Quinta Avenida, continue north to **Calle Corazón,** a short leafy alley with a great *artesanía* store called **Pachamama** and a popular sandwich shop called **Hot.**

Keep walking north on Quinta Avenida, crossing busy Avenida Constituyentes. On the northwest corner, pop into **Ah Cacao** for premium chocolate drinks and sweets.

Just past Calle 28, be sure to take a look at the terrific *artesanía* in **La Sirena** and high-end fashions and accessories at **Pineda Covalín.**

Take Calle 28 east to **Playa Tukán,** another excellent beach and home to the popular beach clubs **Mamita's** and **Kool.** This is one of Playa's best stretches of shoreline.

Cut through the latter to Calle 30, and stop for a refreshing meal at **Cueva del Chango,** a lovely semi-outdoor restaurant that's popular with locals and tourists alike.

Afterward, head back to **Quinta Avenida** for a leisurely stroll—or quick cab ride—back to the ferry.

certainly one of the most stylish of the bars in this up-and-coming area. Order anything under the sun from the bar, and munch on unlikely Mexican-Japanese fusion snacks and meals.

At sunset, the 2nd-floor patio at **Hotel Deseo** (5 Av. at Calle 12, tel. 984/879-3620, www.hoteldeseo.com, 5pm-2am daily) transforms into a sleek lounge, with DJs spinning urban beats and a reliable crowd of local and foreign hipsters. A candlelit stone stairway leads from the street to the open-air terrace, where a long swimming pool is surrounded by queen-size cushions and billowing curtains. There's food service until midnight, and the pool-side bar stirs up creative cocktails.

One of Playa's only gay clubs, **Club 69** (off 5 Av. between Calles 4 and 6, tel. 984/876-9466, 9pm-4am daily) doesn't get interesting until after 1am, and sometimes later. There are regular drag shows and exotic dancers, and, of course, music and dancing. Drinks are so-so and the place could use a good scrub, but it's not bad considering Playa's thin pickings for gay travelers. The entrance is easy to miss—look for the 7-Eleven mini-mart on the west side of Quinta Avenida, then follow the rainbow sign down an alley.

A Playa institution for nearly 30 years, the **Blue Parrot** (Calle 12 at the beach, tel. 984/206-3350, www.blueparrot.com, 8pm-2am daily, free before 10pm, US$8.50 after 10pm) has sand floors, swing bar seats, a candlelit *palapa* lounge, and a small dance floor, all within earshot of the crashing waves. DJs play everything from old-school rock to underground electronica; scantily clad fire dancers perform nightly at 11pm.

A **cluster of small bars** (5pm-midnight daily) on 5 Avenida between Calles 26 and 30 makes this area easy to wander over to after dinner. Among several worth checking out are **La Fe, Rufino, Santa Remedio,** the

© LEA PRADO

Playa's pedestrian-only Quinta Avenida (5th Avenue) has it all, from fine dining and boho shops to open-air bars and tourist traps.

Brazilian-style **La Choperia,** and **La Casa del Hábano,** a cigar shop by day and cocktails and hookah joint at night.

Nightclubs

Coco Bongo Playa (Av. 10 at Calle 12, tel. 984/803-5939, www.cocobongo.com.mx, 10:30pm-4:30am Mon.-Sat., US$50-60 including open bar) is a satellite of the famous nightclub in Cancún. Like the original, Coco Bongo Playa features a slew of celebrity impersonations, from Kiss to Beyoncé, plus acrobats, light shows, and multiple DJs to keep everyone dancing. The space here is fairly small, but the crowds can be huge and boisterous—tons of fun, assuming you're not claustrophobic. At last check, Tuesday was Ladies Night; check Facebook for current promos, and with your hotel concierge about VIP tickets and party-hopper tours. Shows begin at 11:30pm.

There are two more clubs nearby, which either benefit from or are overshadowed by

the crowds amassing outside Coco Bongo. Next door to Coco Bongo is another Cancún offshoot, **Palazzo** (Av. 10 at Calle 12, tel. 984/803-0730, www.palazzodisco.com, 10pm-5am daily, US$30-50), a sister club to The City and Palazzo Cancún in the Zona Hotelera. It offers a somewhat more traditional techno nightclub scene, while aiming to inject old-school glamour through its decor and image. Across the street, **La Santera** (Av. 10 at Calle 12, tel. 984/803-2856, http://lasantera.com, 10pm-3:30am daily, US$20-25) is going for an edgier ambience and has a host of "resident DJs."

And, of course, you can always find a party at **Señor Frog's** (ferry pier, tel. 984/803-3498, 9am-3am daily) and **Carlos n' Charlie's** (Paseo del Carmen, southern end of 5 Av., tel. 984/803-3498, 10am-1am daily), both near the Cozumel ferry pier. These bars are a fixture in Mexican beach towns and are famous for their yard-long drinks, dancing on the tables, and nonstop parties.

SHOPPING

Playa del Carmen offers some of the best shopping on the Riviera Maya, and Quinta Avenida is where it's at.

Artesanía

There are numerous souvenir shops along Quinta Avenida, from small to gargantuan, open all day every day. For something more unique, try the following stores.

La Sirena (5 Av. at Calle 26, tel. 984/803-3422, lasirenaplayadelcarmen@hotmail.com, 9am-10pm daily) is a boutique specializing in Mexican folk art. Italian shop owner Patrizia personally selects the exceptional pieces—whimsical skeleton art, colonial statuettes of La Virgen de Guadalupe, tin-framed mirrors, bright shawls—and you're sure to find something you can't resist.

Packed with high-end Mexican folk art, **Pachamama** (Calle Corazón near 5 Av., tel. 984/803-3355, 9am-11pm daily) is a sure thing if you're willing to drop a load of pesos. Skeleton art and hipster clothes from Mexico City figure prominently.

Specialty Items

Pineda Covalín (5 Av. between Calle 26 and 28, www.pinedacovalin.com, 10am-11pm daily) has gorgeous high-end accessories, including purses, scarves, and wallets, made from silk and other fabrics printed with traditional Mexican and indigenous images. There's a Pineda Covalín shop in Cozumel's airport, but it's past the security check and much smaller than this one.

Opening onto a leafy courtyard, **Galería de Arte** (5 Av. near Calle 6, no phone, 10am-10pm daily) is a collection of about a dozen galleries featuring modern art paintings, sculptures, and wood carvings. Items are by no means cheap, but can be quite special.

For cigars, stop by **Havana Cigar Co.** (5 Av. btwn Calles 10 and 12, tel. 984/803-1047, 9am-11pm daily). Cuban and Mexican *puros* are sold individually (US$5-15) or by the box (US$55-450).

Shopping Centers

At the southern end of Quinta Avenida, **Paseo del Carmen** (10am-10pm daily) is a shady outdoor shopping center with high-end clothing boutiques, jewelry stores, art galleries, and restaurants. Its series of modern fountains make it an especially pleasant place to window-shop or enjoy a nice lunch after a morning at the beach. A **large multi-story shopping center** on Quinta Avenida just south of Avenida Constituyentes was near completion at the time of research.

SPORTS AND RECREATION

You might wonder why anyone would come to Playa for sports and recreation when there's so much of the same in Cozumel. For one thing, the conditions are different in each location: For divers and snorkelers, the current in Playa is less powerful than in Cozumel, and there's easy access to inland cenotes (amazing freshwater caverns). Kiteboarding and stand-up paddling are affected by wind and currents, too, of course, and Playa is somewhat more forgiving to beginners. Playa has excellent golfing, and there's a wider variety of spas and gyms. And because Playa del Carmen has a little of everything, couples and families can plan a day trip here, but not necessarily be bound at the hip the entire time.

Scuba Diving

Diving prices in Playa del Carmen are reasonable, and fairly uniform from shop to shop. Two-tank reef dives cost US$75-90, cenote trips are around US$120, and open-water certification courses run US$400-425. Gear is included in the courses but may be charged separately for fun dives (US$15-20/day). Additional fees, like marine park and cenote admissions, may also apply.

Tank-Ha Dive Center (Calle 10 btwn 5 and 10 Avs., tel. 984/873-0302, www.tankha.com, 8am-10pm daily) is one of the longest-operating shops in Playa and a PADI Gold Palm resort and instructor training facility.

Dive Mike (Calle 8 btwn 5 Av. and the beach,

tel. 984/803-1228, www.divemike.com, 7am-9pm daily) is a very friendly, professional, and reasonably priced shop. Check out its excellent website for additional info and pictures.
Phantom Divers (1 Av. Nte. at Calle 14, tel. 984/879-3988, www.phantomdivers.com, 8am-8pm Mon.-Sat., 8am-7pm Sun.) is one of a handful of locally owned dive shops offering lower-than-average prices. Cash only.
Yucatek Divers (15 Av. btwn Calles 2 and 4, tel. 984/803-1363, www.yucatek-divers.com, 7:30am-5pm daily) is a longtime shop with instruction available in several languages. Notably, all fun dives are led by instructors.
Scuba Playa (Calle 10 btwn 1 and 5 Avs., tel. 984/803-3123, www.scubaplaya.com, 8am-8pm daily) specializes in small groups and offers a six-dive package that includes two tanks apiece in Cozumel, the cenotes, and the reef.

Snorkeling
In Playa itself it's best to go snorkeling with a boat tour, since the snorkeling right off the beach isn't too rewarding. There are also numerous cenotes near Playa that make for unique snorkeling, including several you can visit on your own.

Most of Playa's dive shops offer guided snorkeling tours to excellent sites. Ocean trips cost US$30-50, while cenote trips are US$50-75, all gear included. Be sure to clarify how many reefs or cenotes you'll be visiting and for how long. A wetsuit is strongly recommended, even if it means paying extra to rent one. Cenotes can be quite cold, while sunburn is a serious concern in the open ocean; wetsuits protect against both, as well as against accidental scrapes and cuts.

Dani Sailing (Kool Beach Club, end of Calle 28, cell. tel. 984/155-2015, http://danisailing.com, 9am-5pm daily) offers fun catamaran trips with an hour spent sailing and another hour snorkeling. Or rent snorkel gear and a kayak or stand-up paddleboard (US$15-20/hour) and find a spot of your own. Instruction is available. Look for the small shop where Calle 28 hits the beach.

Sociedad Cooperativa Turística Playa del Carmen (Playa El Recodo, end of Calle 14, no phone, 7am-6pm daily) is a local fisherman's cooperative offering snorkeling tours from a kiosk on the beach (US$30/50 pp for one/two sites).

Wind Sports
Kiteboarding, sailboarding, and sailing have grown in popularity along the Caribbean, a trickle-down effect from the world-famous wind belt on the Gulf coast northwest of here. You can catch at least some breeze almost any time of the year, but the strongest, most consistent winds blow November-March.

Ikarus (5 Av. and Calle 20, tel. 984/803-3490, www.kiteboardmexico.com, 9am-10pm daily) is a full-service kiteboarding retail shop and school. Classes are typically conducted at Isla Blanca, in the massive flat-water Chacmochuch Lagoon north of Cancún, which is ideal for kiting but nearly two hours by car or bus from Playa del Carmen. Transport from Cancún is included in the high season, and simple lodging is offered at Isla Blanca (US$10 pp tent, US$50 s/d). Private classes are US$95 per hour or US$450 for six hours, while groups are US$70 per hour per person (maximum 3 to a group) or US$350 for six hours. Equipment is included for students or can be rented separately (US$95/day). Classes are mainly held November-May, when the conditions are best.

Dani Sailing (Kool Beach Club, end of Calle 28, cell. tel. 984/155-2015, http://danisailing.com, 9am-5pm daily) offers catamaran rentals and tours, with or without snorkeling, as well as kiteboarding rentals and instruction. Prices vary.

Stand-Up Paddling and Kayaking
Stand Up Paddle Playa del Carmen (cell. tel. 984/168-0387, www.suppdc.com) is a one-man operation offering hour-long lessons for US$65 (US$50 pp for 2 people) at the beach nearest you, with an hour's free rental afterward to practice your skills. There's no fixed storefront so reservations are recommended;

otherwise, look for SUP gear near the pier at Avenida Constituyentes or near Fusion beach bar (end of Calle 6). Rental gear is available (US$20/hour, US$65/day).

Do-it-all beach sports outfit **Dani Sailing** (Kool Beach Club, end of Calle 28, cell. tel. 984/155-2015, http://danisailing.com, 9am-5pm daily) rents kayaks (US$15/hour single, US$20/hour double) and stand-up paddleboards (US$20/hour). Hour-long instructional courses (US$20) are available for anyone new to "SUPing."

Swimming with Dolphins

With swimming pens set up in the ocean, **Delphinus Riviera Maya** (Hwy. 307 Km. 282, toll-free Mex. tel. 800/335-3461, toll-free U.S./Can. tel. 888/526-2230, www.delphinus.com.mx, US$109-499) is about as good as it gets for performing dolphins. There are various packages, from 30-minute group interactions to hour-long one-on-one encounters. Check the website for complete descriptions, photos, and a 15 percent discount for booking online. Prices are a bit higher at Delphinus Riviera Maya, mainly because round-trip transportation is included. Ticket prices also include a locker, towel, and goggles.

Sportfishing

Playa de Carmen has excellent sportfishing and bottom fishing, with plentiful wahoo, dorado, mackerel, snapper, barracuda, and—especially April-June—sailfish and marlin. Trips depend mostly on the size and power of the boat that's used, but a four- to five-hour trip for 1-6 people usually costs US$200-250, including tackle and drinks. Many dive shops offer tours, as does **Sociedad Cooperativa Turística Playa del Carmen** (Playa El Recodo, end of Calle 14, no phone, 7am-6pm daily).

Golf

The **Golf Club at Playacar** (Paseo Xaman-Há opposite Hotel Viva Azteca, tel. 998/193-2010, www.palace-resorts.com, 6am-sundown daily) is a challenging 7,144-yard championship course designed by Robert Van Hagge

and located in Playacar, the upscale hotel and residential development south of Playa del Carmen proper. Greens fees are US$180 per adult, US$120 after 2pm, and US$80 per child under age 17 (accompanied by adult), including cart, snacks, and drinks; free hotel pickup is included for full-price rounds. Reserve at least a day in advance November-January.

Skydiving

Gleaming white beaches and brilliant turquoise seas make the Riviera Maya a spectacular place for skydiving. If you're up for it, **Sky Dive Playa** (Plaza Marina, just south of the ferry dock, tel. 984/873-0192, www.skydive.com.mx, 9am-4pm Mon.-Sat.) has been throwing travelers out of planes at 10,000 feet since 1996. You freefall for 4,500 feet—about 45 seconds—then the chute opens for a seven- to eight-minute ride down to a soft landing on the beach. Tandem dives (you and an instructor, US$250) are scheduled every hour; walk-ups are accepted, but reservations are highly recommended. For an additional US$150, cameramen also can be booked to freefall alongside you to record your jump.

Tours

Alltournative (Hwy. 307 Km 287, tel. 984/803-9999, toll-free Mex. tel. 800/466-2848, toll-free U.S. tel. 877/437-4990, toll-free Can. and other countries tel. 877/432-1569, www.alltournative.com, 9am-7pm daily, US$119-129 adult, US$79-99 child under 12) offers a variety of full-day conservation-minded tours, including a combination of activities like canoeing, ziplines, off-road bicycling, caving, and snorkeling, plus visits to the Tulum or Cobá archaeological zones—even to a small Maya village. Guides speak English, Italian, French, German, Dutch, and Spanish, and there are several informational kiosks on Quinta Avenida.

AeroSaab (Playa Del Carmen Airport, 20 Av. Sur near Calle 1, tel. 998/865-4225, www.aerosaab.com) offers stunning panoramic flights of Playa del Carmen and the Riviera Maya (US$183-1,013, 4-6 passengers,

15 minutes-2 hours), as well as scenic full-day tours to places like Chichén Itzá, Isla Holbox, and Mérida/Uxmal (US$296-520 pp). Trips are in four- to six-seat Cessna airplanes and typically require a minimum of 2-4 people. These flights are offered using Cozumel's airport too, but are less expensive from Playa.

Spas and Gyms

El Jardín de Shangri La (Calle 38 at Calle Flamingo, tel. 984/801-1295, www.jardindeshangrila.com, 7am-9pm Mon.-Sat., noon-5pm Sun., US$15/class, multi-class packages available) is a large jungly plot with a palapa-roofed area for yoga and meditation classes. It also hosts "community meditation" on Friday (voluntary donation) and "tribal yoga" with drumming on Saturday (US$20). Check online for the class schedule and upcoming workshops and events.

The Gym (Av. 1 near Calle 16 Bis, tel. 984/873-2098, www.thegymplaya.com, 6am-10pm Mon.-Fri., 7am 7pm Sat., 8am-5pm Sun.) is a modern facility offering state-of-the-art equipment and a host of classes, including yoga, Pilates, spinning, and martial arts. There are personal trainers on-site, too. Day passes are US$15; multiday and monthly passes also are available.

You can get a **massage on the beach** at various locations, including at a large no-name spa on Playa El Recodo (entrance at the end of Calle 14, no phone, 7am-6pm daily, US$18 for 70 minutes).

The well-tended **Unidad Deportiva Villanueva Madrid** (10 Av. near Calle 30, 6am-10:30pm daily) is Playa del Carmen's public sporting facility, with a gym, tennis and basketball courts, track, and soccer field. All have night lighting and are open to the public free of charge, but you need to bring your own gear.

FOOD

Playa del Carmen has restaurants and eateries for all tastes and budgets. Those on Quinta Avenida are pricier, of course, many for good reason. Cheaper eats tend to be off the main drag.

Mexican

La Cueva del Chango (Calle 38 near 5 Av., tel. 984/147-0271, www.lacuevadelchango.com, 8am-11pm Mon.-Sat., 8am-2pm Sun., US$5-15) means The Cave of the Monkey, but there's nothing dim or primitive about it: The covered dining area has lighthearted decor (and a back patio ensconced in leafy vegetation), while the menu features crepes, empanadas, and innovative items like eggs with polenta and *chaya*. It's often packed with Playa's upper crust, though the prices make it accessible to all.

Carboncitos (Calle 4 btwn Avs. 5 and 10, tel. 984/873-1382, US$5-15) is a traveler favorite in Playa, serving terrific Mexican food (and some things you may be missing from home, like fresh salads) in a friendly and welcoming setting. Prices and portions are reasonable by Playa standards, and the restaurant gets the little things right, like tasty guacamole and homemade salsas.

Frutiyogurth (Plaza Pelícanos, Av. 10 near Calle 10, tel. 984/803-2516, www.frutiyogurth.com.mx, 8:30am-10:30pm daily, US$3-7) is a bustling little eatery, serving classic Mexican *tortas* (sandwiches) piled high with fillings like chipotle chicken and *milanesa* (chicken-fried steak), plus a monster selection of fresh juices and smoothies.

An old-school Mexican coffee shop that's popular with locals, **Café Andrade** (Calle 8 near 20 Av., tel. 998/846-8257, 7am-11pm daily, US$2-5) serves up mean breakfast and dinner plates with tacos, *chilaquiles,* mole, enchiladas—you name it, they've probably got it. Lunch specials include soup, a main dish, dessert, and a half pitcher of fresh juice for just six bucks.

Seafood

Unassuming and refreshingly untouristy, **La Pesca** (30 Av. near Av. Constituyentes, no phone, noon-10pm daily, US$5-15) specializes in super-fresh seafood, including hefty fish and shrimp plates, tasty ceviche, and great fish tacos. It's a bit of a hike from the center and has a view of a supermarket parking lot, but it is a tasty way to get off Quinta Avenida.

Ula-Gula (5 Av. at Calle 10, 2nd Fl., tel. 984/879-3727, 4:30pm-midnight daily, US$9-25) serves outstanding gourmet meals in an appealing dining area overlooking Quinta Avenida. The seafood is the real standout here, whether appetizers like tuna with wasabi and soy sauce, or the fish of the day prepared with a parsley Gorgonzola sauce. For dessert, try the chocolate fondant—a small chocolate cake filled with rich chocolate syrup and accompanied by ice cream.

On a fun, busy block at the north end of Playa, **El Diez** (5 Av. at Calle 30, 1pm-midnight daily, US$10-25) is an Argentinean steak house, borrowing the nickname of Argentina's larger-than-life footballer, Diego Maradona. The specialties here are grilled meats and fresh seafood, but the long menu also includes items like burgers, salads, and empanadas. Service can be a bit slow, but the large outdoor dining area is perfect for enjoying the goings-on.

Other Specialties

John Gray's Place (Calle Corazón near Calle 14, tel. 984/803-3689, www.johngrayrestaurantgroup.com, 1pm-5pm and 6pm-11pm Mon.-Sat., US$15-30) is an offshoot of the original John Gray's Kitchen in Puerto Morelos, widely considered one of the best restaurants on the Riviera Maya. The kid lives up to expectations, expertly fusing gourmet American cuisine with flavors from around the world, like tuna carpaccio with wasabi cream and sweet soy sauce, or spicy crab cakes with cilantro-leek fondue.

Although occasionally missing the mark, old-timer **Babe's Noodles and Bar** (Calle 10 btwn 5 Av. and 10 Av., tel. 984/803-0056, www.babesnoodlesandbar.com, 1pm-11pm Mon.-Sat., US$6-14) still serves up delicious Thai-fusion meals in a hip bistro setting. Dishes come in half and full orders. Don't miss a chance at ordering the *limonmenta,* an awesome lime-mint slushy. It's not a huge place, so you may have to wait for a table during high season, or if you prefer, head to its sister

restaurant down the street (5 Av. btwn Calles 28 and 30, cell. tel. 984/120-2592, 5pm-11pm Mon.-Sat.).

100% Natural (5 Av. btwn Calles 10 and 12, tel. 984/873-2242, 7am-11pm daily, US$6-12) serves mostly vegetarian dishes and a large selection of fresh fruit juices. Service can be hit or miss, but the food is fresh and well prepared. Tables are scattered through a leafy garden area and covered patio—great for taking a break from the sun.

If you're looking for cheap eats, check out the string of **hole-in-the-wall eateries** (Av. 10 btwn Calles 8 and 10, US$1.25-4) across the street from Plaza Pelícanos. Here you'll have your choice of tacos, *tortas* (Mexican-style sandwiches), crepes, pizza by the slice, and smoothie stands, at decent prices. Most are open 9am-10pm daily.

Cafés and Bakeries

Two doors down from Starbucks, **Café Sasta** (5 Av. btwn Calles 8 and 10, 7am-11pm daily, US$1.50-5) is putting up the good fight, with old-time charm and a tempting display of muffins, scones, cupcakes, and cheesecake to go along with the full coffee menu. Seating is available indoors and outdoors.

Chocolate lovers will melt over ◖**Ah Cacao** (5 Av. at Av. Constituyentes, tel. 984/803-5748, www.ahcacao.com, 7:15am-11:30pm daily, US$2-5), a chocolate café where every item on the menu—from coffees to cakes—is homemade from the finest of beans. A sister shop (Calle 30 near 5 Av., tel. 984/879-4179, 7am-11:30pm daily) is located up the street from Playa Tukán.

You'll smell **Hot** (Calle Corazón at Calle 14, www.thehotbakingcompany.com, 7am-10pm daily, US$4.50-10) a block away—this café bakes fresh breads and pastries all day. Most people end up staying for more than just a brownie, though—the menu full of sandwiches prepared on whole-wheat or sunflower-seed bread is almost impossible to resist. The shady outdoor eating area is a great place to enjoy a leisurely breakfast, too.

Ferry tickets to Cozumel are sold from booths at the foot of the pier in Playa del Carmen.

© GARY CHANDLER

Groceries

Walmart (Calle 8 btwn Avs. 20 and 25, 7am-midnight daily) is located right behind city hall—how's that for a metaphor?—with everything from clothes, shoes, and snorkel gear to groceries, prepared food, and a full pharmacy. Liquor sales end at 11pm.

INFORMATION AND SERVICES

Tourist Information

There is no tourist information office in Playa, but the **tourist police** have a kiosk on the central plaza (5 Av. at Av. Juárez, 24 hours), which often is stocked with brochures and maps.

Quinta (www.allrivieramaya.com) and **Sac-Be** (www.sac-be.com) are free monthly magazines that usually offer a handful of useful articles, listings, and events calendars.

Emergency Services

Hospiten Riviera Maya (Hwy. 307 s/n, tel. 984/803-1002, www.hospiten.com, 24 hours) is a private hospital offering modern, high-quality medical service at reasonable rates. Many of the doctors have U.S. training and speak English, and are accustomed to treating foreign visitors and expats. It is located along the east side of the highway on the southern side of Playa.

Playa also has a hyperbaric chamber, operated by **Playa International Clinic** (10 Av. at Calle 28 Nte., tel. 984/803-1215, emergency tel. 984/873-1365, 9am-8pm Mon.-Fri., 9am-2pm and 5pm-7pm Sat.).

Prescriptions are required for many antibiotics now, unlike years past. **Farmacias del Ahorro** (10 Av. at Calle 10, 9am-10pm daily) has a full pharmacy on the 1st floor and a **free walk-in clinic** on the 2nd floor, where a doctor can write prescriptions after a short interview or exam; the clinic is closed 3pm-5pm and weekends.

The **tourist police** (tel. 984/877-3340, or 060 from any pay phone) have an office on Avenida Juárez and 15 Avenida, and informational kiosks along Quinta Avenida, theoretically operating 24 hours a day.

Money
Banamex (Calle 12 at 10 Av., 9am-4pm Mon.-Fri.) and **Banorte** (Plaza Pelícanos, 10 Av. btwn Calles 8 and 10, 9am-6pm Mon.-Fri., 10am-2pm Sat.) are full-service banks with ATMs and foreign exchange. There also are several freestanding **ATMs** around town.

Media and Communications
The **post office** (Calle 2 at Av. 20, 9am-4pm Mon.-Fri., 9am-noon Sat.) is easy to miss—look for the dilapidated building near the *combi* terminal.

Internet cafés have gone from ubiquitous to nearly obsolete, thanks to the proliferation of mobile devices and the availability of free Wi-Fi at most hotels. Among the remaining locations include **Playa.Net** (Calle 10 near 10 Av., 9am-3pm and 4pm-10pm Mon.-Sat., US$1.25/hour), **Telcel** (10 Av. btwn Av. Juárez and Calle 2, 9am-10pm Mon.-Sat., US$1/hour), and the overpriced **Markitos** (5 Av. at Calle 20, 9am-11pm daily, US$3.25/hour).

Immigration
Playa del Carmen's **immigration office** (Plaza Antigua mall, 2nd Fl., Calle 10, tel. 998/881-3560, 9am-1pm Mon.-Fri.) is located on the road to Playacar. Avoid using it, however, as the one in Cancún is more efficient. A tourist visa extension, or *prórroga,* can take a week or more in Playa and involves considerable documentation; in Cancún, the same process is simplified and takes as little as two hours.

GETTING THERE
Ferry
Passenger ferries to Playa del Carmen (US$13 each way, 30 minutes) leave from the passenger ferry pier across from the central plaza. **UltraMar** (www.granpuerto.com.mx) and **Mexico Water Jets** (www.mexicowaterjets.com.mx) alternate departures and charge the same amount, though UltraMar's boats are newer. Their ticket booths are opposite each other partway down the pier, with the time of the next departure displayed prominently. The ticket seller may try to sell you a round-trip ticket, but there's no savings in doing so; better to buy a *sencilla* (one-way ticket) and wait to see which company's ferry is departing when you're ready to return. Between the two companies, there are ferries every 1-2 hours on the hour 6am-9pm daily.

Car ferries operated by **Transcaribe** (tel. 987/872-7688 or 987/872-7671 in Cozumel, www.transcaribe.net) depart the international pier in Cozumel for the Calica dock south of Playa del Carmen at 6am, 11am, 4pm, and 8:30pm Monday-Saturday and at 8am and 8pm on Sunday. Returning ferries leave Calica at 4am, 8am, 1:30pm, and 6pm Monday; 1:30pm and 6pm Tuesday and Friday; 8am, 1:30pm, and 6pm Wednesday, Thursday, and Saturday; and 6am and 6pm on Sunday. The trip takes about an hour and 15 minutes and costs US$60 for a passenger car including driver, and US$5.50 per additional passenger. Reservations are available online, by phone, or at the pier, and are strongly recommended.

GETTING AROUND
Playa del Carmen is a walking town, although the steady northward expansion is challenging that description. The commercial part of Quinta Avenida now stretches over 40 blocks and keeps getting longer. Cabs are a good option, especially if your time is short.

Taxi
Taxis around town cost US$2-5, or a bit more if you use a taxi stand or have your hotel summon one. All taxi drivers carry a *tarifário*—an official fare schedule—which you can ask to see if you think you're getting taken for a ride (so to speak). Prices do change every year or two, so ask at your hotel what the current rate is, and always be sure to agree on the fare with the driver before setting off.

Car
Playa has myriad car rental agencies, and prices can vary considerably. Major agencies like

PLAYA DEL CARMEN BUS SCHEDULES

Terminal Turística (5 Av. and Av. Juárez, tel. 984/873-0109, ext. 2501, toll-free Mex. tel. 800/702-8000) is located near the ferry dock and has frequent service north to Cancún and south to Tulum, and most locations in between. Long-distance buses use the Terminal Alterna. Most Tulum-bound buses stop at the turnoffs for destinations along the way, including **Paamul** (US$1.25-3.50, 15 minutes), **Puerto Aventuras** (US$1.50-3.50, 20 minutes), **Xpu-Há** (US$2-4, 25 minutes), **Akumal** (US$2.50-4.50, 30 minutes), **Xel-Há** (US$3-5, 30 minutes), and **Hidden Worlds** and **Dos Ojos** (both US$3-5, 40 minutes).

Most Chetumal-bound buses stop at **Carrillo Puerto** (US$6.75-9.50, 2-2.5 hours) and **Bacalar** (US$13.50-18.25, 4.5 hours).

Most Cancún-bound buses stop at **Puerto Morelos** (US$2-5.50, 35 minutes), but *not* the airport or Cancún's Zona Hotelera.

Destination	Price	Duration	Schedule
Cancún	US$2.75-8	1 hr	every 15-30 mins 12:30am-11:59pm
Cancún Int'l Airport	US$10	1 hr	every 30-60 mins 5am-8pm
Chetumal	US$16-21	4.5 hrs	every 60-90 mins 4:10am-11:30pm
Tulum	US$3.25-5.50	1 hr	every 15-30 mins 1am-11:40pm
Xcaret (main entrance)	US$0.85-4	25 mins	every 30-60 mins 6:10am-11:30pm

Terminal Alterna (Calle 20 btwn Calles 12 and 12 Bis, tel. 984/803-0944, toll-free Mex. tel. 800/702-8000) departures include:

Destination	Price	Duration	Schedule
Campeche	US$42.25-44.50	6.5-8 hrs	10am, 11:30am, 4:40pm, 8pm
Chichén Itzá	US$10.75-22.50	4 hrs	6:10am, 7:30am, and 8am
Cobá	US$6-7.75	2 hrs	every 30-90 mins 6:10am-5:50pm
Mérida	US$28-34	4.5-5.5 hrs	every 60-90 mins 4am-11:59pm
Palenque	US$52.25-62.50	12 hrs	take San Cristóbal bus
San Cristóbal (Chiapas)	US$66.50-79	17-19 hrs	5:15pm, 6:45pm, 7:15pm, and 9:55pm
Valladolid	US$9-12.50	2.5 hrs	every 30-60 mins 6am-6:30pm, plus 4am

DAY TRIPS

Hertz, National, Avis, and Executive are the most reliable and often have great deals if you reserve online.

Parking in Playa in the high season can be a challenge, especially south of Avenida Constituyentes. Parking lots around town include one on Calle 2 at 10 Avenida (8am-10pm daily) and another at Calle 14-bis and 10 Avenida (8am-10pm daily), charging around US$1 per hour or US$9 per day.

Archaeological Zones

If you can drag yourself away from the beaches and diving on Isla Cozumel, a short trip inland will bring you to three of the Yucatán Peninsula's most intriguing ancient ruins—Tulum, Cobá, and Chichén Itzá. Each is quite different from the other, and together they form an excellent introduction to Maya archaeology and architecture. Venturing inland also will give you an opportunity to sneak a peek at how ordinary Yucatecans, including modern-day Maya, live today.

TULUM ARCHAEOLOGICAL ZONE

The Maya ruins of **Tulum** (8am-5pm daily, US$4.75) is one of Mexico's most scenic archaeological sites, built atop a 12-meter (40-foot) cliff rising abruptly from turquoise Caribbean waters. The structures don't compare in grandeur to those of Cobá, Uxmal, or elsewhere but are interesting and significant nevertheless.

Tulum is the single most frequently visited Maya ruin in the Yucatán Peninsula, receiving thousands of visitors every day, most on package tours from nearby resorts. (In fact, it's second only to Teotihuacán, near Mexico City, as the country's most-visited archaeological site.) For that reason, the first and most important piece of advice for independent travelers regarding Tulum is to **arrive early.** It used to be that the tour bus madness didn't begin until 11am, but it creeps earlier and earlier every year. Still, if you're there right at 8am, you'll have the ruins mostly to yourself for an hour or so—which is about all you need for this small site—before the hordes descend. Guides can be hired at the entrance for around US$35 for

1-4 people. Bring your swimsuit if you fancy a morning swim: This is the only Maya ruin with a great little beach right inside the archaeological zone.

History

Tulum was part of a series of Maya forts and trading outposts established along the Caribbean coast from the Gulf of Mexico as far south as present-day Honduras. Its original name was Zamá-Xamanzamá or simply Zamá (derived from *zamal,* or dawn) but was later called Tulum, Yucatec Maya for fortification or city wall, in reference to the thick stone barrier that encloses the city's main structures. Measuring 380 by 165 meters (1,250 by 540 feet), it's the largest fortified Maya site on the Quintana Roo coast (though small compared to most inland ruins).

Tulum's enviable patch of seashore was settled as early as 300 BC, but it remained little more than a village for most of its existence, overshadowed by the Maya city of Tankah a few kilometers to the north. Tulum gained prominence between the 12th and 16th centuries (the Late Post-Classic era), when mostly non-Maya immigrants repopulated the Yucatan Peninsula following the general Maya collapse several centuries prior. Tulum's strategic location and convenient beach landing made it a natural hub for traders who plied the coast in massive canoes measuring up to 16 meters (52 feet) long, laden with honey, salt, wax, animal skins, vanilla, obsidian, amber, and other products.

It was during this Post-Classic boom period that most of Tulum's main structures were built. Although influenced by Mayapán

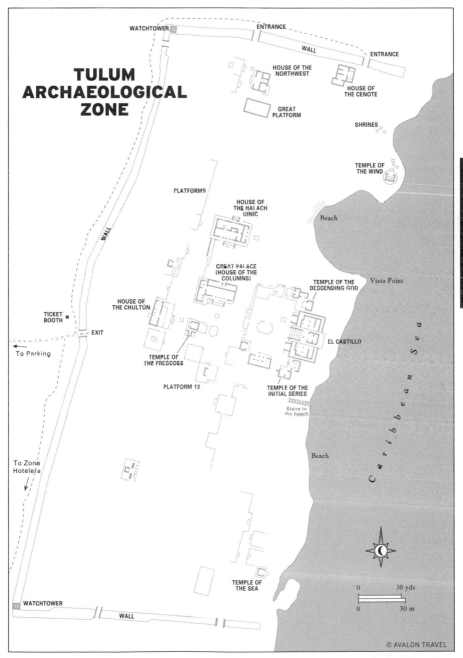

TULUM ARCHAEOLOGICAL ZONE

WATCHTOWER

ENTRANCE

WALL

ENTRANCE

HOUSE OF THE NORTHWEST

HOUSE OF THE CENOTE

GREAT PLATFORM

SHRINES

TEMPLE OF THE WIND

PLATFORMS

HOUSE OF THE HALACH UINIC

Beach

GREAT PALACE (HOUSE OF THE COLUMNS)

TEMPLE OF THE DESCENDING GOD

Vista Point

HOUSE OF THE CHULTÚN

TICKET BOOTH

EXIT

To Parking

TEMPLE OF THE FRESCOES

EL CASTILLO

PLATFORM 13

TEMPLE OF THE INITIAL SERIES

Stairs to the beach

To Zona Hotelera

Beach

TEMPLE OF THE SEA

WATCHTOWER

WALL

Caribbean Sea

| 0 | 30 yds |
| 0 | 30 m |

© AVALON TRAVEL

THE MAYA COLLAPSE

Something went terribly wrong for the Maya between the years AD 800 and 900. Hundreds of Classic Maya cities were abandoned, monarchies disappeared, and the population fell by millions, mainly due to death and plummeting birthrates. The collapse was widespread, but was most dramatic in the Southern Lowlands, a swath of tropical forest stretching from the Gulf of Mexico to Honduras and including once-glorious cities such as Palenque, Tikal, and Copán. (Archaeologists first suspected a collapse after noticing a sudden drop-off in inscriptions; it has been confirmed through excavations of peasant dwellings from before and after that period.)

There are many theories for the collapse, varying from climate change and epidemic diseases to foreign invasion and peasant revolt. In his carefully argued book *The Fall of the Ancient Maya* (Thames and Hudson, 2002), archaeologist and professor of anthropology at Pennsylvania State University David Webster suggests it was a series of conditions, rather than a single event, that led to the collapse.

To a certain degree, it was the very success of Maya cities during the Classic era that set the stage for their demise. Webster points to a population boom just before the collapse, which would have left agricultural lands dangerously depleted just as demand spiked. Classic-era farming techniques were ill-suited to meet the challenge; in particular, the lack of draft animals kept productivity low, meaning Maya farmers could not generate large surpluses of corn and other food. (Even if they could, storage was difficult given the hot, humid climate.) The lack of animals also limited how far away farmers could cultivate land and still be able to transport their crops to the city center; as a result, available land was overused. As Webster puts it, "too many farmers [growing] too many crops on too much of the landscape left the Classic Maya world acutely vulnerable to an environmental catastrophe, such as drought or crop disease."

Certain kingdoms reached their tipping point before others (prompting some to launch 11th-hour military campaigns against weakened rivals), but few escaped the wave of malnutrition, disease, lower birthrates, and outright starvation that seems to have swept across the Maya world in the 9th century. Kings and nobility would have faced increasing unrest and insurrection—after all, their legitimacy was based on their ability to induce the gods to bestow rain, fertility, and prosperity—further destabilizing the social structure and food supply.

The collapse was not universal, of course, and the fall of lowland powers gave other city-states an opportunity to expand and gain influence. But the Maya world was dramatically and permanently changed by it; the grand cities built by the Classic Maya were abandoned to the jungle, most never to be reoccupied, and, as Webster notes, "Cortés and his little army almost starved in 1525 while crossing a wilderness that had supported millions of people seven centuries earlier."

© LIZA PRADO

a stately pyramid at Muyil archaeological zone, just inside the Sian Ka'an Biosphere Reserve

© LIZ PRADO

Archaeologists aren't really sure what purpose these miniature structures (dubbed the "Shrines") at Tulum's Temple of the Wind served.

(the reigning power at the time) and Central Mexican city-states, from which many of Tulum's new residents had emigrated, Tulum's structures mostly exemplify "east coast architecture," defined by austere designs with relatively little ornamentation and a predominantly horizontal orientation (compared to high-reaching pyramids elsewhere). Ironically, construction in these later eras tended to be rather shoddy, thanks in part to improvements in stucco coverings that meant the quality of underlying masonry was not as precise. Today, with the stucco eroded away, Tulum's temples appear more decayed than structures at other sites, even those built hundreds of years prior.

The Spanish got their first view of Tulum, and of mainland indigenous society, on May 7, 1518, when Juan de Grijalva's expedition along the Quintana Roo coast sailed past the then brightly colored fortress. The chaplain of the fleet famously described the city as "a village so large that Seville would not have appeared larger or better." Tulum remained an important city and port until the mid-1500s, when European borne diseases decimated its population. The once-grand city was effectively abandoned and, for the next three centuries, slowly consumed by coastal vegetation. In 1840, Spanish explorers referred to an ancient walled city known as Tulum, the first recorded use of its current name; two years later the famous American/English team of John Lloyd Stephens and Frederick Catherwood visited Tulum, giving the world its first detailed description and illustrations of the dramatic seaside site. During the Caste War, Tulum was occupied by members of the Talking Cross cult, including the followers of a Maya priestess known as the Queen of Tulum.

House of the Cenote

The path from the ticket booth follows Tulum's wall around the northwest corner to two low corbel arch entryways. Using the second entrance (closest to the ocean), you'll first see the Casa del Cenote. The two-room structure, with a third chamber added later, is less impressive than the gaping maw of its namesake cenote. The water is not drinkable, thanks to saltwater intrusion, but that may not have been the case a half millennium ago; it's unlikely Tulum could have grown to its size and prominence without a major water source, not only for its own residents but passing traders as well. Cenotes were also considered apertures to Xibalba, or the underworld, and an elaborate tomb discovered in the floor of the House of the Cenote suggests it may have had ceremonial function as well.

Temple of the Wind

Following the path, the next major structure is the Temple of the Wind, perched regally atop a rocky outcrop overlooking a picturesque sandy cove. If it looks familiar, that's because it appears on innumerable postcards, magazine photos, and tourist brochures. (The view is even better from a vista point behind El Castillo, and of course from the ocean.) The name derives from the unique circular base upon which the structure is built: In Central Mexican cosmology, the circle is associated with the god of the wind, and its presence here (and at other ruins, like San Gervasio on Isla Cozumel) is evidence of the strong influence that Central Mexican migrants/invaders had on Post-Classic Maya societies.

Temple of the Descending God

One of Tulum's more curious structures is the Temple of the Descending God, named for the upside-down winged figure above its doorway. Exactly who or what the figure represents is disputed among archaeologists—theories include Venus, the setting sun, the god of rain, even the god of bees (as honey was one of the coastal Maya's most widely traded products). Whatever the answer, it was clearly a deeply revered (or feared) deity, as the same image appears on several of Tulum's buildings, including the upper temple of Tulum's main pyramid. The Temple of the Descending God also is notable for its cartoonish off-kilter position, most likely the result of poor construction.

El Castillo

Tulum's largest and most imposing structure is The Castle, a 12-meter-high (40-foot) pyramid constructed on a rocky bluff of roughly the same height. Like many Maya structures, El Castillo was built in multiple phases. The first iteration was a low broad platform, still visible today, topped by a long palace fronted by a phalanx of stout columns. The second phase consisted of simply filling in the center portion of the original palace to create a base for a new and loftier temple on top. In the process, the builders created a vaulted passageway and inner chamber, in which a series of intriguing frescoes were housed; unfortunately, you're not allowed to climb onto the platform to see them. The upper temple (also off-limits) displays Central Mexican influence, including snakelike columns similar to those found at Chichén Itzá and grimacing Toltec masks on the corners. Above the center door is an image of the Descending God. Archaeologists believe a stone block at the top of the stairs may have been used for sacrifices.

Temple of the Frescoes

Though quite small, the Temple of the Frescoes is considered one of Tulum's most archaeologically significant structures. The name owes to the fading but remarkably detailed paintings on the structure's inner walls. In shades of blue, gray, and black, they depict various deities, including Chaac (the god of rain) and Ixchel (the goddess of the moon and fertility), and a profusion of symbolic imagery, including corn and flowers. On the temple's two facades are carved figures with elaborate headdresses and yet another image of the Descending God. The large grim-faced masks on the temple's corners are believed to represent Izamná, the Maya creator god.

Halach Uinic and the Great Palace

In front of El Castillo are the remains of two palatial structures: the House of the Halach Uinic and the Great Palace (also known as the House of the Columns). Halach Uinic is a Yucatec Maya term for king or ruler, and this structure seems to have been an elaborate shrine dedicated to Tulum's enigmatic Descending God. The building is severely deteriorated, but what remains suggests its facade was highly ornamented, perhaps even painted blue and red. Next door is the Great Palace, which likely served as residential quarters for Tulum's royal court.

Practicalities

Tulum's massive parking lot and strip-mall-like visitors complex ought to clue you in to the number of tourists that pass through here every day. (Did we mention to get here early?) You'll find a small museum and bookshop amid innumerable souvenir shops and fast-food restaurants. (If this is your first visit to a Maya ruin, don't be turned off by all the hubbub. Tulum is unique for its excessive and obnoxious commercialization; most sites have just a ticket booth and restrooms.)

The actual entrance and ticket booth are about one kilometer (0.6 mile) from the visitors center; it's a flat mild walk, but there are also **trolleys** that ferry guests back and forth for US$2.25 per person round-trip (kids under 10 ride free).

Getting There

BUS

From Playa del Carmen, there are morning buses to Tulum (US$3-6, 1 hour) every 10-30 minutes 6:10am-noon. *Combis* (vans) make the same trip even more frequently for US$4.25; return service is also frequent. Be sure to let the driver know you want to get off at *las ruinas;* it's a short walk from the highway to the entrance to the site, and back again when you're ready to leave.

CAR

Tulum archaeological zone is a quick 62 kilometers (38 miles) south of Playa del Carmen on Highway 307 (and about a kilometer, or 0.6 mile, north of the town of Tulum). There are two signed entrances to the archaeological zone; the one farther south is newer and better, leading directly to the main parking lot (parking US$4).

COBÁ ARCHAEOLOGICAL ZONE

An hour's drive inland from Tulum, the Maya ruins of **Cobá** (8am-5pm daily, US$4) don't have Tulum's stunning Caribbean view and beach, but its structures are much larger and more ornate—in fact, Cobá's main pyramid is the second tallest in the Yucatán Peninsula, and it's one of few you are still allowed to climb. The ruins are also surrounded by lakes and thick forest, making it a great place to see birds, butterflies, and tropical flora. Cobá is not nearly as crowded as Tulum (and is much larger), but it's still a good idea to arrive as early as possible to beat the ever-growing crowds.

History

Cobá was settled as early as 100 BC around a collection of small lagoons; it's a logical and privileged location, as the Yucatán Peninsula is virtually devoid of rivers, lakes, or any other aboveground water. Cobá developed into an important trading hub, and in its early existence had a particularly close connection with the Petén region of present-day Guatemala. That relationship would later fade as Cobá grew more intertwined with coastal cities like Tulum, but Petén influence is obvious in Cobá's high steep structures, which are reminiscent of those in Tikal. At its peak, around AD 600-800, Cobá was the largest urban center in the northern lowlands, with some 40,000 residents and over 6,000 structures spread over 50 square kilometers (31 square miles). The city controlled most of the northeastern portion of the Yucatán Peninsula during the same period before being toppled by the Itzás of Chichén Itzá following a protracted war in the mid-800s. Following a widespread Maya collapse—of which the fall of Cobá was not the cause, though perhaps an early warning sign—the great city was all but abandoned, save as a pilgrimage and ceremonial site for the ascendant Itzás. It was briefly reinhabited in the 12th century, when a few new structures were added,

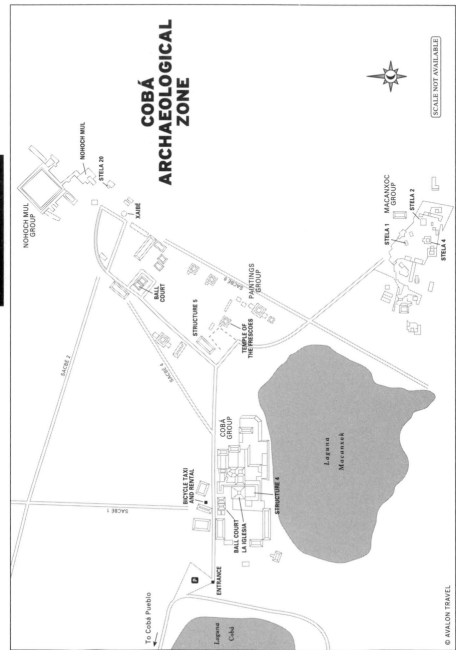

COBÁ ARCHAEOLOGICAL ZONE

SCALE NOT AVAILABLE

NOHOCH MUL GROUP

NOHOCH MUL

STELA 20

XAIBÉ

BALL COURT

STRUCTURE 5

SACBE 8

PAINTINGS GROUP

TEMPLE OF THE FRESCOES

SACBE 2

SACBE 4

SACBE 1

MACANXOC GROUP

STELA 2

STELA 1

STELA 4

COBÁ GROUP

BICYCLE TAXI AND RENTAL

STRUCTURE 4

BALL COURT

LA IGLESIA

Laguna Macanxok

ENTRANCE

P

To Cobá Pueblo

Laguna Cobá

© AVALON TRAVEL

and the other marches in the opposite direction, empty-jawed, returning for more. The vegetation decays in their nests, and the fungus that grows on the compost is an important staple of the ants' diet—a few scientists even claim this makes leaf-cutter ants the world's second species of agriculturists. Only particular types of leaves will do, and the columns can be up to a kilometer (0.6 mile) long.

© GARY CHANDLER

Cobá is home to the Yucatán Peninsula's second tallest Maya pyramid—one of very few you're still allowed to climb.

but had been abandoned again, and covered in a blanket of vegetation, by the time of the Spanish conquest.

Flora and Fauna

The name Cobá (Water Stirred by the Wind in Maya) is surely a reference to the group of shallow lagoons here (Cobá, Macanxoc, Xkanha, and Sacakal). The archaeological site and the surrounding wetlands and forest are rich with birdlife—herons, egrets, motmot, parrots, and the occasional toucan are not uncommon. Arrive early to see the most birds—at the very least you'll get an earful of their varied songs and cries. Later, as the temperature climbs, you'll start to see myriad colorful butterflies, including the large deep-blue *morphidae* and the bright yellow-orange barred sulphur.

If you look on the ground, you'll almost certainly see long lines of leaf-cutter ants. One column carries freshly cut leaves to the burrow,

Cobá Group

Passing through the entry gate, the first group of ruins you encounter is the Cobá Group, a collection of over 50 structures and the oldest part of the ancient city. Many of Cobá's *sacbeob* initiate here. Its primary structure, **La Iglesia** (The Church), rises 22.5 meters (74 feet) from a low platform, making it Cobá's second-highest pyramid. The structure consists of nine platforms stacked atop one another and notable for their round corners. Built in numerous phases beginning in the Early Classic era, La Iglesia is far more reminiscent of Tikal and other Petén-area structures than it is of the long palaces and elaborate facades typical of Puuc and Chenes sites. Visitors are no longer allowed to climb the Iglesia pyramid due to the poor state of its stairs, but it is crowned with a small temple where archaeologists discovered a cache of jade figurines, ceramic vases, pearls, and conch shells.

The Cobá Group also includes one of the city's two **ball courts,** and a large acropolis-like complex with wide stairs leading to raised patios. At one time these patios were connected, forming a long gallery of rooms that likely served as an administrative center. The best-preserved structure in this complex, **Structure 4,** has a long vaulted passageway beneath its main staircase; the precise purpose of this passageway is unclear, but it's a common feature in Cobá and affords a close look at how a so-called Maya Arch is constructed.

The Cobá Group is directly opposite the stand where you can rent bicycles or hire bike taxis. Many travelers leave it for the end of their visit, after they've turned in their bikes.

DAY TRIPS

IF YOU'VE GOT EXTRA TIME . . .

Having made it all the way to Cobá and visited the magnificent ruins there, a few places nearby are worth exploring if you've got the time and energy:

COBÁ CENOTES

A cluster of three well-maintained and well-run **cenotes** (no phone, 8am-5pm daily) make a great stop in their own right, but are especially attractive after a few hours at the ruins. **Choo-Ha, Tamcach-Ha,** and **Multun-Ha** are southwest of Cobá and are operated jointly (US$5/$7/$10 for 1/2/3 cenotes); a fourth cenote called **Nohoch-Ha** is a bit farther and requires a separate entrance fee (US$2). Each is slightly different—one has a high roof and platform for jumping, another is wide and low—but all are impressive enclosed chambers bristling with stalactites and filled with cool crystalline water that's heaven on a hot day. Cement or wooden stairways lead down to the pools; showers and changing areas are available at Choo-Ha. To get there, continue past Cobá ruins on the road to Tepich and follow the signs.

RESERVA DE MONOS ARAÑAS PUNTA LAGUNA

As evening approaches, it's the perfect time to visit the **Punta Laguna Spider Monkey Reserve** (cell. tel. 985/107-9182, 7:30am-5:30pm daily, US$5), a protected patch of forest that's home to various families of boisterous spider monkeys, as well as smaller groups of howler monkeys and numerous bird species. A short path winds through the reserve, passing a small unexcavated Maya ruin and a large lagoon where you can rent canoes (US$8.50). There's also a zipline and a place to rappel into a cenote, but it's typically reserved for large groups. Your best chance of spotting monkeys is by going in late afternoon, and by hiring one of the guides near the entrance (US$10 pp, minimum 2). The reserve (whose official name is Otoch Ma'ax Yetel Kooh, Yucatec Maya for House of the Spider Monkey and Puma) is operated by a local cooperative, whose members live in the nearby village and serve as guides; most speak at least some English. Be sure to wear good walking shoes and bring plenty of bug repellent. The reserve is located 18 kilometers (11 miles) north of Cobá, on the road toward Nuevo X'can.

Nohuch Mul Group

From the Cobá Group, the path winds nearly two kilometers (1.2 miles) through dense forest to Cobá's other main group, Nohoch Mul. The name is Yucatec Maya for Big Mound—the group's namesake pyramid rises an impressive 42 meters (138 feet) above the forest floor, the equivalent of 12 stories. (It was long believed to be the Yucatán Peninsula's tallest structure until the main pyramid at Calakmul in Campeche was determined to be some 10 meters higher.) Like La Iglesia in the Cobá Group, Nohoch Mul is composed of several platforms with rounded corners. A long central staircase climbs steeply from the forest floor to the pyramid's lofty peak. A small temple at the top bears a fairly well-preserved carving of the Descending God, an upside-down figure that figures prominently at Tulum but whose identity and significance is still unclear. (Theories vary widely, from Venus to the God of Bees.)

Nohoch Mul is one of few Maya pyramids that visitors are still allowed to climb, and the view from the top is impressive—a flat green forest spreading almost uninterrupted in every direction. A rope running down the stairs makes going up and down easier.

Where the path hits Nohoch Mul is **Stela 20,** positioned on the steps of a minor structure, beneath a protective *palapa* roof. It is one of Cobá's best-preserved stelae, depicting a figure in an elaborate costume and headdress, holding a large ornate scepter in his arms—both signifying that he is an *ahau,* or high lord or ruler. The figure, as yet unidentified, is standing on the backs of two slaves or captives, with another two bound and kneeling at his feet. Stela 20 is also notable for the date inscribed on it—November 30, 780—the latest Long Count date yet found in Cobá.

Xaibé and the Ball Court

Between the Cobá and Nohoch Mul Groups are several smaller but still significant structures. Closest to Nohuch Mol is a curiously conical structure that archaeologists have dubbed **Xaibé,** a Yucatec Maya word for crossroads. The name owes to the fact that it's near the intersection of four major *sacbeob,* and for the same reason, archaeologists believe it may have served as a watchtower. That said, its unique design and imposing size suggest a grander purpose. Round structures are fairly rare in Maya architecture, and most are thought to be astronomical observatories; there's no evidence Xaibé served that function, however, particularly since it lacks any sort of upper platform or temple. Be aware that the walking path does not pass Xaibé—you have to take the longer bike path to reach it.

A short distance from Xaibé is the second of Cobá's **ball courts.** Both courts have imagery of death and sacrifice, though they are more pronounced here: a skull inscribed on a stone in the center of the court, a decapitated jaguar on a disc at the end, and symbols of Venus (which represented death and war) inscribed on the two scoring rings. This ball court also had a huge plaque implanted on one of its slopes, with over 70 glyphs and dated AD 465; the plaque in place today is a replica, but the original is under a *palapa* covering at one end of the court, allowing visitors to examine it more closely.

Paintings Group

The Paintings Group is a collection of five platforms encircling a large plaza. The temples here were among the last to be constructed in Cobá and pertain to the latest period of occupation, roughly AD 1100-1450. The group's name comes from paintings that once lined the walls, though very little color is visible now,

unfortunately. Traces of blue and red can be seen in the upper room of the **Temple of the Frescoes,** the group's largest structure, but you aren't allowed to climb up to get a closer look.

Although centrally located, the Paintings Group is easy to miss on your way between the more outlying pyramids and groups. Look for a sign for **Structure 5,** where you can leave your bike (if you have one) and walk into the group's main area.

Macanxoc Group

From the Paintings Group, the path continues southeasterly for about a kilometer (0.6 mile) to the Macanxoc Group. Numerous stelae have been found here, indicating it was a place of great ceremonial significance. The most famous of these monuments is **Stela 1,** aka the Macanxoc Stela. It depicts a scene from the Maya creation myth—"the hearth stone appears"—along with a Long Count date referring to a cycle ending the equivalent of 41.9 billion, billion, billion years in the future. It is the most distant Long Count date known to have been conceived and recorded by the ancient Maya. Stela 1 also has reference to December 21, 2012, when the Maya Long Count completed its first Great Cycle, equivalent to 5,125 years. Despite widespread reports to the contrary, there is no known evidence, at Cobá or anywhere, that the Maya believed (much less predicted) that the world would end on that date.

Practicalities

Cobá's main groups are quite spread apart, and visiting all of them adds up to several kilometers. Fortunately, you can rent a bicycle (US$3) or hire a *triciclo* (US$9 for 1 hour, US$15 for 2 hours) at a large stand a short distance past the entryway, opposite the Cobá Group. Whether you walk or ride, don't forget a water bottle, comfortable shoes, bug repellent, sunscreen, and a hat. Watch for signs and stay on the designated trails. Guide service is available—prices are not fixed but average US$52 per group (1.5 hours, up to 6 people). Parking at Cobá is US$4.

DAY TRIPS

Getting There

BUS

From Playa del Carmen, there are morning buses to Cobá (US$6.50-8.50, 2-2.5 hours) at 6:10am, 7:30am, 8am, 8:45am, 9am, and 10am (plus 10:30am on weekends), but just one return bus at 3:10pm (plus 4:50pm on weekends). There usually are additional second-class departures, but you should double-check at the bus station. Alternatively, there are frequent *combis* (vans) between Playa and Tulum (US$3.50, 1 hour) and Tulum and Cobá (US$4.25, 1 hour), from early morning to past sunset.

CAR

Driving to Cobá is easy, with smooth and scenic roads that cut through pretty farmland and small towns. Keep your speed down, however, as there are innumerable *topes* (speed bumps) and occasional people and animals along the shoulder.

From Playa del Carmen, take Highway 307 south to Tulum (63 kilometers/39 miles). At a well-marked intersection at the entrance to Tulum town, turn west onto the Cobá-Tulum road. From there it's 45 kilometers (28 miles) to a large roundabout just outside Cobá village and ruins. Several roads intersect here, so be sure you take the right one.

◖ CHICHÉN ITZÁ ARCHAEOLOGICAL ZONE

Chichén Itzá (8am-5pm daily, US$14.75 including sound and light show) is a monumental archaeological site, remarkable for both its size and scope. The ruins include impressive palaces, temples, and altars, as well as the largest-known ball court in the Maya world. One of the most widely recognized (and heavily visited) ruins in the world, it was declared a World Heritage Site by UNESCO in 1988 and one of the New Seven Wonders of the World in 2007. In 2012, INAH (Instituto Nacional de Antropología e Historia) partnered with Google to photograph—by bicycle—the site for Google Street View maps.

History

What we call Chichén Itzá surely had another name when it was founded. The name means Mouth of the Well of the Itzá but the Itzá, an illiterate and semi-nomadic group of uncertain origin, didn't arrive here until the 12th century. Before the Itzá, the area was controlled—or at least greatly influenced—by Toltec migrants who arrived from central Mexico around AD 1000. Most of Chichén's most notable structures, including its famous four-sided pyramid, and images like the reclining *chac-mool,* bear a striking resemblance to structures and images found at Tula, the ancient Toltec capital, in the state of Hidalgo. Before the Toltecs, the area was populated by Maya, evidenced by the Puuc- and Chenes-style design of the earliest structures here, such as the Nunnery and Casa Colorada.

The three major influences—Maya, Toltec, and Itzá—are indisputable, but the exact chronology and circumstances of those groups' interaction (or lack thereof) is one of the most hotly contested issues in Maya archaeology. Part of the difficulty in understanding Chichén Itzá more fully is that its occupants created very few stelae and left few Long Count dates on their monuments. In this way Chichén Itzá is different from virtually every other ancient city in the Yucatán. It's ironic, actually, that Chichén Itzá is the most widely recognized "Maya" ruin considering it was so deeply influenced by non-Maya cultures, and its history and architecture are so atypical of the region.

Chichén Itzá's influence ebbed and flowed over its many centuries of existence and occupation. It first peaked in the mid-9th century, or Late Classic period, when it eclipsed Cobá as the dominant power in the northern Yucatán region. The effects of a widespread collapse of Maya cities to the south (like Calakmul, Tikal, and Palenque) reached Chichén Itza in the late 900s, and it too collapsed abruptly. The city rose again under Toltec and later Itzá influence, but went into its final decline after an internal dispute led to the rise of Mayapán, which would come to control much of the Yucatán Peninsula. Chichén Itzá was all but abandoned

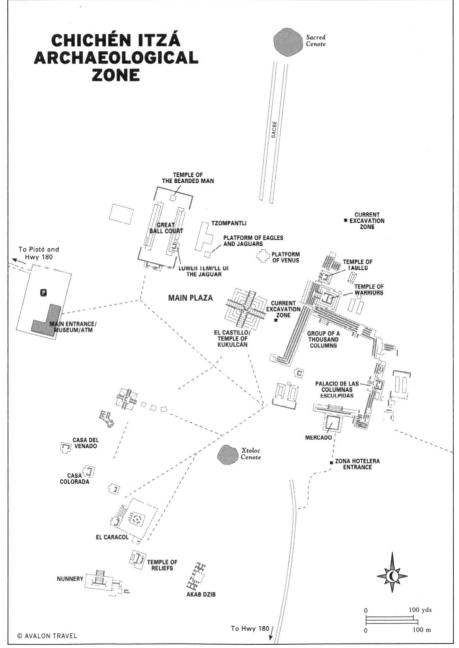

CHICHÉN ITZÁ ARCHAEOLOGICAL ZONE

Sacred Cenote

SACBÉ

DAY TRIPS

TEMPLE OF
THE BEARDED MAN

CURRENT
■ EXCAVATION
ZONE

GREAT
BALL COURT

TZOMPANTLI

PLATFORM OF EAGLES
AND JAGUARS

TEMPLE OF
TABLEO

To Pisté and
Hwy 180

PLATFORM
OF VENUS

LOWER TEMPLE OF
THE JAGUAR

TEMPLE OF
WARRIORS

P

MAIN PLAZA

CURRENT
EXCAVATION
ZONE

MAIN ENTRANCE/
MUSEUM/ATM

EL CASTILLO/
TEMPLE OF
KUKULCÁN

GROUP OF A
THOUSAND
COLUMNS

C

PALACIO DE LAS
COLUMNAS
ESCULPIDAS

CASA DEL
VENADO

MERCADO

Xtoloc
Cenote

CASA
COLORADA

■ ZONA HOTELERA
ENTRANCE

EL CARACOL

TEMPLE OF
RELIEFS

NUNNERY

AKAB DZIB

0   100 yds
0   100 m

To Hwy 180

© AVALON TRAVEL

© H.W. PRADO

a reclining *chac-mool* figure flanked by serpents, at the incomparable Chichén Itzá archaeological zone

by the early 1200s, though it remained an important religious pilgrimage site even after the arrival of the Spanish.

El Castillo/Temple of Kukulcán

The most dramatic structure in Chichén Itzá is El Castillo (The Castle), also known as the Temple of Kukulcán. At 24 meters (79 feet), it's the tallest structure on the site, and certainly the most recognizable. Dating to around AD 850, El Castillo was built according to strict astronomical guidelines. There are nine levels, which, divided by the central staircase, make for 18 platforms, the number of months in the Maya calendar. Each of the four sides has 91 steps, which added together, along with the platform on top, total 365—one for each day of the year. And there are 52 inset panels on each face of the structure, equal to the number of years in each cycle of the Calendar Round.

On the spring and autumn equinoxes (March 21 and September 22), the afternoon

sun lights up a bright zigzag strip on the outside wall of the north staircase as well as the giant serpent heads at the base, giving the appearance of a serpent slithering down the steps. Chichén Itzá is mobbed during those periods, especially by spiritual-minded folks seeking communion with the ancient Maya. The effect also occurs in the days just before and after the equinox, and there are significantly fewer people blocking the view.

Climbing El Castillo used to be a given for any visit to Chichén Itzá, and the views from its top level are breathtaking. However, an elderly tourist died in 2005 after tumbling from near the top of the pyramid to the ground. The accident, combined with longtime warnings from archaeologists that the structure was being irreparably eroded by the hundreds of thousands of visitors who climbed it yearly, prompted officials to close it off. Pyramids at other sites have been restricted as well, and it's looking more and more like a standard policy at Maya archaeological zones.

Deep inside El Castillo and accessed by way of a steep, narrow staircase are several chambers; inside one is a red-painted, jade-studded bench in the figure of a jaguar, which may have served as a throne of sorts. You used to be able to climb the stairs to see the chambers and throne—a fascinating, albeit humid and highly claustrophobic affair—but access was closed at the same time climbing the pyramid was prohibited.

Great Ball Court

Chichén Itzá's famous Great Ball Court is the largest ball court in Mesoamerica by a wide margin. The playing field is 135 meters (443 feet) by 65 meters (213 feet), with two parallel walls 8 meters high (26 feet) and scoring rings in impossibly high perches in the center. The players would've had to hit a 12-pound rubber ball through the rings using only their elbows, wrists, and hips. They wore heavy padding and the game likely lasted for hours. At the game's end, the captain of one team—or even the whole team—was apparently sacrificed, possibly by decapitation. There's disagreement about *which* team got the axe, however. Some say it was the losers—otherwise the game's best players would constantly be wiped out. Some argue that it was the winners, and that being sacrificed would have been the ultimate honor. Of course, it's likely the game varied from city to city and evolved over the many centuries it was played. Along the walls, reliefs depict the ball game and sacrifices.

On the outside of the ball court, the **Lower Temple of the Jaguar** has incredibly fine relief carvings depicting the Maya creation myth. An upper temple is off-limits to visitors, but is decorated with a variety of carvings and remnants of what were likely colorful murals.

The Platforms

As you make your way from the ball court to the Temple of Warriors, you'll pass the gruesome **Tzompantli** (Wall of Skulls). A low T-shaped platform, it is decorated on all sides with row upon row of carved skulls, most with eyes staring out of the large sockets. Among the skulls are images of warriors holding the heads of decapitated victims, skeletons intertwined with snakes, and eagles eating human hearts (a common image in Toltec design, further evidence of their presence here). It is presumed that ceremonies performed on this platform culminated in a sacrificial death for the victim, the head then left on display, perhaps with others already in place. It's estimated that the platform was built AD 1050-1200. Nearby, the **Platform of Venus** and **Platform of Eagles and Jaguars** are smaller square structures, each with low stairways on all four sides, which were likely used for ritualistic music and dancing.

Sacred Cenote

This natural well is 300 meters (984 feet) north of the main structures, along the remains of a *sacbé* (raised stone road) constructed during the Classic period. Almost 60 meters (197 feet) in diameter and 30 meters (98.4 feet) down to the surface of the water, it was a place for sacrifices, mostly to Chaac, the god of rain, who was believed to live in its depths. The cenote has been dredged

and scoured by divers numerous times, beginning as early as 1900, and the remains of scores of victims, mostly children and young adults, have been recovered, as well as innumerable jade and stone artifacts. (Most are now displayed at the Museo Nacional de Antropología in Mexico City.) On the edge of the cenote is a ruined sweat bath, probably used for purification rituals before sacrificial ceremonies. The name Chichén Itzá (Mouth of the Well of the Itzá) is surely derived from this deeply sacred cenote, and it remained an important Maya pilgrimage site well into the Spanish conquest.

Temple of Warriors and Group of a Thousand Columns

The Temple of Warriors is where some of the distinctive reclining *chac-mool* figures are found. However, its name comes from the rectangular monoliths in front, which are carved on all sides with images of warriors. (Some are also prisoners, their hands tied behind their backs.) This temple is also closed to entry, and it can be hard to appreciate the fading images from the rope perimeter. You may be able to get a closer look from the temple's south side, where you can easily make out the figures' expressions and dress (though access is sometimes blocked there as well). The south side is impressive for its facade, too, where a series of well-preserved human and animal figures adorn the lower portion, while above, human faces emerge from serpents' mouths, framed by eagle profiles, with masks of Chaac, the hook-nosed god of rain, on the corners.

The aptly named Group of a Thousand Columns is adjacent to the Temple of Warriors. It's perfectly aligned cylindrical columns likely held up a grand roof structure.

Across the plaza, the **Palacio de las Columnas Esculpidas** (Palace of Sculptured Columns) also has cylindrical columns, but with intricate carvings, suggesting this was the ceremonial center of this portion of the complex. Continuing through the trees, you'll reach the **Mercado** (market). The name is purely speculative, though it's easy to imagine

CENOTE HOPPING

The states of Quintana Roo and Yucatán are dotted with hundreds of cenotes–pools of shimmering blue water fed by a vast underground freshwater river system. Some look like large ponds, others are deep sinkholes, and others occupy gaping caverns or have dramatic rock formations above and below the surface. Many cenotes are open to the public, and their cool clear water is perfect for swimming, snorkeling, and scuba diving. Facilities range from simple restrooms and snorkel rental to full-service "cenote parks" with guided tours.

QUINTANA ROO

All along the highway from Cancún to Tulum, south to the Costa Maya, and inland to Cobá are signs for cenotes–dozens in all, and that's just the ones open to the public. Many are connected by underground channels, making them especially popular among divers (though still great for swimming and snorkeling).

- **Ruta de los Cenotes:** Sure, some spots along the "Cenote Route" are tourist traps, but others are sublime, like Siete Bocas, a huge eerie cavern filled with shimmering water, and Lucerno Verde, a gorgeous open-air pool filled with freshwater turtles and fish.

- **Jardín de Edén:** The best and biggest of a cluster of cenotes near Playa Xpu-Há, with a large cavern that forms a dramatic overhang.

- **Cenote Cristalino:** Next to Jardín de Edén, Cristalino also has an overhanging cliff, but a smaller swimming area.

- **Cenote Manatí:** Near Tankah Tres, this is actually a series of connected cenotes and lagoons that wind inland through a tangled scrub forest.

- **Dos Ojos** and **Hidden Worlds:** Side-by-side full-service cenote parks with equipment, guides, and spectacular caverns.

- **Gran Cenote:** A gorgeous cavern with natural arches and stalactite formations, located east of Tulum on the road to Cobá.

- **Aktun-Há:** Past Gran Cenote, this innocuous-looking cenote (commonly called Car Wash) has stunning cavern formations below the surface.

- **Cenote Choo-Ha:** One of four dramatic cenotes southwest of Cobá, with a high domed ceiling and iridescent blue water.

YUCATÁN

Cenotes in the state of Yucatán are more widely scattered and tend to be classic deep circular sinkholes, with or without domelike roofs.

- **Sacred Cenote:** Perhaps the most famous cenote is the one at Chichén Itzá, a massive sinkhole 60 meters (197 feet) across and 25 meters (82 feet) from the edge to the water's surface, into which the ancient Maya cast figurines, jewelry, even sacrificial victims.

- **Cenote Ik-Kil:** Just three kilometers (1.9 miles) from Chichén Itzá, this huge deep cenote can be crowded as a result, but it's still a dramatic place to cool off after the ruins.

- **Cenote Yokdzonot:** Also nearby Chichén Itzá, this little-known gem is all the more rewarding for being operated by a cooperative of enterprising local women.

- **Cenote X'Canché:** This pretty 12-meter-deep (39 feet) cenote is a great addition to Ek' Balam archaeological site, located a kilometer (0.6 mile) down a forest path from the ruins.

- **Cenotes de Dzitnup:** Twin cenotes just outside the town of Valladolid, both with huge domed ceilings and large swimmable pools beneath.

- **Cenotes de Cuzamá:** Getting to these three cenotes via horse-drawn carts is half the fun. Two have slippery ladders leading down to their cool azure waters.

- **Cenote Kankirixché:** South of Mérida and considered one of the peninsula's prettiest cenotes. It's not hard to see why, with its cool turquoise water, dangling tree roots, and a roof bristling with stalactites.

a breezy bustling market here, protected from the sun under a wood and *palapa* roof built atop the structure's remarkably high columns.

Osario, El Caracol, and the Nunnery

From the market, bear left (away from El Castillo, just visible through the trees) until you meet the path leading to the site's southern entrance. You'll pass the **Osario** (ossuary), also known as the Tomb of the High Priest. Like a miniature version of El Castillo, the pyramid at one time had four stairways on each side and a temple at the crest. From the top platform, a vertical passageway leads into a chamber where seven tombs were discovered, along with numerous copper and jade artifacts indicating the deceased were of special importance (and hence the temple's name). Continuing on, you'll pass two more large structures, **Casa del Venado** (House of the Deer) and **Casa Colorada** (Red House).

The highlight of this portion of Chichén Itzá is **El Caracol** (The Snail Shell), also known as the Observatory, and perhaps the most graceful structure at Chichén Itzá. A two-tiered circular structure is set atop a broad rectangular platform, with window slits facing south and west, and another aligned according to the path of the moon during the spring equinoxes. Ancient astronomers used structures like this one to track celestial events and patterns—the orbits of the Moon and Venus, and the coming of solar and lunar eclipses, for example—with uncanny accuracy.

Beyond El Caracol is the **Nunnery,** so-named by Spanish explorers who thought it looked like convents back home. Judging from its size, location, and many rooms, the Nunnery was probably an administrative palace. Its exuberant facades show strong Chenes influence, another example of the blending of styles in Chichén Itzá.

DAY TRIPS

©LIZA PRADO

Chichén Itzá's famous observatory is known as El Caracol (The Snail Shell) for the unique circular staircase inside.

Sound and Light Show

Though it was closed for retooling at the time of research, the site puts on a nightly high-tech sound and light show at 7pm in the winter (Oct.-Apr.) and at 8pm in the summer (May-Sept.). The fee to enter is included in the general admission; if you'd like to see the show the night before you visit the ruins, buy a US$10 partial entrance—*not* the show-only ticket—and keep your stub for credit the next morning. (Just tell the ticket seller your plan, and you'll get the right ticket. If you're only interested in the show and want to skip the ruins, the price is US$6.) The sound and light show is presented in Spanish, but for an additional US$3.25 you can rent headphones with translations in English, French, German, and Italian.

Practicalities

The grounds are open 8am-5pm daily. Admission is US$14.75 per person, plus US$3.75 to enter with a video camera; parking is US$1.80. The fee includes entrance to the ruins and the sound and light show, but there is no discount if you don't go to the latter.

Guides can be hired at the entrance according to fixed and clearly marked prices: US$42 for a two-hour tour in Spanish, US$50 in English, French, Italian, or German. Prices are per group, which can include up to eight people. Tips are customary and not included in the price. The visitors center has restrooms, an ATM, free luggage storage, a café, a bookstore, a gift shop, and an information center.

Getting There
BUS

Buses to and from the coast stop at Chichén Itzá itself, and at the small town of Pisté, about 2.5 kilometers (1.6 miles) from the entrance to the ruins. First-class buses are more expensive and less frequent, but much preferred for safety, comfort, and reliability.

From Playa del Carmen, there are second-class departures for Chichén Itzá (US$11, 5 hours) at 6:10am and 7:30am Monday-Saturday (6:10am only on Sun.), and a first-class bus at 8am daily (US$24, 4 hours). There's one first-class return bus at 4:30pm.

CAR

Chichén Itzá lies adjacent to Highway 180, 200 kilometers (124 miles) west of Cancún and 268 kilometers (167 miles) from Playa del Carmen. For drivers, the quickest way to get there is via the *cuota,* a large modern freeway extending from Cancún most of the way to the city of Mérida, with a well-marked exit for Chichén Itzá and Pisté. There's a price for speed and convenience, though: The toll from Cancún is an eye-opening US$33 each way. You can take the old *carretera libre* (free highway) instead; it's in reasonably good condition but takes much longer, mainly because you pass through numerous small villages and seemingly innumerable *topes* (speed bumps).

Ecoparks and Nature Reserves

If you like Cozumel's Parque Chankanaab, you're sure to enjoy the bigger and better eco-parks on the Riviera Maya, including Xcaret, Xel-Há, and the newest addition to the family, Xplor. Each is slightly different but all are family friendly and quite well operated, making for a memorable, albeit expensive, outing. All have packages that include transportation from Playa del Carmen; alternatively, if you want to save US$20 per person on transportation, *combis* (shuttle vans) are an easy way to get to these parks (though you'll have to walk to the entrances from the highway turnoff). Southbound *combis* line up on Calle 2 near 20 Avenida, with service 24 hours a day (every 10 minutes until 11pm, then every 30 minutes). Fares are US$1.25-$3 (10-50 minutes), depending on your destination.

© J.W. PRADO

A day at Xcaret ends with an extravagant performance in the park's huge stadium, ranging from folkloric dancing to a Maya ball game.

To return, flag down a *combi* heading north along the highway.

◉ XCARET

Just five kilometers (3.1 miles) south of Playa, **Xcaret** (Hwy. 307 Km. 282, tel. 998/883-0470, www.xcaret.com.mx, 8:30am-9:30pm daily, US$79/39.50 adult/child, US$139/69.50 adult/child including transportation and buffet) is a mega-eco-park offering water activities like snorkeling in underground rivers and swimming with dolphins and sharks; up-close animal viewing areas including jaguar and puma islands, a butterfly pavilion, and an aquarium; a phenomenal folk art museum that's brimming with *artesanía* from around Mexico; and spectacular shows, like a Maya ball game, regional dances, and music performances. Xcaret is thoroughly touristy and pre-packaged, yes, but also surprisingly well done and a worthwhile day trip, especially for families. There are numerous packages

and prices, including combo visits with sister parks Xplor and Xel-Há; be sure you know what you're getting (and not getting) when you book. Discounts are available for booking online.

XEL-HÁ

Built around a huge natural inlet, **Xel-Há** (Hwy. 307, 9 kilometers/5.6 miles north of Tulum, tel. 984/105-6981, www.xel-ha.com, 8:30am-6pm daily, US$79 adult all-inclusive, US$119 adult with round-trip transportation, 50 percent off child 5-11, under 5 free) is all about being in and around the water. Activities include snorkeling, snuba, tubing, and interactive programs with dolphins, manatees, and stingrays. Although it doesn't compare to snorkeling on the reef, there's a fair number of fish darting about, and it makes for a fun easy introduction for children and beginners. Check the website for online deals and combo packages with sister resorts Xcaret and Xplor.

© H.W. PRADO

Xcaret is a fun family-friendly park, but it can get quite crowded.

XPLOR

The newest of the Xcaret company's family of ecoparks, **Xplor** (Hwy. 307 Km. 282, toll-free Mex. tel. 01-800/212-8951, toll-free U.S./Can. tel. 888/922-7381, www.xplor.travel, 9am-5pm Mon.-Sat., US$109 adult admission, US$139 including transportation, 50 percent off child 5-11, child under 5 not admitted) is adjacent to the mother ship and focused on adventure activities. The park has a zipline circuit with 14 segments, including tandem lines and a splashdown in the mouth of a cavern. Other activities include swimming and rafting through caverns bristling with stalactites, and driving amphibious ATVs through the forest and underground passages. Admission includes lockers, showers, buffet lunch, and fresh-made juices and smoothies.

SIAN KA'AN BIOSPHERE RESERVE

Sian Ka'an is Yucatec Mayan for "where the sky is born," and it's not hard to see how the original inhabitants arrived at such a poetic name.

The unkempt beaches, blue-green sea, bird-filled wetlands and islets, and humble accommodations are manna for bird-watchers, artists, snorkelers, and kayakers. It also happens to be one of the best fly-fishing spots in the world, with all three flatwater Grand Slam catches: bonefish, tarpon, and permit.

The reserve was created in 1986, designated a UNESCO World Heritage Site in 1987, and expanded in 1994. It now encompasses around 1.3 million acres of coastal and mangrove forests and wetlands, and some 113 kilometers (70 miles) of pristine coral reefs just offshore. A huge variety of flora and fauna thrive in the reserve, including four species of mangrove, many medicinal plants, and about 300 species of birds, including toucans, parrots, frigate birds, herons, and egrets. Monkeys, foxes, crocodiles, and boa constrictors also populate the reserve and are spotted by locals and visitors with some regularity. Manatees and jaguars are the reserve's largest animals but also the most reclusive: You need sharp eyes and a great deal of luck to spot either one. More than 20 Maya

DAY TRIPS

© LIZA PRADO

dolphin spotting in Sian Ka'an Biosphere Reserve, south of Tulum

ruins have been found in the reserve, though most are unexcavated.

Sights
MUYIL ARCHAEOLOGICAL ZONE
The most accessible Maya site within the Sian Ka'an reserve is **Muyil** (Hwy. 307, 25 kilometers/15.5 miles south of Tulum, 8am-5pm daily, US$3), on the western edge of the park. Also known as Chunyaxché, it is one of the oldest archaeological sites in the Maya world, dating back to 300 BC and occupied continuously through the conquest. It's believed to have been primarily a seaport, perched on a limestone shelf near the edge of Laguna Muyil; it is connected to the Caribbean via a canal system that was constructed by ancient Maya traders and still exists today.

Only a small portion of the city has been excavated, so it makes for a relatively quick visit. There are six main structures ranging from two-meter-high (6.6-foot) platforms to the impressive **Castillo**. At 17 meters (56 feet), it is one of the tallest structures on the peninsula's

Caribbean coast. The Castillo is topped with a unique solid round masonry turret from which the waters of the Caribbean Sea can be seen. Unfortunately, climbing to the top is prohibited.

A *sacbé* (raised stone road) runs about a half kilometer (0.3 mile) from the center of the site to the edge of the **Laguna Muyil**. Part of this *sacbé* is on private property, however, so if you want to access the lagoon from the ruins—you also can get to it by car—there is an additional charge of US$3.50 per person. Along the way, there is a lookout tower with views over Sian Ka'an to the Caribbean.

Once you arrive at the water's edge, it's possible to take a **boat tour** (US$45 pp) that crosses both Muyil and Chunyaxche Lagoons, which are connected by a canal that was carved by the ancient Maya in order to reach the ocean. It's a pleasant way to enjoy the water, and you'll also get a view of several otherwise inaccessible ruins along the lagoons' edges and through the mangroves, with the final stop being **Xlapak ruins,** a small site thought to have been a

DAY TRIPS

© LIZA PRADO

Mangrove forests are a great place to kayak, canoe, and spot wildlife.

trading post. If arriving by car, look for signs to Muyil Lagoon on Highway 307, just south of the similarly named archaeological site. More thorough tours of this part of Sian Ka'an can be booked in Tulum.

(BAHÍA DE LA ASCENSIÓN

Ascension Bay covers about 20 square kilometers (12.4 square miles), and its shallow flats and tangled mangrove islands teem with bonefish, tarpon, and huge permit—some of the biggest ever caught, in fact. It is a fly fisher's dream come true, and it has been attracting anglers from around the world since the mid-1980s. Don't fly-fish? No worries: The spin fishing is also fantastic, while the offshore reef yields plenty of grouper, barracuda, dorado, tuna, sailfish, and marlin.

Sports and Recreation

SPORTFISHING

Sportfishing is world-class in and around Sian Ka'an—it's hard to go wrong in the flats and mangrove islands, or with the Caribbean

lapping at its shores. Recommended outfits include **Pesca Maya** (7 kilometers/4.3 miles north of Punta Allen, tel. 998/848-2496, toll-free U.S. tel. 888/894-5642, www.pescamaya.com, 8am-7pm daily); the **Palometa Club** (Punta Allen, north of the central plaza, toll-free U.S. tel. 888/824-5420, www.palometa-club.com, 8am-6pm daily); and **Club Grand Slam** (near the entrance to Punta Allen, US tel. 984/139-2930, www.grandslamfishing-lodge.com). Rates start at around US$400 for a private full-day tour, including lunch and admission and license fees. Variations like renting gear, adding people, and half-day options can also be arranged.

BIRD-WATCHING

Sian Ka'an is also an excellent place for bird-watching. Trips to Bird Island and other spots afford a look at various species of water birds, including male frigates showing off their big red balloon-like chests in the winter. Tours often combine bird-watching with snorkeling and walking around one or more bay islands.

Prices are typically per boat, so don't be shy to approach other travelers in town about forming a group.

In Tulum, operators to consider include **CESiaK** (Hwy. 307 just south of the Tulum ruins turnoff, tel. 984/871-2499, www.cesiak.org, 9am-2pm and 4pm-8pm daily); **Community Tours Sian Ka'an** (Tulum, Calle Osiris Sur near Calle Sol Ote., tel. 984/871-2202, www.siankaantours.org, 7am-9pm daily); and, if your budget permits, **Visit Sian Ka'an** (Sian Ka'an Biosphere Reserve, Carr. Tulum-Punta Allen Km. 15.8, cell. tel. 984/141-4245, www.visitsiankaan.com), which offers customized private tours.

KAYAKING
The tangled mangrove forests, interconnected lagoons, and scenic bays make Sian Ka'an ideal for kayaking. **CESiaK** (Hwy. 307 just south of the Tulum ruins turnoff, tel. 984/871-2499, www.cesiak.org, 9am-2pm and 4pm-8pm daily) offers kayak tours (US$50, 3 hours) and rentals for do-it-yourself exploration (US$25/35 s/d, 3 hours). **Community Tours Sian Ka'an**

(Calle Osiris Sur near Calle Sol Ote., tel. 984/871-2202, www.siankaantours.org, 7am-9pm daily) is another good option.

Getting There
To get to Sian Ka'an and Punta Allen as a day trip, catch an early ferry from Cozumel to Playa del Carmen. From there, unless you're joining an organized tour, a rental car is necessary. Once you pick up your car, head south on Highway 307 to the entrance of Tulum town. A well-marked intersection directs you east (and then south) through Tulum's beach area and Zona Hotelera; in about eight kilometers (5 miles) you'll reach the *el arco* (the arch), marking the reserve boundary, where you register and pay a US$4 per person park fee. From there it's 56 kilometers (35 miles) by dirt road to Punta Allen. The road is much improved from years past, and an ordinary car can make it in 2-3 hours. It can be much more difficult after a heavy rain, however. Be sure to fill the tank in Tulum—there is no gas station along the way or in Punta Allen, though some locals sell gas from their homes.

BACKGROUND

The Land

The history of Cozumel, and the entire Yucatán Peninsula, is deeply intertwined with its unique geology and ecology. From the ancient Maya to modern-day tourism, the land and its resources have shaped the course of Yucatecan events. And the Yucatán, in turn, has been witness and party to major developments in Mexican history, from serving as the stage upon which the early Spanish conquest was conducted to helping rescue a moribund Mexican economy in the 1980s.

GEOGRAPHY

Cozumel is roughly 48 kilometers (30 miles) long and 16 kilometers (10 miles) wide, making it Mexico's third-largest island, after two islands in the Sea of Cortez. Geologically, Cozumel is a flat limestone shelf whose highest point is just 15 meters (49 feet) above sea level. It is separated from the mainland by the Cozumel Channel, which is 16 kilometers (10 miles) across and over 400 meters (1,300 feet) deep. Like the rest of the Yucatán Peninsula, Cozumel is dotted with cenotes and underground caverns, and is home to the fifth-longest cave system in the world. Cozumel has some beautiful stretches of natural beaches, but much of its shoreline is made up of ironshore, a hard and extremely jagged type of rock formed

© LIZA PRADO

HURRICANE ALLEY

Hurricanes are part of life in the Caribbean, and the entire western Atlantic seaboard. They begin as tropical depressions off the coast of Africa and are pushed by trade winds across the Atlantic Ocean. The storms, fueled by water evaporation, strengthen dramatically as they enter the warm Caribbean waters. That's also where the trade winds weaken, and local wind patterns, mostly northward and eastward, cause hurricanes to turn predictably northward.

Cozumel doesn't experience as many hurricanes as islands farther east, but has had its fair share of direct hits. For years, Hurricane Gilbert was the storm everyone remembered; it roared ashore in 1988 with 160 mile-per-hour winds and 17-foot storm surge. Then, in 2005, Cozumel was hit with two Category 5 storms—Emily and Wilma—just 90 days apart. Wilma

was particularly destructive; not only was it the most intense hurricane recorded to that point, it was extremely slow moving, coming to a virtual standstill over Cozumel for nearly 24 hours. The years since have set records for the number and intensity of storms, unleashing heavy surf and destructive winds, even on areas not directly hit.

Practically all climate scientists believe global climate change plays a significant role in the growing intensity of hurricanes. For its part, Cozumel seems to bounce back from each storm with renewed pluck and innovation, using the destruction as an opportunity to upgrade streets, sidewalks, parking, drainage, and more, not least to prove to the millions of tourists who visit yearly that hurricanes aren't a reason to stay away. Based on the ever-growing queue of cruise ships, the message seems to be working.

by erosion of ancient limestone. The island's interior is covered in a low dense forest that remains undeveloped and virtually untouched.

CLIMATE

The weather in Cozumel and much of the Yucatán follows a yearly cycle of rainy season (May-October) and dry season (November-April). Travelers to the region in the dry season will experience warm days, occasional brief storms called *nortes*, and plenty of tourists. In the rainy season, expect spectacular storms and hot, muggy days. The region is especially hot and humid in May and June, when it hovers around 90°F *and* 90 percent humidity.

Hurricane season runs July-November, with most activity occurring mid-August-mid-October. Cloudy conditions and scattered showers are common during this period, occasionally developing into tropical storms. Hurricanes are still relatively rare, but their effects are wide-reaching—even if a storm isn't predicted to hit Cozumel or the

Yucatán, it may send plenty of heavy rain and surf that direction. If a hurricane *is* bearing down, don't try to tough it out; cut short your trip or head inland immediately.

ENVIRONMENTAL ISSUES
Hurricanes

Hurricanes are nothing new to Cozumel, but evidence that global climate change may lead to increased frequency and intensity of Atlantic hurricanes is cause for serious concern. In 2005, two Category 5 storms pummeled the island, including Hurricane Wilma, the most intense storm ever recorded in the Atlantic basin (measured by barometric pressure).

Overdevelopment

Runaway construction is more of a problem along the Riviera Maya than Cozumel, but the island isn't immune to its effects. Cozumel, like the entire Yucatán Peninsula, is made of highly porous limestone with a weblike underground watershed. Contamination is extremely difficult to clean up or even contain, as it spreads

© LIZA PRADO

conch shells, bleached white by the brilliant Riviera Maya sun

quickly in multiple directions via underground currents, including into the ocean. It goes without saying that damage to either Cozumel's reef or its freshwater supply would be a direct and serious blow to the all-important tourist economy.

Flora and Fauna

FLORA
Virtually all of Cozumel's development is along the coast, while the interior is a vast swath of mostly untouched forest and scrubland that is home to several unique species of trees, most of which are of moderate height or smaller, rarely growing more than 10 meters (33 feet) high.

Sapodilla
Cozumel's best known tree is the sapodilla. One of numerous latex-producing trees found in the tropics, the sapodilla's gooey sap, known as chicle, was a hot commodity in the late 19th and early 20th centuries, when it was mixed with sugar to make chewing gum. The ancient Maya used it for much the same purpose—boiling it, shaping it into blocks, then slicing off chunks for chewing, though without sweetener. The sapodilla's fruit is also delicious, and its wood is valued for its hardness and durability.

Chechen
The chechen tree's pretty white bark and graceful posture belie a very unpleasant characteristic: Even a slight brush of its leaves or trunk on skin can cause severe itching, rash, even blistering thanks to a potent poison found in the tree's sap. Also known as the poisonwood tree, chechen has rich durable wood, all the more valuable for the difficulty in harvesting it!

Guaya

This rangy evergreen is part of the lychee nut family and produces clumps of leathery seed pods that contain sweet yellowy pulp and a large round seed. Also known as mamoncillo, the fruit is enjoyed many ways: right off the stem, chilled, or with lime and chile, while the seed can be roasted.

Mangrove

There are at least three types of mangroves in Cozumel: white, red, and botoncillo. Hardy and salt-resistant, mangroves thrive in coastal regions throughout the Riviera Maya and beyond. They are an important food source for numerous sea creatures and a refuge for birds, and play a vital role in filtering water and protecting coastal dunes and soil. But their presence along would-be beach areas makes them a common victim in beachfront developments; thousands of acres of mangroves were torn out to make room for resorts in Cancun, Playa del Carmen, Cozumel, and much of the Riviera Maya. Most of Cozumel's remaining mangroves are in Parque Punta Sur (Faro Celarain) on the island's southern end, and there are NGOs working to protect and reforest mangroves in Cozumel and elsewhere.

Agricultural Species

In addition to the native flora, it's possible to find many agricultural species growing feral around the island, including pineapple, banana, mango, squash, corn, and sweet potato. These are remnants of earlier times when agriculture was more widespread and a necessary practice on an isolated island. Today, with the advent of ferry service and higher-paid jobs in tourism, there are few working fields left.

FAUNA
Land Animals
MAMMALS

The Cozumel raccoon and Cozumel fox, both endemic, are pygmy versions of their mainland counterparts. Island dwarfism (aka insular dwarfism) is a common phenomenon in which populations of certain species are isolated in confined regions (islands are the most common, but it can happen in lakes, caves, etc.) and evolve into smaller species in response to limited space and resources. The Cozumel raccoon is 20 percent smaller and 50 percent lighter than standard raccoons and eats crabs, frogs, lizards, and insects. Only a few hundred individuals are left, making it a critically endangered species, though they're a fairly common sight around Bahia Ciega, on Cozumel's northwest tip, where they boldly beg for food at the pier and parking lot. The Cozumel fox is a pygmy version of mainland gray fox and is also critically endangered; in fact, with no confirmed sightings since 2001, they may already be extinct. Cozumel's other mammals include an endemic harvest mouse, a subspecies of coati (a relative of raccoons), as well as rabbits, armadillos, deer, and wild boars.

BIRDS

Cozumel's most notable bird species is probably the Cozumel thrasher, a type of mockingbird that has the dubious honor of being the most endangered bird in all of Mexico. There have been no confirmed sightings since 2006, though unconfirmed sightings in 2008 and later make scientists reasonably confident the species isn't entirely extinct. The Cozumel thrasher population dropped sharply following Hurricane Gilbert in 1988, and again after Hurricanes Emily and Wilma in 2005. Although thrashers have survived hurricanes for millennia, scientists speculate that the population had grown stressed by predation from boa constrictors, which were introduced in 1971 and have proliferated rapidly since. It certainly didn't help that Gilbert and Wilma were—and remain—the two most intense storms ever recorded in the Atlantic basin.

Cozumel has three other endemic birds: the tiny Cozumel vireo, the large pheasant-like Cozumel curassow, and the zippy Cozumel emerald, a type of hummingbird. Migratory birds commonly spotted on the island include the lesser nighthawk, black skimmer, roseate spoonbill, herons, egrets, ibis, and more.

LIONFISH

The lionfish is a spectacular striped fish with a "mane" of fins and poisonous spines that is changing the underwater landscape of Cozumel and the entire Caribbean. Historically found only in the warm regions of the Pacific and Indian Oceans, lionfish were first sighted in Atlantic waters in 1992 in Biscayne Bay, Florida; it's believed they were released into the wild after a private aquarium was swept into the ocean by Hurricane Andrew. Since then, lionfish have been documented in the Florida Keys, the Bahamas, Cuba, and elsewhere; the first lionfish sighting in Cozumel was in January 2009.

Voracious hunters with no natural predators, lionfish can grow to 20 inches long and devour everything from small reef fish to commercial fish like snapper and juvenile grouper. They thrive at depths of just a few feet to over 500 feet, and their coloring makes them especially well-suited for coral environments. Cozumel's National Marine Park officials have taken proactive efforts to help curb the growth of this invasive fish, garnering widespread community support. There now are fishing tournaments targeting lionfish, and spear-fishing training for local sport divers; experts are even trying, with some success, to "train" wild sharks and mature grouper to prey on lionfish by introducing them into known hunting grounds. Restaurants are doing their part by creating innovative and tasty dishes from lionfish meat.

REPTILES

Cozumel's reptile species include iguanas, which can sometimes be spotted sunning themselves on the warm flat rocks at San Gervasio archaeological site, and caymans, a relative of crocodiles, which live in the lagoon and marsh areas of Parque Punta Sur. Boa constrictors were introduced in 1971 and have spread and multiplied throughout the island, causing considerable harm to local bird and rodent species.

Sea Animals

Cozumel's best-known animals live in the pristine waters surrounding it, protected as a federal maritime reserve.

CORAL REEFS

The spectacular coral reefs that grace Cozumel's waters are made up of millions of tiny carnivorous organisms called polyps. Individual polyps can be less than a centimeter (0.4 inch) long or up to 15 centimeters (6 inches) in diameter. Related to the jellyfish and sea anemone, coral polyps capture prey with tiny tentacles that deliver a deadly sting.

Reef-building polyps have limestone exoskeletons, which they create by extracting calcium from the seawater. Reefs are formed as generation after generation of polyps attach themselves to and atop each other. Different species attach in different ways, resulting in the many shapes and sizes of ocean reefs: delicate lace, trees with reaching branches, pleated mushrooms, stovepipes, petaled flowers, fans, domes, heads of cabbage, and stalks of broccoli. Though made up of individual polyps, coral structures function like a single organism, sharing nutrients through a central gastrovascular system. Even in ideal conditions, most coral grows no more than five centimeters (2 inches) per year.

Reefs are divided into three types: barrier, atoll, and fringing. A barrier reef runs parallel to the coast, with long stretches separated by narrow channels. The Mesoamerican Reef extends 250 kilometers (155 miles) from the tip of Isla Mujeres to Sapodilla Cay in the Gulf of Honduras—only the Great Barrier Reef in Australia is longer. An atoll typically forms around the crater of a submerged volcano. The polyps begin building their colonies along the lip of the crater, forming a circular coral island with a lagoon in the center. The Chinchorro Bank, off the southern coast of Quintana Roo, is the largest coral atoll in the Northern Hemisphere, measuring 48 kilometers long and

© J.W. PEADO

Sea turtles are a universal favorite among divers and snorkelers. They can even be spotted on boat tours when they come to the surface to breath.

14 kilometers wide (30 miles by 9 miles). A fringing reef is coral living on a shallow shelf that extends outward from shore into the sea.

FISH

Cozumel's waters are home to myriad fish species, including parrot fish, candy bass, moray eels, spotted scorpion fish, turquoise angelfish, fairy basslets, flame fish, and gargantuan manta rays. Several species of shark also thrive here and along the Riviera Maya coast, though they're not considered a serious threat to swimmers and divers. Sport fish—sailfish, marlin, and bluefin tuna—also inhabit the outer Caribbean waters.

SEA TURTLES

Tens of thousands of sea turtles of various species once nested on the coastal beaches of Cozumel and the Riviera Maya. Cozumel's nesting grounds are in far better shape than the mainland's, which are increasingly occupied by resorts and other developments. The Mexican government and various ecological organizations are trying hard to save the dwindling turtle population. Turtle eggs are dug up and reburied in sand on safe beaches; when the hatchlings break through their shells, they are brought to a beach and allowed to rush toward the sea in hopes of imprinting a sense of belonging there so that they will later return to the spot. In some cases the hatchlings are scooped up and placed in tanks to grow larger before being released into the open sea. The government is also enforcing tough penalties for people who take turtle eggs or capture, kill, or sell these creatures once they hatch.

History

The first people to have occupied Isla Cozumel for any significant amount of time were probably small groups of Putun and Itzá Indians, who arrived from the present-day Campeche and Tabasco states in the 3rd or 4th century AD. They were accomplished seafarers whose coastal explorations extended clear around the Yucatán Peninsula and as far south as Central America. (Centuries later, the Itzá would take control of large parts of the interior, including a declining Maya capital they made their own: Chichén Itzá.) Over time Cozumel's population and stature grew, serving as an important outpost for indigenous traders of various groups, who plied the coast in dugout canoes laden with salt, honey, and other products.

MAYA RISE AND FALL

Mayan city-states on the mainland also grew in strength and influence during this time, and eventually came to dominate the entire Yucatán Peninsula, including Cozumel, and much of present-day Chiapas, Guatemala, Belize, Honduras, and El Salvador. (The name Cozumel is a Spanish corruption of the Yucatec Maya name Cuzamil, meaning Land of Swallows. It's not known what the earliest groups called the island.) Itzá influence all but disappeared under Maya rule, save for one notable aspect: worship of Ixchel, goddess of the moon, fertility, and childbirth, which the Maya adopted enthusiastically. Cozumel was a major pilgrimage site for Maya women and girls across Mesoamerica, a place to visit at least once in their lives for good fortune in childbirth and motherhood. In fact, archaeologists believe Cozumel was one of the three most important religious sites for early Maya, along with Chichén Itzá and Izamal.

The Maya were the dominant group in the Yucatán Peninsula and beyond until the 9th century AD, when most of the major cities abruptly collapsed. (The exact cause is unknown, though archaeologists suspect overpopulation, environmental degradation, and extended drought were to blame.) Like the rest of the Maya world, Cozumel experienced a massive population decline during that time, followed by centuries of slow recovery. By AD 1200, Cozumel had reemerged as a major trading outpost—many of the structures at the island's main archaeological site, San Gervasio, date to that period—and was growing in population and influence in the 1500s, when the first European contact occurred.

EUROPEAN CONTACT AND CONQUEST

The first European explorers to land on Isla Cozumel did so in 1518. A fleet of four ships, commanded by Juan de Grijalva and sailing from Cuba, reached Cozumel after being pushed off course during an exploratory mission in the Caribbean. The fleet arrived there on May 3, day of the Holy Cross, and Grijalva christened the island Isla de la Santa Cruz. The expedition's priest performed mass on the island, arguably the first Christian service to be held on present-day Mexican territory. A year later, Hernán Cortéz stopped at Cozumel before his famous march into the Mexican mainland and his unlikely capture of the Aztec capital at Teotihuacan, at present-day Mexico City.

In 1520 another expedition brought more than bearded white men and giant ships. Smallpox broke out on Cozumel and elsewhere, killing untold thousands of indigenous people. Cozumel's native population fell from 20,000 to under 3,000 in less than a decade's time. Moreover, as the conquest progressed and the Spanish established cities and ports on the mainland, Cozumel became less important as a stopover and its population shrank further, to just a few hundred people. Pirates took to using Cozumel as a refuge and launching pad for attacks on Spanish merchant ships. Among them was French *corsaire* Pierre de Sanfroy, who is

DECIPHERING THE GLYPHS

For years, scholars could not agree whether the fantastic inscriptions found on Maya stelae, codices, and temple walls were anything more than complex records of numbers and dates. Many thought the text was not "real writing," as it did not appear to reproduce spoken language. Even those who believed the writing to be more meaningful despaired at ever reading it.

Mayanist and scholar Michael D. Coe's *Breaking the Maya Code* (Thames and Hudson, 1992) is a fascinating account of the decipherment of Maya hieroglyphics. Coe describes how, in 1952, reclusive Russian scholar Yuri Valentinovich Knorosov made a crucial breakthrough by showing that Maya writing did in fact convey spoken words. Using a rough alphabet recorded by Fray Diego de Landa (the 16th-century bishop who, ironically, is best known for having destroyed numerous Maya texts), Knorosov showed that ancient texts contain common Yucatec Maya words such as *cutz* (turkey) and *tzul* (dog). Interestingly, Knorosov conducted his research from reproductions only, having never held a Maya artifact or visited an ancient temple. (When he did finally visit Tikal in 1990, Coe says Knorosov wasn't very impressed.)

But Knorosov's findings were met with staunch resistance by some of the field's most influential scholars, which delayed progress for decades. By the mid-1980s, however, decipherment picked up speed; one of many standouts from that era is David Stuart, the son of Maya experts, who went to Cobá with his parents at age eight and passed the time copying glyphs and learning Yucatec Maya words from local playmates. As a high school student he served as chief epigrapher on a groundbreaking exploration in Belize, and at age 18 he received a US$128,000 MacArthur Fellowship (aka "Genius Award") to, as he told Michael Coe, "play around with the glyphs" full-time.

Researchers now know that Maya writing is like most other hieroglyphic systems. What appears at first to be a single glyph can have up to four parts, and the same word can be expressed in pictorial, phonetic, or hybrid form. Depending on context, one symbol can have either a pictorial or phonetic role; likewise, a particular sound can be represented in more than one way. The word *cacao* is spelled phonetically as "ca-ca-u" but is written with a picture of a fish (*ca*) and a comb-like symbol (also *ca*, according to Landa) and followed by -u. One of David Stuart's great insights was that for all its complexity, much of Maya glyphic writing is "just repetitive."

But how do scholars know what the symbols are meant to sound like in the first place? Some come from the Landa alphabet, others are suggested by the pictures that accompany many texts, still others from patterns derived by linguistic analyses of contemporary Maya languages. In some cases, it is simply a hunch that, after applying it to a number of texts, turns out to be right. If this seems like somewhat shaky scientific ground, it is—but not without a means of being proved. The cacao decipherment was confirmed when the same glyph was found on a jar with cacao residue still inside.

Hundreds of glyphs have been deciphered, and most of the known Maya texts can be reliably translated. The effort has lent invaluable insight into Maya civilization, especially dynastic successions and religious beliefs. Some archaeologists lament, not unreasonably, that high-profile glyphic studies divert attention from research into the lives of everyday ancient Maya, who after all far outnumbered the nobility but are not at all represented in the inscriptions. That said, it's impossible not to marvel at how one of the world's great ancient civilizations is revealed in the whorls and creases of fading stone pictures.

© LIZA PRADO

a small Maya ruin inside Parque Punta Sur

said to have occupied Cozumel's small village for several weeks in 1579, making the church his home (including sleeping on the altar) and harassing and terrifying the local townspeople. Colonial administrators in Mérida eventually admitted the island could not be adequately protected and ordered the last residents to be evacuated, first in 1650 and again in 1688. From its heyday as a 20,000-resident city and vital regional trading post shortly before the arrival of Europeans, Cozumel would enter the 18th century virtually abandoned, and remain so for nearly 150 years.

MEXICAN INDEPENDENCE AND THE CASTE WAR

Mexico's war of independence began in 1810 and lasted until 1821. Life in the Yucatán Peninsula changed relatively little under Mexican rule, especially for the region's Maya peasants, whose abuse and oppression continued unchecked. In 1847, Maya peasants rose up in armed revolt against the Yucatán Peninsula's white and mestizo colonizers, in a conflict known as the Caste War. The Maya had long resisted their subjugation, but the Caste War was a far more coordinated and widespread uprising than any previous. Tens of thousands of Maya organized into quasi-armies, with weapons ranging from farm implements to English muskets smuggled through what was then British Honduras (now Belize). The indigenous forces were virtually unstoppable, capturing city after city until only the state capital of Mérida remained. The Maya were marching on Mérida when the seasonal rains, marking the beginning of planting season, began earlier than usual. The Maya peasant-soldiers abandoned the fight to return home and tend their fields, and never regained the upper hand.

Cozumel played little role in the Caste War, although the embattled governor of Yucatán did try to sell the island to Spain in order to raise money for weapons and fortifications (Spain declined). More significantly, Cozumel served as refuge for people fleeing the conflict, notably a small group of Christian Maya who founded El Cedral and a group of 20-plus families from Valladolid who reestablished the village of San Miguel. Both groups proved remarkably industrious, establishing schools, courts, and local governmental bodies. (When the latter community was registered by the state in 1849, it was called San Miguel de Cozumel, the first official use of its present name.) Direct descendants of both groups remain on the island, many in top positions in Cozumel's government and civic life.

BOOM AND BUST

The latter half of the 19th century were boom years for Cozumel and the Yucatán Peninsula, thanks to international demand for two products: rope made from henequen, a species of cactus that thrives in northern Yucatán, and chicle, a type of tree sap used in early chewing gum. Henequen barons built beautiful mansions in Mérida and sent their children to school in Europe, while Cozumel's first hotels were built to accommodate visiting businessmen from Wrigley's and other companies.

The excesses of powerful landholders and institutions, including the Catholic Church, during that time were a source of animosity throughout the country, and eventually led to war. The Mexican Revolution broke out in 1910 and lasted until 1921. Some of the most recognizable names of Mexican history were involved in the revolution, including Emiliano Zapata and Benito Juárez, an indigenous military commander from Oaxaca who would become the country's first post-revolution president. In the late 1930s, President Lázaro Cárdenas undertook a massive nationalization program, claiming the major electricity, oil, and other companies for the state, and created state-run companies like PEMEX. In Yucatán state, Governor Felipe Carrillo Puerto helped establish labor unions, educational centers, and political clubs and decreed that abandoned henequen haciendas be appropriated by the government and redistributed to the poor.

NEW DIRECTION

The henequen and chicle booms were tempered by reforms instituted following the revolution, but were truly quashed by the invention of synthetic alternatives around World War II. But from the collapse of the chicle industry rose the beginnings of Cozumel's present-day economy: tourism. In the 1950s, reports began appearing in American travel magazines extolling Cozumel as a cheap yet lovely alternative to Acapulco. The revolution in Cuba in 1959 helped, forcing American travelers to seek out a new Caribbean vacation spot. Cozumel also became popular as a diving destination in that period, benefiting vicariously from the popularity of Jacques Cousteau and his groundbreaking underwater films.

Tourism in Cozumel grew steadily over the next few decades. Cruise ships began arriving in 1968, and by the mid-1970s Cozumel was on the itineraries of most major cruise lines. The island even enjoyed an unusually long respite from hurricanes: thirteen years, 1975–1988, without a major storm making landfall. Cancún was created around that time, virtually from scratch, and quickly emerged as a world-class tourist destination.

THE LOST YEARS

The rest of Mexico, however, endured some of its most difficult challenges during the same period. By the 1960s the country's political and electoral systems were utterly controlled by one party, the Institutional Revolutionary Party, or PRI. PRI members held every major office in the federal government, and most state governments as well. The party was deeply corrupt and grew increasingly brutal in its treatment of detractors. The most notorious example was the gunning down of scores of student demonstrators—some say up to 250—by security forces in 1968 in Mexico City's Tlatelolco Plaza. The massacre took place at night; by morning the plaza was cleared of bodies and scrubbed of blood, and the government simply denied that it ever happened.

It seemed Mexico couldn't catch a break. The country suffered through a massive devaluation of its currency in the early 1980s and was struck by a massive earthquake in 1985 that killed 9,000 people and left 100,000 homeless. In

1994, implementation of the North American Free Trade Agreement (NAFTA) in 1994 was met simultaneously by another massive devaluation of the peso and an armed uprising by a peasant army called the Zapatistas in the state of Chiapas.

DEFEATING THE PRI

Despite the many crises and conflicts, electoral reforms that had been implemented in the late 1980s and early 1990s finally bore fruit, culminating in the historic 2000 presidential election, in which an opposition candidate—former Coca-Cola executive Vicente Fox of the center-right Partido de Acción Nacional (PAN)—defeated the PRI candidate, ending the PRI's 70-year reign. Fox was succeeded in 2006 by another PAN member, Felipe Calderón Hinojosa, in an election in which the PRI finished a distant third.

Cozumel, meanwhile, was rocked during that period not by political storms but real ones. In 1988, Hurricane Gilbert roared ashore, killing 52 people on Cozumel and setting the record for the most intense storm ever recorded in the Atlantic. In 2005 the island was hit by two Category 5 storms, Emily and Wilma; the latter not only exceeded Gilbert in barometric lows—making it the Atlantic basin's most intense storm ever—but it was especially destructive because it lingered over the island for three full days.

THE DRUG WAR

President Calderón campaigned on a promise to expand Mexico's job market and encourage foreign investment, including new tourism projects in the Yucatán and elsewhere. But it was another pledge—to break up the drug trade and the cartels that controlled it—that consumed his entire presidency and plunged parts of Mexico into a spasm of violence unlike any since the revolution. Mexico's drug war has its roots in the insatiable demand for drugs in the United States. For decades, cocaine, heroin, and other drugs from South America made their way to the United States mainly through the Caribbean on speedboats and small planes.

But as that route was choked off by the U.S. Coast Guard and others, Mexico became an increasingly important conduit. (Drug production also has grown within Mexico itself, especially of marijuana and methamphetamines.) Mexican drug cartels have long operated within defined territories—the Gulf cartel, the Sinaloa cartel, the Juárez cartel, etc.—and did so largely with impunity, thanks to corruption in the police and PRI-controlled local governments. But if corruption encouraged the illicit trade, it also helped keep violence to a minimum; the cartels kept to themselves, and politicians and police turned a blind eye.

In 2006, encouraged by the United States, Calderón dispatched the Mexican military to various northern cities to break up the cartels and their distribution networks. They achieved some initial success—and continue to do so—but the broader effect was to disrupt the balance of power between the cartels, which began vying for valuable routes and territories. Violence erupted with shocking speed and ferocity, with shoot-outs among rival gangs and a gruesome cycle of attacks and reprisals, including decapitations and torture. As many as 60,000 people have died in the conflict, including more than 24,000 in 2011 alone; another 20,000 people remain missing. It's worth noting, at the same time, that tourists are almost never involved: 90 percent of the deaths have been among known gang members, and another 7 percent are police and military. The vast majority of the violence occurs in a few northern and central states, far from Cozumel and the Yucatán Peninsula, which are among the safest places in the whole country.

MEXICO TODAY

In the summer of 2012, Mexico's national soccer team won its first Olympic gold medal, defeating heavily favored Brazil at the London games. It was a small blessing perhaps, in the scheme of things, but one that seemed to lift the country's collective spirit. Later that year, Mexicans elected Enrique Peña Nieto, the PRI candidate, as president. Without turning his back on drug cartel violence, Peña Nieto has focused on addressing drug abuse, unemployment, and corruption on a local level.

And despite the tragedy of the drug war, tourism in Mexico, and the Riviera Maya in particular, has actually increased during the same period. Cozumel now receives over a thousand cruise ships and two million cruise ship passengers every year, and Cancún accounts for 25 percent of the country's foreign visitors. Just as hurricanes are a part of life in Cozumel—and all of Mexico, metaphorically speaking—so is recovery. Cozumel has bounced back from the storms that have hit it, and Mexico is sure to do the same.

Government and Economy

GOVERNMENT
Mexico is a constitutional democracy modeled after that of the United States, including a president (who serves one six-year term), a two-house legislature, and a judiciary branch.

ECONOMY
Oil
The leading industry on the Yucatán Peninsula is oil. Produced by the nationally owned PEMEX, the oil industry is booming along the Gulf coast from Campeche south into the state of Tabasco. Most of the oil is shipped at OPEC prices to Canada, Israel, France, Japan, and the United States. Mexico is also rich in natural gas, much of which is sent to the United States.

Fishing
Yucatecan fisheries also are abundant along the Gulf coast. At one time fishing was not much more than a family business, but today fleets of large purse seiners with their adjacent processing plants can be seen on the Gulf of Mexico. With the renewed interest in preserving fishing grounds for the future, the industry could continue to thrive for many years.

Tourism
Until the 1970s, Quintana Roo's economy amounted to very little. For a few years the chicle boom brought a flurry of activity up and down the state—it was shipped from the harbor of Isla Cozumel. Native and hardwood trees have always been in demand; coconuts and fishing were the only other natural resources that added to the economy—but neither on a large scale.

With the development of an offshore sandbar —Cancún—into a multimillion-dollar resort, tourism became the region's number-one moneymaker. The development of the Riviera Maya (extending from Cancún to Tulum)—and now, the Costa Maya (south of Sian Ka'an to the border of Belize)—only guaranteed the continued success of the economy. New roads now give access to previously unknown beaches and Maya structures. Extra attention is going to archaeological zones ignored for hundreds of years. All but the smallest have restrooms, ticket offices, gift shops, and food shops.

People and Culture

DEMOGRAPHICS

Today, 75-80 percent of the Mexican population is estimated to be mestizo (a combination of the indigenous and Spanish-Caucasian races). Only 10-15 percent are considered to be indigenous peoples. For comparison, as recently as 1870, the indigenous made up more than 50 percent of the population. While there are important native communities throughout Mexico, the majority of the country's indigenous peoples live in the Yucatán Peninsula, Oaxaca, and Chiapas.

RELIGION

The vast majority of Mexicans are Roman Catholic, especially in the generally conservative Yucatán Peninsula. However, a vigorous evangelical movement gains more and more converts every year.

LANGUAGE

The farther you go from a city, the less Spanish you'll hear and the more dialects of indigenous languages you'll encounter. The government estimates that of the 10 million indigenous people in the country, about 25 percent do not speak Spanish. Of the original 125 native languages, 70 are still spoken, 20 of which are classified as Maya languages, including Tzeltal, Tzotzil, Chol, and Yucatec.

Although education was made compulsory for children in 1917, this law was not enforced in the Yucatán Peninsula until recently. Today, schools throughout the peninsula use Spanish-language books, even though many children do not speak the language. In some of the rural schools, bilingual teachers are recruited to help children make the transition.

© LIZA PRADO

Iglesia San Miguel, Cozumel's main Catholic church

POPULATION

Around 100,000 people live on the island of Cozumel, more than three-quarters of which (77,000-plus) live in the main town of San Miguel de Cozumel. Ethnically, the population is overwhelmingly mestizo; there are a small number of indigenous-identified people in El Cedral, descendants of the original 18 Yucatec Maya families who founded that community in the 1840s, and a small number of expats of various races, mostly white North Americans and Europeans. Unlike most Caribbean islands, Cozumel has no history of African slavery, and the Black population there is tiny. Religiously, Cozumel is similar to the rest of Mexico and Latin America, with a majority of people self-identifying as Catholic, but with a significant and growing number of people of Protestant evangelical faiths.

FOOD

It's an island, so of course the specialty in Cozumel is seafood. Whole fish or fillets, lobster or shrimp, deep fried or foil baked—you can get super-fresh and well-prepared seafood at just about any restaurant in town. Ironically, much of the seafood served in Cozumel is not caught around the island because of fishing restrictions under the national marine park.

Instead the catch comes from nearby places like Isla Mujeres or the southern Riviera Maya. You can always find excellent steaks, pork, and chicken, too, because of the proximity to the mainland.

MUSIC

Cozumel is a Caribbean island in many ways, but it doesn't have the rich independent musical traditions of a place like Jamaica or Cuba; local tastes and trends tend to mirror those of Mexico generally. Travelers can find just about any sort of music they like, from electronica at nightclubs, salsa at cantina bars, or classic rock at sports bars.

ARTS AND CRAFTS

Mexico has an incredibly rich colonial- and folk-art tradition. While not considered art to the people who make and use it, traditional indigenous clothing is beautiful, and travelers and collectors are increasingly able to buy it in local shops and markets. Prices for these items can be high, for the simple fact that they are handwoven and can literally take months to complete. Los Cinco Soles, a shop in downtown Cozumel, is an especially good place to purchase pottery, carving, and textiles from around the Yucatán and beyond.

ESSENTIALS

Getting There

Isla Cozumel is easily accessible to visitors. Thousands of people arrive every day—more than two million per year—by ferry from Playa del Carmen, via plane using the island's modern airport, and on huge cruise ships.

AIR

Cozumel International Airport (CZM, tel. 987/872-2081, www.asur.com.mx) is approximately three kilometers (1.9 miles) from Downtown Cozumel. The airport has an ATM in the departures area, AmEx currency exchange at arrivals, and a few magazine stands and duty-free shops. The **airport taxi cooperative** (tel. 987/872-1323) provides private and shared transport to the center and to resorts along the western coast. Prices vary by destination. Private taxis are US$11-21 per person, while shared transport costs US$5-8 per person and utilizes 10-person shuttles or Suburbans; departures are every 5-20 minutes. A taxi stand near the exit sells tickets and has prices prominently displayed.

If you don't mind the time and hassle of traveling from the mainland to Cozumel, consider flying into **Cancún International Airport** (CUN, Carr. Cancun-Chetumal Km. 22, tel. 998/848-7200, www.cancun-airport.com),

© LIZA PRADO

FLYING TO COZUMEL

The following airlines service **Cozumel International Airport** (CZM, tel. 987/872-2081, www.asur.com.mx):

- **Air Canada** (toll-free Mex. tel. 800/719-2827, toll-free U.S./Can. tel. 888/247-2262, www.aircanada.com)
- **American Airlines** (toll-free Mex. tel. 800/904-6000, toll-free U.S./Can. tel. 800/433-7300, www.aa.com)
- **Continental** (airport tel. 987/872-0847, toll-free Mex. tel. 800/900-5000, toll-free

U.S./Can. tel. 800/864-8331, www.continental.com)

- **Delta** (toll-free Mex. tel. 800/123-4710, toll-free U.S. tel. 800/221-1212, www.delta.com)
- **Frontier Airlines** (toll-free U.S. tel. 800/432-1359, www.frontierairlines.com)
- **United Airlines** (toll-free Mex. tel. 800/900-5000, toll-free U.S./Can. tel. 800/864-8331, www.united.com)
- **US Airways** (toll-free Mex. tel. 800/843-3000, toll-free U.S. tel. 800/428-4322, www.usairways.com)

which typically has cheaper fares. If you choose this option, plan on taking a bus (US$10.50, 1 hour, every 40 minutes 10am-10:15pm daily) or taxi (US$33/95 shared/private, 45 minutes) to Playa del Carmen and catching the ferry to Isla Cozumel from there (US$13 each way, 30 minutes, every 1-2 hours 7am-10pm daily).

Departure Tax

There is a US$48 departure tax to fly out of Mexico—most airlines incorporate the tax into their tickets, but it's worth setting aside some cash just in case.

FERRY

Passenger ferries from Playa del Carmen to Cozumel (US$13 each way, 30 minutes) leave from the pier at the end of Calle 1 Sur. They arrive in Cozumel's passenger ferry pier, which is across from the central plaza. **UltraMar** (www.granpuerto.com.mx) and **Mexico Water Jets** (www.mexicowaterjets.com.mx) alternate departures every 1-2 hours and charge the same amount, though UltraMar's boats are newer. In both Playa and Cozumel, their ticket booths are side by side at or near the piers, with the time of the next departure displayed prominently. The ticket seller will try to sell you a round-trip ticket, but there's no disadvantage to buying a *sencilla* (one-way ticket) and waiting to see which ferry has the next departure

when you're ready to return. Between the two companies, ferries depart Playa del Carmen on the hour every 1-2 hours 7am-10pm daily; in Cozumel, passenger ferries return to Playa del Carmen on the hour every 1-2 hours 6am-9pm daily.

Car ferries operated by **Transcaribe** (tel. 987/872-7688 or 987/872-7671 in Cozumel, www.transcaribe.net) depart from the Calica dock south of Playa del Carmen at 4am, 8am, 1:30pm, and 6pm Monday; 1:30pm and 6pm Tuesday and Friday; 8am, 1:30pm, and 6pm Wednesday, Thursday, and Saturday; and 6am and 6pm on Sunday. Returning from Cozumel, the ferry leaves from the international pier at 6am, 11am, 4pm, and 8:30pm Monday-Saturday and at 8am and 8pm on Sunday. The trip takes about 75 minutes and costs US$60 for a passenger car including driver plus US$5.50 per additional passenger. Reservations are available online, by phone, or at the pier, and are strongly recommended. **Note:** Many insurance carriers do not cover rental cars while they are transported on ferries in Mexico. Although it's unlikely the vehicle ferry will sink, find out whether your insurance covers it before assuming this risk.

CRUISE SHIP

Isla Cozumel receives up to 30 cruise ships per week in the high season, some carrying as many

the car ferry connecting Playa del Carmen and Cozumel

© LIZA PRADO

as 5,000 people. Many sail out of Miami and Fort Lauderdale, stopping at Key West before continuing to the island. Cruise ships use three designated piers: Punta Langosta (Av. Rafael Melgar at Calle 9 Sur), TMM International Pier (Carr. Costera Sur, 3.4 kilometers/2 miles south of town), and Puerta Maya (Carr. Costera Sur, 3.8 kilometers/2.3 miles south of town, www.puertamaya.com). For a schedule of cruise ship arrivals, check out www.cozumelinsider.com/cruiseships.

Cruise ships stopping in Cozumel vary in services, amenities, activities, and entertainment. Pools, restaurants, nightclubs, and cinemas are commonplace. Fitness centers and shops also make ship life convenient. To hone in on the type of cruise you'd like to go on, research options on the Internet, in the travel section of your local newspaper, and by contacting your travel agent.

If your budget is tight, consider traveling standby. Ships want to sail full and are willing to cut their prices—sometimes up to 50 percent—to do so. Airfare usually is not included. **Note:** Once you're on the standby list, you likely will have no choice of cabin location or size.

BUS

Although there are no long-distance buses on Cozumel, you can buy tickets for buses leaving Playa del Carmen for destinations throughout the Yucatán Peninsula and beyond at **Ticket Bus** (Calle 2 at Av. 10 Sur, tel. 987/869-2553, 8am-9pm Mon.-Sat., 10am-8pm Sun.). There is no extra charge for the service.

Getting Around

In town, you can easily walk anywhere you like. For the rest of the island, you'll need a car (or moped or bike), or else take a taxi. There's no public bus service, thanks in large part to opposition by the island's powerful taxi union. It is a shame, really, since it would be so convenient and economical to have a fleet of buses making loops around the island.

TAXI

Taxis are everywhere—you can easily flag one down on Avenida Rafael Melgar, near the main passenger pier, and around the plaza. If you want to be picked up at a specific place and time, call the **taxi union office** (Calle 2 btwn Avs. 5 and 10, tel. 987/872-0041, 24 hours daily). Cabs typically charge US$3.25 around town and US$5.75 from the center to the airport, for up to four people. For hotels and beach clubs on the western shore south of town, you'll pay US$5-$20, depending on the distance. Fares to the east side are a bit more, from US$12.50-$30, while San Gervasio and Punta Sur cost US$50-60. A trip around the island runs US$85. Most taxi stands have the current fares prominently displayed; always agree on a price before getting into a taxi.

CAR

There's a lot to see around Cozumel, including plenty of unmarked spots where you might want to pull over and take a closer look. Having wheels of your own makes this sort of exploring possible, and can make your time on Cozumel more enjoyable and memorable.

Car Rental

The best rates (and best vehicles) are typically found online with the major international rental chains like Hertz, Thrifty, and Avis. They're especially convenient if you're coming and going by air, though all have offices in town, too. Cozumel has a few local agencies with good rates as well. A few tips:

- If you're booking online, it's best to book on the car rental company's own website rather than a travel website. The prices are usually the same, and if there are any problems, the rental office can't pass the blame to another website.

- Ask your credit card company if your card provides free collision (liability) insurance on rental cars abroad. (Most do.) Unlike ordinary insurance, you'll have to pay any charges upfront and then file for reimbursement once you return. The coverage is usually better, though, with zero deductible and coverage even on dirt roads. There occasionally are restrictions, such as on the length of the rental period, and remember you have to actually use the card to pay for the rental in order to get the benefit!

- Car rental agencies make most of their money off the insurance, not the vehicle. That's why they push so hard for you to buy coverage. They'll warn you that with credit card insurance you'll have to pay 100 percent of any damages upfront; this is technically true, but it will be reimbursed when you file a claim back home. The agency may require you to authorize a larger "hold" on your card, as much as US$5000, for potential damages. This is no big deal—it's not an actual charge—but that amount will be unavailable for other purchases. Consider bringing two or more credit cards, especially if your credit limit is low. **Note:** This hold often entails leaving a blank credit card imprint, ostensibly to cover the deductible if there is any damage. Be sure that this is returned to you when you return the car.

- Third-party damage insurance is required by law, and rental agencies are technically required to provide it. Lately, however, rental agencies say third-party coverage is free for anyone who also purchases collision insurance. But if you decline their collision insurance (because you get it through your credit card), suddenly there's a charge for third-party coverage. Credit cards typically do not offer third-party coverage, so you end up having to pay it. It's less expensive than collision insurance, but still a bummer to pay.

- Travel with a copy of your credit card's car rental insurance coverage as well as the insurance requirements of the car rental agency itself. Both are typically available online. These will prove very useful when/if the agent tries to convince you to buy unnecessary insurance coverage.

Before you drive off, the attendant will review the car for existing damage—definitely accompany him or her on this part, and don't be shy about pointing out every nick, scratch, and ding. Other things to confirm before driving off include:

- There is a spare tire (preferably a full-size, not temporary, one) and a working jack and tire iron.

- All doors lock and unlock, including the trunk.

- The headlights, brake lights, and turn signals work.

- All the windows roll up and down properly.

- The proper—and current—car registration is in the car. In some cases, your car rental contract serves as the registration.

- The amount of gas in the tank—you'll have to return it with the same amount.

- There is a 24-hour telephone number for the rental agency in case of an emergency.

Highways and Road Conditions

The distance around the island—on paved roads, and including the northwestern arm that dead-ends after Cozumel Country Club—is approximately 93 kilometers (58 miles). Driving without stopping, it takes a little under two hours to circumnavigate the island. If doing this, consider going counterclockwise so there's nothing between your vehicle and the ocean, especially on the east side. Biking around the island is possible but challenging, given the strong crosswinds.

Cozumel has three **PEMEX gas stations** (7am-midnight daily). Two are in town on Avenida Benito Juárez (at Avs. Pedro Joaquin Coldwell and 75), and the third is four kilometers (2.5 miles) south of town on the Carretera Costera Sur across from Puerta Maya, the main cruise ship pier.

Note: Most streets are one-way in town; if you're driving, be aware that *avenidas* (avenues) run north-south and have the right-of-way over *calles* (streets), which run east-west. Once you leave town, there is a single road that circles the entire island.

Ángeles Verdes

The "Green Angels" (tel. 078) are teams of uniformed trained mechanics who ply the main roads in green trucks offering free roadside assistance to anyone whose vehicle has become stranded or disabled. In Cozumel, there are usually at least two teams on duty 8am-7pm daily; they drive in opposite directions on the coastal road, stopping wherever needed. Most of the mechanics speak at least some English, and will truly seem heaven-sent if your rental car breaks down or gets stuck on a sandy shoulder. Services are free, but parts and gas, if needed, are extra.

Driving Scams

Most police in Cozumel are honest and conscientious, and harassing travelers is very uncommon. As long as you are a careful and defensive driver, it is very unlikely you'll have any interaction with the police. Most travelers who

TRAVELING WITH IMPORTANT DOCUMENTS

The last thing you need when you're on the road is to lose your passport, tourist card, credit cards, or other important documents. It can happen, though, and if it does, here are steps you can take beforehand to make life easier in such a situation:

- Write down your credit card and ATM numbers and the 24-hour service numbers; store them in a safe place, including online (i.e., email them to yourself).

- Scan and/or make copies of your passport, tourist card, and airline tickets; store them online.

- Give a copy of these documents to someone you trust back home. If you have a travel companion, give him or her a copy too.

- Carry a copy of your passport and tourist card in your purse or wallet and leave the originals in the hotel safe or locked in your bag; they're a lot more likely to be lost or stolen on the street than taken by hotel staff.

- When you move from place to place, carry your passport and important documents in a travel pouch, always under your clothing.

are pulled over actually have done something wrong—speeding, running a stop sign, turning on red. In those situations, remain calm and polite. If you have an explanation, definitely give it; it is not uncommon to discuss a given situation with an officer. Who knows, you may even convince him you're right—it's happened to us!

Of greater concern are gas station attendants. Full service is the norm here—you pull up, tell the person how much you want, and he or she does the rest. A common scam is for one attendant to distract you with questions about wiper fluid or gas additives while another starts the pump at 50 or 100 pesos. Before you answer any questions, be sure the attendant resets, or "zeroes," the pump before starting to pump.

HITCHHIKING

Hitchhiking is not recommended for either men or women. If you have no choice but to hitch a ride, opt for a pickup truck, where you can sit in the back (and jump out, if necessary).

TOURS

Regional travel agents and tour operators offer a vast range of organized trips. You pay extra, of course, but all arrangements and reservations are made for you—from guides and transportation to hotels and meals. Special-interest trips also are common—dive trips, sportfishing trips, and archaeological tours. Ask around or surf the Internet, and you'll find a world of organized adventure.

Visas and Officialdom

PASSPORTS

All U.S. citizens traveling to Mexico by air, land, or sea are required to have a passport. Canadians may travel to Mexico without a passport; they simply need an official photo ID and proof of citizenship, such as an original birth certificate. All other nationalities must have a valid passport.

VISAS AND TOURIST CARDS

Citizens of most countries, including the United States, Canada, and members of the E.U., do not need to obtain a visa to enter Mexico. All foreigners, however, are issued a white tourist card when they enter, with the number of days that they are permitted to stay in the country written at the bottom, typically

30-60 days. If you plan to stay for more than a month, ask the official to give you the amount of time you need; the maximum stay is 180 days.

Hold onto your tourist card! It must be returned to immigration officials when you leave Mexico. If you lose it, you'll be fined and may not be permitted to leave the country (or even the immigration office) until you pay.

To extend your stay up to 180 days, head to the nearest immigration office a week *before* your tourist card expires. Be sure to bring it along with your passport. There, you'll fill out several forms, go to a bank to pay the US$25 processing fee, make photocopies of all the paperwork (including your passport, entry stamp, tourist card, and credit card), and then return to the office to get the extension. For every extra 30 days requested, foreigners must prove that they have US$1,000 available, either in cash or travelers checks, or simply by showing a current credit card. The process can take anywhere from a couple of hours to a week, depending on the office.

CUSTOMS

Plants and fresh foods are not allowed into Mexico, and there are special limits on alcohol, tobacco, and electronic products. Archaeological artifacts, certain antiques, and colonial art cannot be exported from Mexico without special permission.

Above all, do not attempt to bring marijuana or any other narcotic in or out of Mexico. Jail is one place your trusty guidebook won't come in handy.

Returning home, you will be required to declare all items you bought in Mexico. Citizens of the United States are allowed to reenter with US$800 worth of purchases duty-free; the figure for other travelers varies by country.

CONSULATES

The consulates in Cancún and Mérida handle passport issues (replacing a lost one, adding pages, etc.) and can help their citizens if they are in a serious or emergency situation, including hospitalization, assault, arrest, lawsuits, or death. There also is a U.S. consular agent on Isla Cozumel. Consulates usually do not help resolve common disputes—with tour operators or hotels, for example.

Foreign consulates and consular agencies in the region include:

AUSTRIA
Cancún: Av. Tulum at Calle Pecari, tel. 998/884-5431, claudiaemx@yahoo.com.mx, 9am-2pm Monday-Friday
Mérida: Av. Colón Norte 501-C, tel. 999/925-6386, bulnesa@prodigy.net.mx, 9:30am-1pm and 5pm-8pm Monday-Friday

BELGIUM
Cancún: Plaza Tropical, Av. Tulum 192, Local 59, tel. 998/892-2512, www.diplomatie.be, 10am-2pm Monday-Friday

BELIZE
Chetumal: Calle Ramon F. Iturbe No. 476, tel. 983/832-5764, conbelizeqroo@gmail.com, 9am-1pm Monday-Friday
Mérida: Calle 53 between Calles 56 and 58, tel. 999/928-6152, consbelize@dutton.com.mx, 9am-1pm Monday-Friday

CANADA
Cancún: Plaza Caracol, Blvd. Kukulcán Km. 8.5, Local 330, tel. 998/883-3360, www.canada.org.mx, 9am-5pm Monday-Friday

CUBA
Cancún: Pecari 17, tel. 998/884-3423, www.cubadiplomatica.cu/mexico, 9am-1pm Monday-Friday
Mérida: Calle 1-D between Calles 42 and 44, tel. 999/944-4216, www.cubadiplomatica.cu/mexico, 8:30am-1:30pm Monday-Friday

DENMARK
Cancún: Omni Hotel, Blvd. Kukulcán Km. 16.5, tel. 998/881-0600, apresidencia@grupocancun.net, 9am-1pm Monday-Friday

FINLAND
Cancún: Edificio Popolnah, Av. Nader 28-1, tel. 998/884-1600, notariacancun@prodigy.net. mx, 9am-2pm and 5pm-8pm Monday-Friday **Mérida:** Calle 86-B No. 595-B, tel. 999/984-0399

FRANCE
Mérida: Calle 60 btwn Calles 41 and 43, tel. 999/930-1500, consuladofrancia@sipse.com. mx, 9am-5pm Monday-Friday

GERMANY
Cancún: Calle Punta Conocó 36, tel. 998/884-5333, konsul_d@yahoo.com.mx, 9am-noon Monday-Friday
Mérida: Calle 49 between Calles 30 and 32, tel. 999/944 3752, konsulat@jerommel.de, 9am-noon Monday-Friday

GUATEMALA
Cancún: Edificio Barcelona, Av. Nader 148, 998/884-8296, 9am-1pm Monday-Friday
Chetumal: Avenida Héroes de Chapultepec 356, tel. 983/832 3045, 9am-1pm Monday-Friday

IRELAND
Cancún: Av. Cobá 15, tel. 998/112-5436, consul@gruporoyale.com, 9am-1pm Monday-Friday

ITALY
Cancún: Parque Las Palapas, Alcatraces 39, tel. 998/884-1261, conitaca@prodigy.net.mx, 9am-2pm Monday-Friday

NETHERLANDS
Cancún: Pabellón Caribe, Av. Nichupté MZ 2, SM 19, tel. 998/884-8672, nlconsulcancun@prodigy.net.mx, 9am-1pm Monday-Friday
Mérida: Calle 64 btwn Calles 47 and 49, tel. 999/924-3122, pixan2003@prodigy.net.mx, 8am-5pm Monday-Friday

NORWAY
Cancún: Calle Venado 30, tel. 998/887-4412, 9am-1pm Monday-Friday

SPAIN
Cancún: Edificio Oasis, Blvd. Kukulcán at Calle Cenzontle, tel. 998/848-9918, consules@oasishotel.com.mx, 10am-1pm Monday-Friday
Mérida: Calle 8 btwn Calles 5 and 7, tel. 999/948-0181, 10am-1pm Monday-Friday

SWEDEN
Cancún: Omni Hotel, Blvd. Kukulcán Km. 16.5, tel. 998/881-0600, katiavara@omnicancun.com.mx, tel. 998/881-0600, 9am-6pm Monday-Friday

SWITZERLAND
Cancún: above Rolandi's restaurant, Av. Cobá 12, tel. 998/884-8446, 9am-2pm Monday-Friday

UNITED KINGDOM
Cancún: The Royal Sands Resort, Blvd. Kukulcán Km 13.5, tel. 998/881-0100, http://ukinmexico.fco.gov.uk/en, 9am-3pm Monday-Friday

UNITED STATES
Cancún: Torre La Europea, Blvd. Kukulcán Km. 13, tel. 998/883-0272, cancunagency@gmail.com, 8am-1pm Monday-Friday, appointment required for some services
Isla Cozumel: Plaza Villamar, central plaza, tel. 987/872-4574, usgov@cozumel.net, noon-2pm Monday-Friday
Mérida: Calle 60 No. 338-K btwn Calles 29 and 31, tel. 999/942-5700, www.merida.usconsulate.gov, 7:30am-4:30pm Monday-Friday, appointment required for some services
Playa del Carmen: The Palapa, Calle 1 btwn Avs. 15 and 20, tel. 984/873-0303, playausca@gmail.com, 9am-1pm Monday-Friday

UNDERAGE TRAVELERS

In the United States, anyone under 18 traveling internationally without *both* parents or legal guardians must present a signed, notarized letter from the parent(s) or guardian(s) granting the minor permission to leave the country. This requirement is aimed at preventing international abductions, but it causes frequent and major disruptions for vacationers.

Conduct and Customs

CLOTHING

Perhaps the single most-abused social custom in Mexico is the use of shorts. Mexicans rarely wear them outside the home or off the beach, while many foreign travelers seem to have packed nothing but. There is a bit more flexibility in beach areas, but it's worth getting in the habit of wearing long pants or skirts whenever going to dinner, attending performances, and especially when entering churches and government offices, where shorts and tank tops are inappropriate.

Topless and nude sunbathing are not customary on Mexican beaches, and are rarely practiced in Cozumel and other areas frequented by Americans and Canadians. However, on beaches popular with Europeans, especially Playa del Carmen and Tulum, it is more commonplace. Wherever you are, take a look around to help decide whether baring some or all is appropriate.

PHOTOGRAPHING LOCALS

No one enjoys having a stranger take his or her picture for no good reason, and indigenous people are no different. The best policy is simply not to take these photographs unless you've first asked the person's permission and he or she has agreed. **Tip:** If the potential subject of your photo is a vendor, buy something and *then* ask if you can take a photo—you're more likely to get a positive response.

GREETINGS

Even a small amount of Spanish can go a long way in showing respect and consideration for the people you encounter. Make a point of learning basic greetings like *buenos días* (good morning) and *buenas tardes* (good afternoon) and using them in passing, or as preface to a conversation; it is considered somewhat impolite to launch into a discussion without greeting the other person first.

Tips for Travelers

OPPORTUNITIES FOR STUDY AND VOLUNTEERING

On Isla Cozumel, **Dirección Municipal de Ecología y Medio Ambiente** (Calle 11 at Av. 65, tel. 987/872-5795) is the governmental agency that monitors Cozumel's sea turtles and manages related volunteer opportunities. Travelers often help monitor sea turtle nests and help release hatchlings into the sea. Nesting season runs May-September, and during that period volunteers join biologists on nighttime walks of Cozumel's beaches, locating and marking new nests and helping to move vulnerable eggs to protected hatcheries. July-November, volunteers help release hatchings into the sea. This typically happens at sundown, and involves encouraging turtles to move toward the water (without touching them) and scaring off birds in search of an easy meal. Proficiency in Spanish is useful but not required.

Cozumel Volunteer Connection (tel. 987/869-0504, www.cozumelinsider.com/acs) coordinates a variety of volunteer opportunities for travelers—from ocean conservation and beach clean-up to working in women's shelters and with children in crisis.

While there are no Spanish-language schools on Cozumel, Playa del Carmen is becoming a popular place to study Spanish, with several schools, plenty of options for cultural and historical excursions, and, of course, great beaches and nightlife. Top schools include:

Solexico (Calles 6 btwn 35 and 40 Avs., tel. 984/873-0755, www.solexico.com) is a highly recommended school with a welcoming campus and reputation for professionalism. Classes

© GARY CHANDLER

Have child, will travel.

are offered one-on-one or in groups no larger than five, and for 15, 20, 25, or 40 hours per week (US$190-625/week). All levels of courses are offered, including instruction geared toward professionals who have regular contact with Spanish speakers.

International House (Calle 14 Nte. btwn 5 and 10 Avs., tel. 984/803-3388, www.ihrivieramaya.com, 7am-9pm Mon.-Fri., 9am-1pm Sat.) occupies a pretty and peaceful colonial home, with a large classroom, garden, and café on-site. Group classes (US$220/week) meet 20 hours per week with a maximum of 8 students, though typically just 3-4, and can be paired with instruction in things like diving, Mexican cooking, and Latin dancing. Private and two-person classes are also available, as well as custom courses for medical professionals, teachers, and other groups.

TRAVELERS WITH DISABILITIES

Mexico has made many improvements for the blind and people in wheelchairs—many large stores and tourist centers have ramps or elevators, and a growing number of hotels also have rooms designed for guests with disabilities. That said, Mexico is still a hard place to navigate if you have a disability. Definitely ask for help—for what Mexico lacks in infrastructure, its people often make up for in graciousness.

TRAVELING WITH CHILDREN

Mexico is a great place to take kids, whether youngsters or teenagers. The variety of activities and relative ease of transportation help keep everyone happy and engaged. Cozumel and the Riviera Maya are especially family friendly, with several different ecoparks, outdoors activities like snorkeling and kayaking, and miles of beaches. Perhaps best of all, Mexico is a country where family is paramount, so kids—even fussy ones—are welcome just about everywhere.

SENIOR TRAVELERS

Seniors should feel very welcome and safe visiting Cozumel. Mexico is a country that affords great respect to *personas de la tercera edad* (literally "people of the third age"), and especially in the tradition-minded Yucatán Peninsula. But as anywhere, older travelers should take certain precautions. Cozumel can be extremely hot and humid, especially May-July. Seniors should take extra care to stay cool and hydrated. Exploring the Maya ruins also can be hot, not to mention exhausting. Bring water and snacks. Travelers with balance or mobility concerns should think twice about climbing any of the pyramids or other structures. They can be deceptively treacherous, with steps that are steep, uneven, and slick.

Isla Cozumel and Playa del Carmen have state-of-the-art hospitals, staffed by skilled doctors, nurses, and technicians, many of whom speak English. Most prescription medications are available in Mexico, often at discount prices. However, pharmacists are woefully under-trained, and you should always double-check the active ingredients and dosage of any pills you buy here.

GAY, LESBIAN, AND TRANSGENDER TRAVELERS

While openly gay women are still rare in Mexico, gay men are increasingly visible in large cities and certain tourist areas. Playa del Carmen, for instance, has a visible gay presence and a number of gay-friendly venues. Nevertheless, many locals—even in large cities—are not accustomed to open displays of homosexuality and may react openly and negatively. Many hotel attendants also simply don't understand that two travel companions of the same gender may prefer one bed—in some cases they will outright refuse to grant the request. Some couples find it easier to book a room with two queen-size beds and just sleep in one.

GREEN TOURISM

Tourists can contribute significantly—positively and negatively—to the health of Cozumel's reef and marine life. Most coral grows very slowly and is extremely sensitive to abuse; when you are snorkeling or diving, be careful not to kick the coral with your fins, knock it with your tank, and certainly do not stand on it or break off any pieces. Likewise, avoid kicking up sand or sediment, which can settle on coral and stunt or even kill it. Feeding fish and other marine life also is harmful.

Cozumel has limited fresh water and electricity, and tourists are encouraged to conserve as much as possible. Many hotels give guests the option of reducing the frequency that towels and linens are changed and laundered, and, of course, you should never leave on lights and especially air-conditioning while you're out.

Health and Safety

SUNBURN

Common sense is the most important factor in avoiding sunburn. Use waterproof and sweatproof sunscreen with a high SPF. Reapply regularly—even the most heavy-duty waterproof sunscreen washes off faster than it claims to on the bottle (or gets rubbed off when you use your towel to dry off). Be extra careful to protect parts of your body that aren't normally exposed to the sun—a good way to cover every inch is to apply sunscreen *before* you get dressed—and give your skin a break from direct sun every few hours. Remember that redness from a sunburn takes several hours to appear—that is, you can be sunburned long before you *look* sunburned.

If you get sunburned, treat it like any other burn by running cool water over it for as long and as often as you can. Do not expose your skin to more sun. Re-burning the skin can result in painful blisters that can easily become infected. There are a number of products designed to relieve sunburns, most with aloe extracts. Finally, be sure to drink plenty of water to keep your skin hydrated.

HEAT EXHAUSTION AND HEAT STROKE

The symptoms of heat exhaustion are cool moist skin, profuse sweating, headache, fatigue, and drowsiness. It is associated with dehydration and commonly happens during or after a strenuous day in the sun, such as while visiting ruins. You should get out of the sun, remove any tight or restrictive clothing, and sip a sports drink such as Gatorade. Cool compresses and raising your feet and legs helps, too.

Heat exhaustion is not the same as heat stroke, which is distinguished by a high body temperature, a rapid pulse, and sometimes delirium or even unconsciousness. It is an extremely serious, potentially fatal condition, and victims should be taken to the hospital immediately. In the meantime, wrap the victim in wet sheets, massage the arms and legs to increase circulation, and do not administer large amounts of liquids. Never give liquids if the victim is unconscious.

DIARRHEA

Diarrhea is not an illness in itself, but your body's attempt to get rid of something bad—bacteria, parasites, or amoebae—in a hurry. No fun, it is usually accompanied by cramping, dehydration, fever, and, of course, frequent trips to the bathroom.

If you get diarrhea, it should pass in a day or two. Anti-diarrheals such as Lomotil and Imodium A-D will plug you up but don't cure you—use them only if you can't be near a bathroom. The malaise you feel from diarrhea typically is from dehydration, not the actual infection, so be sure to drink plenty of fluids—a sports drink such as Gatorade is best. If it's especially bad, ask at your hotel for the nearest *laboratorio* (laboratory or clinic), where the staff can analyze a stool sample for around US$5 and tell you if you have a parasitic infection or a virus. If it's a common infection, the lab technician will tell you what medicine to take. Be aware that medicines for stomach infection are seriously potent, killing not only the bad stuff but the good stuff as well; they cure you but leave you vulnerable to another infection. Avoid alcohol and spicy foods for several days afterward.

A few tips for avoiding stomach problems include:

- Only drink bottled water. Avoid using tap water even for brushing your teeth.

- Avoid raw fruits or vegetables that you haven't disinfected and cut yourself. Lettuce is particularly dangerous since water is easily trapped in the leaves. Also, as tasty as they look, avoid the bags of sliced fruit sold from street carts.

- Order your meat dishes well done, even if it's an upscale restaurant. If you've been to a market, you'll see that meat is handled very differently here.

INSECTS

Insects are not of particular concern in Cozumel, certainly not as they are in other parts of the tropics. Mosquitoes are common, but are not known to carry malaria. Dengue fever, also transmitted by mosquitoes, is present but still rare. Certain destinations are more likely to be buggy, like forested archaeological zones and coastal bird-watching areas, and travelers should bring and use insect repellent there, if only for extra comfort.

CRIME

Cozumel and the Yucatán Peninsula are generally quite safe, and few travelers report problems with crime of any kind. You may find illicit drugs relatively easy to obtain in Playa del Carmen, but bear in mind that drug crimes are prosecuted vigorously in Mexico (especially ones involving foreigners), and your country's embassy can do very little to help. Sexual assault and rape have been reported by women at nightclubs, sometimes after having been slipped a "date rape" drug. While clubs are raucous and sexually charged by definition, women should be especially alert to the people around them and wary of accepting drinks from strangers. In all areas, commonsense precautions are always recommended, such as taking a taxi at night instead of walking (especially if you've been drinking) and avoiding flashing your money and valuables, or leaving them unattended on the beach or elsewhere. Utilize the safety deposit box in your hotel room, if one is available; if you rent a car, get one with a trunk so your bags will not be visible through the window.

Information and Services

MONEY

Accessing your money is not difficult in Cozumel, especially near the central plaza. **HSBC** (Av. 5 Sur at Calle 1, 9am-6pm Mon.-Fri., 9am-3pm Sat.), **Bancomer** (Av. 5 Sur btwn Av. Juárez and Calle 1, 8:30am-4pm Mon.-Fri.), and **Banorte** (Av. 5 Nte. btwn Av. Juárez and Calle 2, 9am-5pm Mon.-Fri., 9am-2pm Sat.) all have ATMs and exchange foreign cash.

Currency and Exchange Rates

Mexico's official currency is the peso, divided into 100 centavos. It is typically designated with the symbol $, but you may also see MN$ (*moneda nacional,* or national currency) or M$. We've listed prices in their U.S. dollar equivalent.

U.S. dollars and E.U. euros are accepted in the shopping districts of Cozumel and Playa del Carmen. However, you'll want and need pesos everywhere else, as most shopkeepers appreciate visitors paying in the local currency.

At the time of research, US$1 was equal to M$12, slightly less for Canadian dollars, and M$16.25 for euros.

ATMs

ATMs are easily accessible in Downtown Cozumel though tougher to find elsewhere on the island; they are without question the easiest, fastest, and best way to manage your money. Be aware that you may be charged a transaction fee by the ATM (US$1-3 typically) as well as your home bank (as much as US$5). It's worth asking your bank if it partners with a Mexican bank, and whether transaction fees are lower if you use that bank's cash machines.

Travelers Checks

With the spread of ATMs, travelers checks have stopped being convenient for most travel, especially in a country as developed as Mexico. If you do bring them, you will have to exchange them at a bank or a *casa de cambio* (exchange booth).

Credit Cards

Visa and MasterCard are accepted at all large hotels and many medium and small ones, upscale restaurants, main bus terminals, travel agencies, and many shops throughout Mexico. American Express is accepted much less frequently. Some merchants tack on a 5-10 percent surcharge for any credit card purchase—ask before you pay.

Cash

It's a good idea to bring a small amount of U.S. cash, on the off chance that your ATM card suddenly stops working; a US$200 reserve should be more than enough for a two-week visit. Stow it away with your other important documents, to be used only if necessary.

Tax

A 12 percent value-added tax (*IVA* in Spanish) applies to hotel rates, restaurant and bar tabs, and gift purchases. When checking in or making reservations at a hotel, ask if tax has already been added. In some cases, the tax is 17 percent.

Bargaining

Bargaining is common and expected in street and artisans' markets, but try not to be too aggressive. Some tourists derive immense and almost irrational pride from haggling over every last cent, and then turn around and spend several times that amount on beer or snacks. The fact is, most bargaining comes down to the difference of a few dollars or even less, and earning those extra dollars is a much bigger deal for most artisans than spending them is to most tourists.

Tipping

While tipping is always a choice, it is a key supplement to many workers' paychecks. In fact,

USEFUL TELEPHONE NUMBERS

EMERGENCIES
- Emergencies: 066 or 060
- Emergency Ambulance: 065 or 987/872-1058
- Ángeles Verdes (free roadside assistance): 078 or 800/903-9200

MEDICAL ASSISTANCE
- Centro Médico de Cozumel: 987/872-9400
- Clínica-Hospital San Miguel: 987/872-0103 or 987/872-6104

- Hyperbaric Medical Center: 987/872-1430
- Farmacia Similares: 987/869-2440

POLICE
- Tourist Police: 987/872-0409
- Municipal Police (non-emergency): 987/872-0409
- State Police: 987/872-0599

GENERAL
- Directory Assistance: 044
- Taxi: 987/872-1130 or 987/872-1167

for some—like baggers at the grocery store—the tip is the *only* pay they receive. And while dollars and euros are appreciated, pesos are preferred. (**Note:** Foreign coins can't be changed to pesos, so are useless to workers.) Average gratuities in the region include:

- Archaeological zone guides: 10-15 percent if you're satisfied with the service; for informal guides (typically boys who show you around the site), US$1-2 is customary.

- Gas station attendants: around US$0.50 if your windshield has been cleaned, tires have been filled, or the oil and water have been checked; no tip is expected for simply pumping gas.

- Grocery store baggers: US$0.25-0.50.

- Housekeepers: US$1-2 per day; either left daily or as a lump sum at the end of your stay.

- Porters: about US$1 per bag.

- Taxi drivers: Tipping is not customary.

- Tour guides: 10-15 percent, and don't forget the driver—US$1-2 is typical.

- Waiters: 10-15 percent; make sure the gratuity is not already included in the bill.

COMMUNICATIONS AND MEDIA
Postal Service
Mailing letters and postcards from Mexico is neither cheap nor necessarily reliable. Delivery times vary greatly, and letters get "lost" somewhat more than postcards. Letters (under 20 grams) and postcards cost US$1 to the United States and Canada, US$1.20 to Europe and South America, and US$1.35 to the rest of the world. Visit the Correos de México website (www.correosdemexico.com.mx) for pricing on larger packages and other services.

Cozumel's **post office** (Av. Rafael Melgar at Calle 7, 9am-5pm Mon.-Fri., 9am-1pm Sat.) is next to Punta Langosta shopping center.

Telephone
Ladatel—Mexico's national phone company—maintains good public phones on Cozumel and throughout the country. Plastic phone cards with little chips in them are sold at most mini-marts and supermarkets in 30-, 50-, 100-, and 200-peso denominations. Ask for a *tarjeta* Ladatel—they are the size and stiffness of a credit card, as opposed to the

PHONE CALLS

LONG-DISTANCE DIRECT DIALING
- Domestic long-distance: 01 + area code + number
- International long-distance (United States only): 001 + area code + number
- International long-distance (rest of the world): 00 + country code + area code + number

LONG-DISTANCE COLLECT CALLS
- Domestic long-distance operator: 02
- International long-distance operator (English-speaking): 09

MEXICAN LANDLINE TO MEXICAN CELL PHONE
- Within the same area code: 044 + 3-digit area code + 7-digit phone number

- Different area code: 045 + 3-digit area code + 7-digit phone number

MEXICAN CELL PHONE TO MEXICAN CELL PHONE
- Within the same area code: 7-digit number only
- Different area code: 3-digit area code + 7-digit number

INTERNATIONAL LANDLINE/ CELL PHONE TO A MEXICAN CELL PHONE
- From U.S. or Canada: 011 + 52 + 1 + 3-digit area code + 7-digit number
- From other countries: international access code + 52 + 1 + 3-digit area code + 7-digit number

---

thin cards used for cell phones. Insert the card into the phone, and the amount on the card is displayed on the screen. Rates and dialing instructions (in Spanish and English) are inside the phone cabin. At the time of research, rates were roughly US$0.10 per minute for local calls, US$0.40 per minute for national calls, and US$0.50 per minute for calls to the United States and Canada.

A number of Internet cafés offer inexpensive **Web-based phone service,** especially in the larger cities where broadband connections are fastest. Rates tend to be significantly lower than those of Ladatel, and you don't have to worry about your card running out.

Beware of phones offering "free" collect or credit card calls; far from being free, their rates are outrageous.

If you've got an unlocked GSM cell phone, you can purchase a local SIM card for around US$15, including US$5 credit, for use during your trip. Calls are expensive, but text messaging is relatively cheap, including to the United States; having two local phones/chips can be especially useful for couples or families traveling together.

To call a local Mexican cellular phone from within Mexico, dial 044 plus the area code and number. If you're calling a Mexican cellular phone that's registered out of the area you're calling from, use the 045 prefix instead. If you're calling a Mexican mobile phone from outside Mexico, add a 1 between the country code and the area code, and do not use the 044 or 045 prefixes. Be aware that calling a cell phone within Mexico can be very pricey, regardless of where you're calling from.

Internet Access
On Isla Cozumel, there are myriad Internet cafés where you can get online, make international phone calls, burn photos to CDs, and more. **Phonet** (Calle Rosado Salas at Av. 10, 8am-11pm daily) is a quiet, reliable place charging US$0.85 per hour of Internet use and

US$0.35 per minute for calls to the United States and Canada.

Wireless Internet is also becoming popular at all levels of hotels; if you need to stay connected while you're on the road and you're willing to travel with a laptop or tablet, it's easy—and free—to access the Internet.

Newspapers

The most popular daily newspapers in the region are *Novedades Quintana Roo* and *El Diario de Yucatán*. The main national newspapers are also readily available, including *Reforma, La Prensa,* and *La Jornada*. For news in English, you'll occasionally find the *Miami Herald Cancún Edition* in Playa del Carmen and Isla Cozumel.

Radio and Television

Most large hotels and a number of midsize and small ones have cable or satellite TV, which usually includes CNN (though sometimes in Spanish only), MTV, and other U.S. channels. AM and FM radio options are surprisingly bland—you're more likely to find a good *rock en español* station in California than you are in the Yucatán.

MAPS AND TOURIST INFORMATION

There are numerous websites with news, tips, maps, special deals, discussion groups, and other information about Cozumel, including www.thisiscozumel.com, www.cozumelinsider.com, www.cozumelmycozumel.com, www.cozumeltoday.com, and even www.cruiseportinsider.com.

The *Free Blue Guide to Cozumel* has good maps and listings for a range of services, from restaurants to dive shops. Look for the booklet as you get off the ferry.

Maps

A husband-and-wife team creates outstanding and exhaustively detailed maps of Isla Cozumel, Playa del Carmen, inland archeological zones, and other Yucatan Peninsula-specific maps, sold at their website **www.cancunmap. com.** They're as much guidebooks as maps, with virtually every building and business identified, many with short personal reviews, plus useful information like taxi rates, driving distances, ferry schedules, and more. Maps cost around US$10, and often come with a couple of smaller secondary maps.

Dante produces reasonably reliable maps of the entire Yucatán Peninsula; it also operates a chain of excellent bookstores at various archaeological sites.

Most local tourist offices distribute maps to tourists free of charge, though quality varies considerably. Car rental agencies often have maps, and many hotels create maps for their guests of nearby restaurants and sights.

Tourist Offices

The city tourist office has three **information booths** (8am-7pm Mon.-Sat., 9am-2pm Sun.)—in the central plaza, at the international pier, and at Puerta Maya pier. English is spoken at all locations.

Photography and Video

Digital cameras are as ubiquitous in Mexico as they are everywhere else, but memory sticks and other paraphernalia can be prohibitively expensive; bring a spare chip in case your primary one gets lost or damaged. If your chip's capacity is relatively small and you're not bringing your laptop along, pack a couple of blank DVDs and a USB cable to download and burn photos, which you can do at most Internet cafés.

Video is another great way to capture the color and movement of Isla Cozumel and the mainland. Be aware that all archaeological sites charge an additional US$3.75 to bring in a video camera; tripods often are prohibited.

WEIGHTS AND MEASURES
Measurements

Mexico uses the metric system, so distances are in kilometers, weights are in kilograms, gasoline is sold by the liter, and temperatures are given in Celsius. See the chart at the back of this book for conversions from the imperial system.

Time Zone

Isla Cozumel—as well as the rest of the Yucatán Peninsula—is in U.S. Central Standard Time. Daylight Savings Time is recognized April-October.

Electricity

Mexico uses the 60-cycle, 110-volt AC current common in the United States. Bring a surge protector if you plan to plug in a laptop.

RESOURCES

Spanish Glossary

The form of Spanish spoken in Mexico is quite clear and understandable, and far less clipped or colloquial than in other Spanish-speaking countries. That's good news for anyone new to the language and hoping to use their trip to learn more.

abarrotería: small grocery store
amigo, amiga: friend
antojitos: Mexican snacks, such as huaraches, flautas, and quesadillas
artesanías: handicrafts, as distinguished from *artesano, artesana,* the person who makes handicrafts
boleto: ticket, boarding pass
bucear, buzo: to scuba dive, scuba diver
caballero: gentleman
camionera central: central bus station; alternatively, *terminal camionera*
cárcel: jail
colectivo: a shared public taxi or minibus that picks up and drops off passengers along a designated route; alternatively, *combi*
combi: a shared public minibus; alternatively, *colectivo*
comedor: small restaurant
correo: post office
cuadra: city block
cuota: literally "toll," commonly refers to a toll highway
dama: lady
Don, Doña: title of respect, generally used for an older man or woman
farmacia: pharmacy or drugstore

gasolinera: gasoline station
impuestos, I.V.A. (pronounced EE-va): taxes, value-added tax
indígena: indigenous person; commonly, but incorrectly, an indian (*indio*)
jardín: garden or small park
lancha: small motorboat; alternatively, *panga*
larga distancia: long-distance telephone service, or the *caseta* (booth) where it's provided
lonchería: small lunch counter, usually serving juices, sandwiches, and *antojitos* (Mexican snacks)
mescal: alcoholic beverage distilled from the fermented hearts of maguey (century plant)
mordida: slang for bribe; literally, "little bite"
palapa: thatched-roof structure, often open air
panga: small motorboat; alternatively, *lancha*
parque central: town plaza or central square; alternatively, *zócalo*
PEMEX: government gasoline station, acronym for Petróleos Mexicanos, Mexico's national oil corporation
policía: municipal police, alternatively *preventativa*
propina: tip, as at a restaurant or hotel; alternatively, *servicio*
retorno: highway turnaround
temporada: season, as in *temporada alta/baja* (high/low season)
terminal camionera: central bus station; alternatively, *camionera central*
zócalo: town plaza or central square; alternatively, *parque central*

ABBREVIATIONS

Av.: *avenida* (avenue)
Blvd.: *bulevar* (boulevard)
Calz.: *calzada* (thoroughfare, main road)
Carr.: *carretera* (highway)

Col.: *colonia* (subdivision)
Nte.: *norte* (north)
Ote.: *oriente* (east)
Pte.: *poniente* (west)
s/n: *sin número* (no street number)

Spanish Phrasebook

Whether you speak a little or a lot, using your Spanish will surely make your vacation a lot more fun. You'll soon see that Mexicans truly appreciate your efforts and your willingness to speak their language.

Spanish commonly uses 30 letters—the familiar English 26, plus four straightforward additions: ch, ll, ñ, and rr.

PRONUNCIATION

Once you learn them, Spanish pronunciation rules—in contrast to English and other languages—generally don't change. Spanish vowels generally sound softer than in English. (*Note:* The capitalized syllables that follow receive stronger accents.)

Vowels

a   like ah, as in "hah": *agua* AH-gooah (water), *pan* PAHN (bread), and *casa* CAH-sah (house)

e   like eh, as in "hem": *mesa* MEH-sah (table), *tela* TEH-lah (cloth), and *de* DEH (of, from)

i   like ee, as in "need": *diez* dee-EHZ (ten), *comida* ko-MEE-dah (meal), and *fin* FEEN (end)

o   like oh, as in "go": *peso* PEH-soh (weight), *ocho* OH-choh (eight), and *poco* POH-koh (a bit)

u   like oo, as in "cool": *uno* OO-noh (one), *cuarto* KOOAHR-toh (room), and *usted* oos-TEHD (you); when it follows a "q" the u is silent: *quiero* ki-EH-ro (I want); when it follows an "h" or has an umlaut, it's pronounced like "w": *huevo* WEH-vo (egg)

Consonants

b, d, f, k, l, m, n, p, q, s, t, v, w, x, y, z, and ch   pronounced almost as in English; **h** is silent

c   like k, as in "keep": *cuarto* KOOAR-toh (room), *Tepic* tay-PEEK (capital of Nayarit state); when it precedes "e" or "i," pronounce **c** like s, as in "sit": *cerveza* sehr-VEH-sah (beer), *encima* ehn-SEE-mah (atop)

g   like g, as in "gift" when it precedes "a," "o," "u," or a consonant: *gato* GAH-toh (cat), *hago* AH-goh (I do, make); otherwise, pronounce **g** like h, as in "hat": *giro* HEE-roh (money order), *gente* HEN-tay (people)

j   like h, as in "has": *Jueves* HOOEH-vehs (Thursday), *mejor* meh-HOR (better)

ll   like y, as in "yes": *toalla* toh-AH-yah (towel), *ellos* EH-yohs (they, them)

ñ   like ny, as in "canyon": *año* AH-nyo (year), *señor* SEH-nyor (mister, sir)

r   is lightly trilled: *pero* PEH-roh (but), *tres* TREHS (three), *cuatro* KOOAH-troh (four)

rr   like a Spanish r, but with much more emphasis and trill: *burro* (donkey), *carretera* (highway), *ferrocarril* (railroad)

Note: The single exception to the above is the pronunciation of **y** when it's being used as the Spanish word for "and," as in *Eva y Leo.* In such case, pronounce it like the English ee, as in "keep": Eva "ee" Leo (Eva and Leo).

Accent

The rule for accent, the relative stress given to syllables within a given word, is straightforward. If a word ends in a vowel, an "n," or an "s," accent the next-to-last syllable; if not, accent the last syllable.

Pronounce *gracias* GRAH-seeahs (thank you),

orden OHR-dehn (order), and *carretera* kah-reh-TEH-rah (highway) with the stress on the next-to-last syllable.

Otherwise, accent the last syllable: *venir* vay-NEER (to come), *ferrocarril* feh-roh-cah-REEL (railroad), and *edad* eh-DAHD (age).

Exceptions to the accent rule are always marked with an accent sign: (á, é, í, ó, or ú), such as *teléfono* teh-LEH-foh-noh (telephone), *jabón* hah-BON (soap), and *rápido* RAH-pee-doh (rapid).

BASIC AND COURTEOUS EXPRESSIONS

Most Spanish-speakers consider formalities important. Whenever approaching anyone, try to say the appropriate salutation—good morning, good evening, etc. Standing alone, the greeting *hola* (hello) can sound brusque.

Hello. *Hola.*
Good morning. *Buenos días.*
Good afternoon. *Buenas tardes.*
Good evening. *Buenas noches.*
How are you? *¿Cómo está Usted?*
Very well, thank you. *Muy bien, gracias.*
Okay; good. *Bien.*
Not okay; bad. *No muy bien; mal.*
So-so. *Más o menos.*
And you? *¿Y usted?*
Thank you. *Gracias.*
Thank you very much. *Muchas gracias.*
You're very kind. *Muy amable.*
You're welcome. *De nada.*
Good bye. *Adiós.*
See you later. *Hasta luego.*
please *por favor*
yes *sí*
no *no*
I don't know. *No sé.*
Just a moment, please. *Un momento, por favor.*
Excuse me, please (when you're trying to get attention). *Disculpe* or *Con permiso.*
Excuse me (when you've made a mistake). *Lo siento.*
Pleased to meet you. *Mucho gusto.*
Do you speak English? *¿Habla Usted inglés?*

Is English spoken here? *¿Se habla inglés?*
I don't speak Spanish well. *No hablo bien el español.*
I don't understand. *No entiendo.*
How do you say... in Spanish? *¿Cómo se dice... en español?*
What is your name? *¿Cómo se llama Usted?*
My name is... *Me llamo...*
Would you like... *¿Quisiera Usted...*
Let's go to... *Vamos a...*

TERMS OF ADDRESS

When in doubt, use the formal *Usted* (you) as a form of address.

I *yo*
you (formal) *Usted*
you (familiar) *tu*
he/him *él*
she/her *ella*
we/us *nosotros*
you (plural) *ustedes*
they/them *ellos* (all males or mixed gender); *ellas* (all females)
mister, sir *señor*
missus, ma'am *señora*
miss, young lady *señorita*
wife *esposa*
husband *esposo*
friend *amigo* (male); *amiga* (female)
boyfriend; girlfriend *novio; novia*
son; daughter *hijo; hija*
brother; sister *hermano; hermana*
father; mother *padre; madre*
grandfather; grandmother *abuelo; abuela*

TRANSPORTATION

Where is...? *¿Dónde está...?*
How far is it to...? *¿A cuánto está...?*
from... to... *de... a...*
How many blocks? *¿Cuántas cuadras?*
Where (Which) is the way to...? *¿Dónde está el camino a...?*
the bus station *la terminal de autobuses*
the bus stop *la parada de autobuses*
Where is this bus going? *¿Adónde va este autobús?*
the taxi stand *la parada de taxis*

the train station *la estación de ferrocarril*
the boat *el barco* or *la lancha*
the airport *el aeropuerto*
I'd like a ticket to... *Quisiera un boleto a...*
first (second) class *primera (segunda) clase*
roundtrip *ida y vuelta*
reservation *reservación*
baggage *equipaje*
Stop here, please. *Pare aquí, por favor.*
the entrance *la entrada*
the exit *la salida*
the ticket office *la taquilla*
(very) near; far *(muy) cerca; lejos*
to; toward *a*
by; through *por*
from *de*
the right *la derecha*
the left *la izquierda*
straight ahead *derecho; directo*
in front *en frente*
beside *al lado*
behind *atrás*
the corner *la esquina*
the stoplight *el semáforo*
a turn *una vuelta*
here *aquí*
somewhere around here *por aquí*
right there *allí*
somewhere around there *por allá*
street; boulevard *calle; bulevar*
highway *carretera*
bridge *puente*
toll *cuota*
address *dirección*
north; south *norte; sur*
east; west *oriente (este); poniente (oeste)*

ACCOMMODATIONS
hotel *hotel*
Is there a room? *¿Hay cuarto?*
May I (may we) see it? *¿Podría (podríamos) verlo?*
What is the rate? *¿Cuál es la tarifa?*
Is that your best rate? *¿Es su mejor precio?*
Is there something cheaper? *¿Hay algo más económico?*
a single room *un cuarto sencillo*
a double room *un cuarto doble*

double bed *cama matrimonial*
twin bed *cama individual*
with private bath *con baño privado*
hot water *agua caliente*
shower *ducha; regadera*
towels *toallas*
soap *jabón*
toilet paper *papel higiénico*
blanket *cobija*
sheets *sábanas*
air-conditioned *aire acondicionado*
fan *abanico; ventilador*
key *llave*
manager *gerente*

FOOD
I'm hungry *Tengo hambre.*
I'm thirsty. *Tengo sed.*
menu *carta; menú*
order *orden*
glass *vaso*
fork *tenedor*
knife *cuchillo*
spoon *cuchara*
napkin *servilleta*
soft drink *refresco*
coffee *café*
tea *té*
drinking water *agua pura; agua potable*
carbonated water *agua mineral*
bottled uncarbonated water *agua sin gas*
beer *cerveza*
wine *vino*
milk *leche*
juice *jugo*
cream *crema*
sugar *azúcar*
cheese *queso*
snack *antojito; botana*
breakfast *desayuno*
lunch *almuerzo* or *comida*
daily lunch special *comida corrida*
dinner *cena*
the check *la cuenta*
eggs *huevos*
bread *pan*
salad *ensalada*
fruit *fruta*

mango *mango*
watermelon *sandía*
papaya *papaya*
banana *plátano*
apple *manzana*
orange *naranja*
lime *limón*
fish *pescado*
shellfish *mariscos*
shrimp *camarones*
meat (without) *(sin) carne*
chicken *pollo*
pork *puerco*
beef; steak *res; bistec*
bacon; ham *tocino; jamón*
fried *frito*
roasted *asado*
barbecue; barbecued *barbacoa; al carbón*
food to go *comida para llevar; para llevar*
delivery service *servicio a domicilio*

SHOPPING

money *dinero*
money-exchange bureau *casa de cambio*
I would like to exchange travelers
 checks. *Quisiera cambiar cheques de
 viajero.*
What is the exchange rate? *¿Cuál es el tipo
 de cambio?*
How much is the commission? *¿Cuánto
 cuesta la comisión?*
Do you accept credit cards? *¿Aceptan
 tarjetas de crédito?*
money order *giro*
How much does it cost? *¿Cuánto cuesta?*
What is your final price? *¿Cuál es su último
 precio?*
expensive *caro*
cheap *barato; económico*
more *más*
less *menos*
a little *un poco*
too much *demasiado*

HEALTH

Help me please. *Ayúdeme por favor.*
I am ill. *Estoy enfermo.*
Call a doctor. *Llame un doctor.*

Take me to... *Lléveme a...*
hospital *hospital; clinica medica*
drugstore *farmacia*
pain *dolor*
fever *fiebre*
headache *dolor de cabeza*
stomachache *dolor de estómago*
burn *quemadura*
cramp *calambre*
nausea *náusea*
vomiting *vomitar*
medicine *medicina*
antibiotic *antibiótico*
pill; tablet *pastilla*
aspirin *aspirina*
ointment; cream *pomada; crema*
bandage *venda*
cotton *algodón*
sanitary napkins *Kotex*
birth control pills *pastillas anticonceptivas*
contraceptive foam *espuma anticonceptiva*
condoms *preservativos; condones*
contact lenses *pupilentes*
glasses *lentes*
dental floss *hilo dental*
dentist *dentista*
toothbrush *cepillo de dientes*
toothpaste *pasta de dientes*
toothache *dolor de dientes*
delivery service *servicio a domicilio*

POST OFFICE AND COMMUNICATIONS

long-distance telephone *teléfono de larga
 distancia*
I would like to call... *Quisiera llamar a...*
collect *por cobrar*
person to person *persona a persona*
credit card *tarjeta de crédito*
post office *correo*
letter *carta*
stamp *estampilla, timbre*
postcard *tarjeta*
air mail *correo aereo*
registered *registrado*
money order *giro*
package; box *paquete; caja*
string; tape *cuerda; cinta*

Internet *internet*
Internet café *ciber café; ciber*
website *página web*
Web search *búsqueda*
link *enlace*
email *correo electrónico*
Skype *Skype*
Facebook *face*

AT THE BORDER

border *frontera*
customs *aduana*
immigration *migración*
tourist card *tarjeta de turista*
inspection *inspección; revisión*
passport *pasaporte*
profession *profesión*
marital status *estado civil*
single *soltero*
married; divorced *casado; divorciado*
widowed *viudado* (male); *viudada* (female)
insurance *seguro*
title *título*
driver's license *licencia de manejar*

AT THE GAS STATION

gas station *gasolinera*
gasoline *gasolina*
unleaded *sin plomo*
fill it up, please *lleno, por favor*
tire *llanta*
tire repair shop *vulcanizadora*
air *aire*
water *agua*
oil; oil change *aceite; cambio de aceite*
grease *grasa*
My... doesn't work. *Mi... no sirve.*
battery *batería*
radiator *radiador*
alternator *alternador*
generator *generador*
tow truck *grúa*
repair shop *taller mecánico*
tune-up *afinación*
auto parts store *refaccionería*

VERBS

In Spanish, verbs employ mostly predictable forms and come in three classes, which end in *ar, er,* and *ir.* Note that the first-person (*yo*) verb form is often irregular.

to buy *comprar*
I buy, you (he, she, it) buys *compro, compra*
we buy, you (they) buy *compramos, compran*

to eat *comer*
I eat, you (he, she, it) eats *como, come*
we eat, you (they) eat *comemos, comen*

to climb *subir*
I climb, you (he, she, it) climbs *subo, sube*
we climb, you (they) climb *subimos, suben*

Here are more (with irregularities indicated):

to do or make *hacer* (regular except for *hago,* I do or make)
to go *ir* (very irregular: *voy, va, vamos, van*)
to go (walk) *andar*
to love *amar*
to work *trabajar*
to want *desear, querer*
to need *necesitar*
to read *leer*
to write *escribir*
to repair *reparar*
to stop *parar*
to get off (the bus) *bajar*
to arrive *llegar*
to stay (remain) *quedar*
to stay (lodge) *hospedar*
to leave *salir* (regular except for *salgo,* I leave)
to look at *mirar*
to look for *buscar*
to give *dar* (regular except for *doy,* I give)
to carry *llevar*
to have *tener* (irregular but important: *tengo, tiene, tenemos, tienen*)
to come *venir* (similarly irregular: *vengo, viene, venimos, vienen*)

Spanish has two forms of "to be":

to be *estar* (regular except for *estoy*, I am)
to be *ser* (very irregular: *soy, es, somos, son*)

Use *estar* when speaking of location or a temporary state of being: "I am at home." *"Estoy en casa."* "I'm sick." *"Estoy enfermo."* Use *ser* for a permanent state of being: "I am a doctor." *"Soy doctora."*

NUMBERS
zero *cero*
one *uno*
two *dos*
three *tres*
four *cuatro*
five *cinco*
six *seis*
seven *siete*
eight *ocho*
nine *nueve*
10 *diez*
11 *once*
12 *doce*
13 *trece*
14 *catorce*
15 *quince*
16 *dieciseis*
17 *diecisiete*
18 *dieciocho*
19 *diecinueve*
20 *veinte*
21 *veintiuno*
30 *treinta*
40 *cuarenta*
50 *cincuenta*
60 *sesenta*
70 *setenta*
80 *ochenta*
90 *noventa*
100 *cien*
101 *cientiuno*
200 *doscientos*
500 *quinientos*
1,000 *mil*

10,000 *diez mil*
100,000 *cien mil*
1,000,000 *millón*
one half *medio*
one third *un tercio*
one fourth *un cuarto*

TIME
What time is it? *¿Qué hora es?*
It's one o'clock. *Es la una.*
It's three in the afternoon. *Son las tres de la tarde.*
It's 4am. *Son las cuatro de la mañana.*
six-thirty *seis y media*
a quarter till eleven *un cuarto para las once*
a quarter past five *las cinco y cuarto*
an hour *una hora*

DAYS AND MONTHS
Monday *lunes*
Tuesday *martes*
Wednesday *miércoles*
Thursday *jueves*
Friday *viernes*
Saturday *sábado*
Sunday *domingo*
today *hoy*
tomorrow *mañana*
yesterday *ayer*
January *enero*
February *febrero*
March *marzo*
April *abril*
May *mayo*
June *junio*
July *julio*
August *agosto*
September *septiembre*
October *octubre*
November *noviembre*
December *diciembre*
a week *una semana*
a month *un mes*
after *después*
before *antes*

Suggested Reading

The following titles provide insight into the region and the Maya people. A few of these books are more easily obtained in Mexico, but all of them will cost less in the United States. Most are nonfiction, though several are fiction and great to throw into your carry-on for a good read on the plane. Happy reading!

Beletsky, Les. *Travellers' Wildlife Guides: Southern Mexico*. Northampton, MA: Interlink Books, 2006. A perfect companion guide if you plan on bird-watching, diving/snorkeling, hiking, or canoeing your way through your vacation. Excellent illustrations.

Coe, Michael D. *Breaking the Maya Code*. New York: Thames and Hudson, 1999. A fascinating account of how epigraphers, linguists, and archaeologists succeeded in deciphering Maya hieroglyphics.

Coe, Michael D. *The Maya*. New York: Thames and Hudson, 2005. A well-illustrated, easy-to-read volume on the Maya people.

Franz, Carl, and Lorena Havens. *The People's Guide to Mexico*. Berkeley, CA: Avalon Travel, 2012. A humorous guide filled with witty anecdotes and helpful general information for visitors to Mexico. Don't expect any specific city information, just nuts-and-bolts hints for traveling south of the border.

Maya: Divine Kings of the Rain Forest. Cologne: Könemann, 2006. A beautifully compiled book of essays, photographs, and sketches relating to the Maya, past and present. Too heavy to take on the road but an excellent read.

McNay Brumfield, James. *A Tourist in the Yucatán*. Watsonville, CA: Tres Picos Press, 2004. A decent thriller that takes place in the Yucatán Peninsula; good for the beach.

Meyer, Michael, and William Sherman. *The Course of Mexican History*. New York: Oxford University Press, 2006. A concise one-volume history of Mexico.

Nelson, Ralph. *Popul Vuh: The Great Mythological Book of the Ancient Maya*. Boston: Houghton Mifflin, 1974. An easy-to-read translation of myths handed down orally by the Quiche Maya, family to family, until written down after the Spanish conquest.

Sodi, Demetrio M. (in collaboration with Adela Fernández). *The Mayas*. Mexico City: Panama Editorial S.A., 1987. This small book presents a fictionalized account of life among the Maya before the conquest. Easy reading for anyone who enjoys fantasizing about what life *might* have been like before recorded history in the Yucatán.

Stephens, John L. *Incidents of Travel in Central America, Chiapas, and Yucatán*. 2 vols. New York: Cosimo Classics, 2008. Good companions to refer to when traveling in the area. Stephens and illustrator Frederick Catherwood rediscovered many of the Maya ruins on their treks that took place in the mid-1800s. Easy reading.

Underwater Editions. *Cozumel Dive Guide and Log Book*. Mexico, D.F.: Underwater Editions, 2006. Excellent overview of the dive sites around Isla Cozumel, with color maps and photos.

Webster, David. *The Fall of the Ancient Maya*. New York: Thames and Hudson, 2002. A careful and thorough examination of the possible causes of one of archaeology's great unsolved mysteries—the collapse of the Classic Maya in the 8th century.

Internet Resources

www.backyardnature.net/yucatan
Notes and observations by an experienced naturalist about the major plants and animal species in the northern Yucatán Peninsula.

www.cancunmap.com
An excellent source of detailed maps of the Riviera Maya and some inland archaeological zones.

www.cozumelinsider.com
Good website covering Cozumel, including current tourist information and issues important to locals.

www.cozumelmycozumel.com
A website offering a host of information to travelers and people considering a move to Isla Cozumel, moderated by longtime expats.

www.cozumeltoday.com
Website with articles geared toward travelers; affiliated with *Cozumel Today* magazine.

www.cruiseportinsider.com
A good source of information for travelers arriving to Cozumel via cruise ship, including maps and shore excursion descriptions.

www.locogringo.com
Website with extensive business listings for the Riviera Maya.

www.mesoweb.com
Website relating to Mesoamerican cultures, including detailed reports and photos of past and current archaeological digs.

www.mostlymaya.com
Eclectic but informative website on various Maya topics; especially useful for info on Maya languages.

www.playa.info
An established website with lots of travel planning information to Playa and the Riviera Maya. It also has a popular forum for asking questions and sharing tips.

www.qroo.gob.mx
Official website of Quintana Roo state, including information for tourists.

www.thisiscozumel.com
Excellent website for Cozumel, including up-to-date tourist information.

www.travelyucatan.com
Detailed information and practical advice about traveling to and around the Yucatán Peninsula.

www.yucatan.gob.mx
Official website of Yucatán state, including information for tourists.

Index

List of Maps

Acknowledgments

Our sincere thanks, first, to the scores of everyday residents of Isla Cozumel and the Riviera Maya—from dive shop operators to hotel workers to passersby—whose help and patience were essential to researching this book. We're also grateful for the tips and information we received from travelers and expatriates along the way, and from those who contacted us with suggestions and comments.

Our sincere thanks, too, to all the folks at Moon Handbooks who made this book possible. A first edition guidebook is no small undertaking, and we're lucky to have such excellent editorial and production support from everyone at Moon. Thanks, especially, to Kathryn Ettinger for her patience and flexibility as the project took longer than expected, and of course for her sharp editing. Many thanks to Lucie Ericksen and the graphics department,

and to Kat Bennett and the cartography department, for making this book look so great, inside and out, and for adjusting their schedules to ours. And we're grateful to Grace Fujimoto for proposing that we do a stand-alone guide to Isla Cozumel in the first place; it was truly a dream-come-true assignment.

Finally, we're extremely grateful for the support and encouragement we enjoy from friends and family. Thank you especially to Mom and Dad Prado for their help on the ground in Mexico and back home in Colorado, to Grandpa Joe and Grandma Elyse for seeing us down the home stretch, and to Koko—teacher, friend, and babysitter extraordinaire. And of course our life is immeasurably richer for having Eva and Leo in it: There's nothing like having kids to reopen your eyes to the world around you.

www.moon.com

DESTINATIONS | ACTIVITIES | BLOGS | MAPS | BOOKS

MOON.COM is ready to help plan your next trip! Filled with fresh trip ideas and strategies, author interviews, informative travel blogs, a detailed map library, and descriptions of all the Moon guidebooks, Moon.com is all you need to get out and explore the world—or even places in your own backyard. While at Moon.com, sign up for our monthly e-newsletter for updates on new releases, travel tips, and expert advice from our on-the-go Moon authors. As always, when you travel with Moon, expect an experience that is uncommon and truly unique.

KEEP UP WITH MOON ON FACEBOOK AND TWITTER
JOIN THE MOON PHOTO GROUP ON FLICKR

MAP SYMBOLS

Expressway	◖	Highlight	✗	Airfield	⚲	Golf Course
Primary Road	○	City/Town	✈	Airport	Ⓟ	Parking Area
Secondary Road	◉	State Capital	▲	Mountain	◢	Archaeological Site
Unpaved Road	⊛	National Capital	✛	Unique Natural Feature	⚑	Church
Trail	★	Point of Interest			⛽	Gas Station
Ferry	•	Accommodation	⟆	Waterfall	☁	Glacier
Railroad	▾	Restaurant/Bar	▲	Park		Mangrove
Pedestrian Walkway	▪	Other Location	▣	Trailhead		Reef
Stairs	⋀	Campground	⚐	Skiing Area		Swamp

CONVERSION TABLES

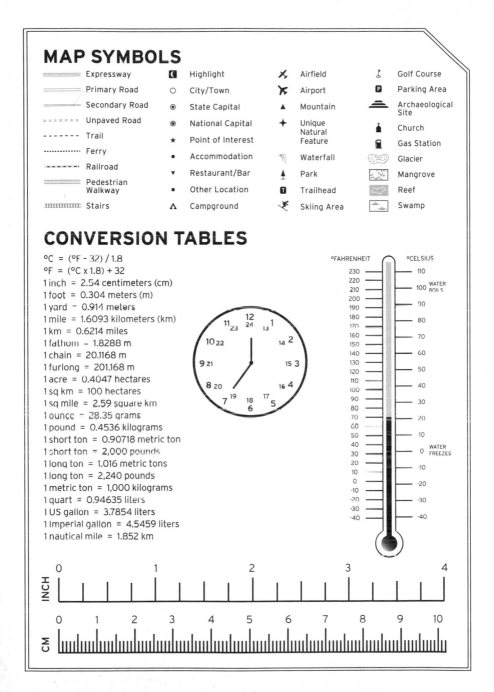

°C = (°F - 32) / 1.8
°F = (°C x 1.8) + 32
1 inch = 2.54 centimeters (cm)
1 foot = 0.304 meters (m)
1 yard = 0.914 meters
1 mile = 1.6093 kilometers (km)
1 km = 0.6214 miles
1 fathom = 1.8288 m
1 chain = 20.1168 m
1 furlong = 201.168 m
1 acre = 0.4047 hectares
1 sq km = 100 hectares
1 sq mile = 2.59 square km
1 ounce = 28.35 grams
1 pound = 0.4536 kilograms
1 short ton = 0.90718 metric ton
1 short ton = 2,000 pounds
1 long ton = 1.016 metric tons
1 long ton = 2,240 pounds
1 metric ton = 1,000 kilograms
1 quart = 0.94635 liters
1 US gallon = 3.7854 liters
1 Imperial gallon = 4.5459 liters
1 nautical mile = 1.852 km

MOON COZUMEL

Avalon Travel
a member of the Perseus Books Group
1700 Fourth Street
Berkeley, CA 94710, USA
www.moon.com

Editor and Series Manager: Kathryn Ettinger
Copy Editor: Ann Seifert
Graphics and Production Coordinator: Lucie Ericksen
Cover Designer: Lucie Ericksen
Map Editor: Kat Bennett
Cartographer: Kat Bennett
Indexer: Greg Jewett

ISBN-13: 978-1-61238-708-6
ISSN: 2331-9585

Printing History
1st Edition – January 2014
5 4 3 2 1

Front cover photo: Isla de la Pasión, a popular beach retreat on Isla Cozumel's northwest shore © Gary Chandler

Title page photo: Shells come in all shapes and sizes and are a popular souvenir © H.W. Prado
Color interior photos: pages 6, 7, 8 top-left and bottom, 9 bottom, 11 top and bottom-left, 12, 16, 18, 20 right, 23: © Liza Prado; pages 8 top-right, 9 top, 10, 11 bottom-right, 15, 16, 17, 22: © H.W. Prado; page 19: © 123rf.com; page 20 left: © Gary Chandler

Printed in Canada by Friesens

KEEPING CURRENT

If you have a favorite gem you'd like to see included in the next edition, or see anything that needs updating, clarification, or correction, please drop us a line. Send your comments via email to feedback@moon.com, or use the address above.